Beneath the Tamarind Tree

Beneath the Tamarind Tree

A STORY OF COURAGE, FAMILY, AND THE LOST SCHOOLGIRLS OF BOKO HARAM

ISHA SESAY

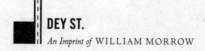

DEY ST.
An Imprint of WILLIAM MORROW

BENEATH THE TAMARIND TREE. Copyright © 2019 by Isha Sesay. All rights reserved. Printed in the United States of America. No part of this book may be used or reproduced in any manner whatsoever without written permission except in the case of brief quotations embodied in critical articles and reviews. For information, address HarperCollins Publishers, 195 Broadway, New York, NY 10007.

HarperCollins books may be purchased for educational, business, or sales promotional use. For information, please email the Special Markets Department at SPsales@harpercollins.com.

A hardcover edition of this book was published in 2019 by Dey Street, an imprint of William Morrow.

FIRST DEY STREET PAPERBACK EDITION PUBLISHED 2020.

Designed by Paula Russell Szafranski
Tamarind leaves artwork © MariPo/Shutterstock

Library of Congress Cataloging-in-Publication Data has been applied for.

ISBN 978-0-06-268661-9

20 21 22 23 24 LSC 10 9 8 7 6 5 4 3 2 1

To my beloved mother, Kadi;
your faith continues to guide me

You came back to me

You left me

I waited for you

You are mine

You are mine

You are mine

—TONI MORRISON, *Beloved*

Beneath the Tamarind Tree

CHAPTER ONE

THE SINGING WAS SO SOFT AT FIRST, I THOUGHT MY MIND WAS PLAY-ing tricks. I stopped unpacking my frayed leather duffel and stood completely still. With my head half-cocked, my neck craning, I waited, expectant, in my bare hotel room. Then I heard it again. This time, the haunting medley of voices filling the air was unmis-takable. But who was singing?

I was in Yola, northern Nigeria, in December 2016, counting down the hours till I set off on a pilgrimage of sorts—to witness the long-awaited return home of the twenty-one Chibok girls. Just a few weeks earlier, much of the world had been stunned by their sudden release, after years in Boko Haram captivity. Now the girls were finally returning to families and to a community desperate to welcome them back to the very place from which they'd been stolen. Their homecoming was under way and I was covering the emotional journey for CNN.

A host of thoughts ran through my head as I tried to make sense of the music. I knew the CNN team was staying in the same hotel as the girls. I also knew the building was on lockdown, surrounded by a ring of armed Nigerian security forces—access was severely restricted, so it was unlikely that a choir had made its way onto the grounds.

The singing got louder, even more joyful. The harmonies pulled at me, insistent, drawing me out from the safety of my room. I was no longer wearing my hastily purchased abaya, a long, loose-fitting garment typically worn by women in parts of the Muslim world. The dark, shapeless cloak was meant to mask my body-hugging jeans and T-shirt, sparing me from the likelihood of disapproving looks in this predominantly Muslim, conservative corner of Nigeria. Wearing the abaya was also my attempt to blend in and maintain a lower profile. After more than a decade on CNN International, I had become an easily recognizable face to viewers throughout Africa. Now I was worried my appearance might trigger unwanted publicity, which in turn could create unforeseen dangers. After all, the threat of Boko Haram attacks was still very much an active concern and part of day-to-day life in this region of Nigeria.

But for now, offended sensibilities were the farthest thing from my mind. I needed to find out who was singing. My heart raced as I turned the key to unlock my room and stepped out into the white-tiled corridor. The hallway was empty. I found only the glow of the midafternoon West African sun coupled with rising voices in the near distance. I stood in the golden light, letting the waves of sound wash over me, while I tried to figure out which way to go. As the row of rooms to my right offered up only silence, I was pretty certain the exuberant echoes were coming from the other direction.

I had barely taken ten steps when Mel, the bodyguard assigned to me by CNN, blocked my path. He'd been given the unenviable task of tracing my every move throughout this assignment. We'd first worked together in 2014, and now, more than two years later, he'd become all too familiar with my habit of agreeing to stay in one place only to then wander off from that very spot. It felt like he was starting to develop eyes at the back of his head because he was always hovering nearby whenever I tried to break away.

"Mel, who's singing?" I asked.

A warm smile slowly unfurled across his broad face, uncovering the wide gap between his top front teeth. "It's the girls," he replied.

The girls! I excitedly repeated to myself. The sound of rhythmic clapping now joined the melding voices. I could feel their energy and emotions rising and I had to find them. But since we hadn't been at the hotel long, I was confused, without any clear idea of which way to go. From the look on my face, Mel knew exactly what I was thinking. Before I could even get the words out, he spoke. "I know where they are. Come with me."

From the very first moment, two years earlier, when I'd learned that Boko Haram militants had stormed a girls' boarding school in northeastern Nigeria and made off into the darkness with 276 girls, the search for the missing Chibok girls had dominated my life. On the night they disappeared, April 14, 2014, I was on the other side of the world, in Atlanta, Georgia, where I'd been living and working as a CNN anchor and correspondent for close to a decade, thousands of miles away from the continent I'd grown up on. During my career as a broadcast journalist, I'd covered hundreds of stories: some tales of tragedy and injustice, others of devastated hopes and unfulfilled dreams. Yet no other story struck me with such force, or took such deep and permanent root within my being, as the abduction of the Chibok girls.

In the early days of the story, details of what had happened in that far-flung town trickled out slowly, and what emerged made this tragedy all the more personal for me. The missing girls were poor, born to parents of limited education and opportunities, from homes without distinction, relegated to the overlooked margins of Nigeria's status-conscious society. The mere fact that these girls were still going to school in the first place, in a region distinguished for being home to one of the largest out-of-school populations in the world, made each and every one of them heroic in my eyes. They knew that education could change the trajectory of their lives, and just as important, improve the livelihoods of their loved ones. They may have been born into a world with narrow expectations for them, but these girls were striving for so much more. I instantly recognized the course of their preabduction lives because in many ways, it mirrored a story I had known my whole life. Like the Chibok girls, my mother, Kadiatu Abibatu Conteh, had also wanted more, and this desire had set her on a unique path decades earlier in neighboring Sierra Leone. Her choices and determination, in turn, had given me the life I have now.

My mother was born to poor, uneducated parents in Rotifunk, a small, underdeveloped town in Sierra Leone's southeast. Like Chibok, it has long been a place of dusty roads lit at night primarily by star-filled skies. My grandmother, Mammy Iye, sold fresh peppers, homemade peanut butter, and peppermints in the loud, bustling local market, while my grandfather, Pa Amadou Conteh, was far more devoted to his Muslim faith than making money. The family home lacked electricity and running water, which meant my mother's childhood was framed by trips to the river to fill buckets and studying by lamplight, much like millions of other women and girls throughout Chibok and other parts of Africa today. Added to these physical hardships were emotional trials. My grandfather's other wife, Mammy Yenken, devoted her energies to haranguing Pa Conteh to stop him from paying my mother's school fees. Yet in spite of the constant tussle between progress and deep-seated tradition within her home, and notwithstanding the lack of female role models to inspire and guide her, young Kadi excelled in school and went on to win scholarships and awards. This success took her farther and farther away from her family's rural beginnings, and ultimately across the Atlantic Ocean to England. Thanks to the lottery of life, I was born in London to African parents who were not only highly educated but also progressive thinkers. If not for fate, twinned with my mother's childhood determination, I could just as easily have started off in a place not much different from Chibok and been one of the millions of girls facing countless obstacles to gain an education. Instead, my parents saw educating me as a priority, and I considered the freedom to dream up countless different paths to my future a birthright—all of which cemented the foundation for the life I have today. I am a living testament to the transformative power of education, and that truth never leaves me.

Before being stolen from their school beds, the Chibok girls had essentially been tackling the same journey my mother had made. That fact bound me to them in deep ways. The notion that Islamic militants tore them from their path because of inherent misogyny, combined with an opposition to the formal education of women, made me more than distressed. It also lit a fire within me. As a journalist, I fully committed myself to covering what had happened to the girls from Chibok, and I hoped and prayed that I'd see the day they were returned to their broken community. I believed their grieving families deserved answers to the long-neglected questions of their whereabouts, and I felt strongly that this story shouldn't be allowed to simply slip away from the global consciousness.

When the Chibok girls first disappeared, for what now seems like a brief moment, their plight held the gaze of celebrities worldwide, including then–first lady Michelle Obama, Angelina Jolie, Beyoncé, and Alicia Keys, along with myriad global political leaders. The hashtag #BringBackOurGirls flooded social media platforms. Within this arena, fierce advocates both known and unknown stood shoulder to shoulder literally and technologically with Bring Back Our Girls (BBOG) activists, demanding the Nigerian government do whatever was required to secure the release of the missing and reunite them with their families. In the United States, with the click of a button and the whoosh of a social media posting, everyone, including the global media, was all in.

Until they weren't.

As the flow of information about the hundreds of girls and the details of hostage negotiations ebbed away, so too did the gaze of much of the world. Almost two and a half years later, on October 13, 2016, twenty-one of them were suddenly set free by Boko Haram—the product of months-long secret negotiations led by Zannah Mustapha, a former Nigerian lawyer, and officials within the Swiss embassy in Nigeria. The same team would go on to secure the release of eighty-two more girls months later, in May 2017.

The moment I heard the news of the twenty-one being freed I dropped everything, grabbed a hastily purchased suitcase, and jumped on a plane to Nigeria that same day. This was the moment I'd been waiting for, a chance to shift attention away from the troubling view of these girls as ciphers for loss, a stolen cache of nameless, faceless black bodies. Now the world would share in the triumph of their return.

But instead of a huge worldwide celebration, the coverage was minimal. In America, it seemed the only thing ratings-obsessed news executives were prepared to extensively focus on was the race to the bottom between presidential candidates Donald Trump and Hillary Clinton, who would face off with each other at the beginning of November. Meanwhile, even the limited reporting of the twenty-one girls who'd been released failed to gain traction among the US public. This wasn't simply because of a news cycle in hyperdrive, thanks to the frenzied politics of the moment. There was also something else at play that underpinned the relatively muted reaction to the girls' release. In large sections of US society, the suffering of black and brown people—and in particular, black and brown women—is readily accepted and cast aside, a reality borne out by this nation's history.

People had moved on.

But I remained undeterred.

So here I was, a couple of days before Christmas in Yola, a city in Nigeria's restive northeast, preparing to set off the next morning on a long, dangerous road trip to Chibok. The newly freed twenty-one girls were heading home for the first time since they'd been abducted in 2014. They would be with their loved ones on Christmas day, a holiday of deep significance and celebrated like no other by Chibok's devoutly Christian community. After everything the girls had endured, the prospect of them being welcomed back at this particular time of year filled me with joy. The homecoming also represented a triumph of their families' unfailing Christian faith. I knew from conversations with some of the girls' loved ones over the years that their faith had comforted them and strengthened their hopes of their children one day returning, long after they'd been forgotten by much of the world.

This trip was my chance to bring the Chibok girls' story full circle. It was also an opportunity to try once more to resurrect public interest in this mass abduction. Far too many Americans have viewed Boko Haram as a purely Nigerian problem despite the fact that in 2011 the terror outfit was able to plan and execute a suicide bomb attack on the United Nations' headquarters in Abuja that killed at least eighteen people. Fast-forward a couple of years, and in 2015 the Islamist group pledged allegiance to the Islamic State of Iraq and Syria (ISIS). I'd long believed the United States was in no position to be so dismissive of Boko Haram.

I must admit that I undertook my decision to make the journey with the twenty-one girls with a great deal of pain and difficulty. My mother had suffered a stroke just three weeks earlier and I'd been at her bedside ever since. To follow the girls meant abandoning, at least temporarily, that duty. I was stuck, interrogating my values, my priorities, and loyalties, questions I returned to repeatedly during the journey, each time struck anew by pangs of guilt.

Many times, in fact, I wondered if my effort to present the story of the twenty-one girls' homecoming to the rest of the world was worth such personal torment.

But as I followed Mel to the source of the jubilant singing, everything I felt signaled I'd made the right choice. When I finally stood outside the room where the group was gathered, their beautiful, soaring voices crowded out any lingering doubts. I was exactly where I needed to be.

I knocked gently and waited. Moments later, one of the girls cracked the door, and as she did, the chorus of voices swept past us and filled the passageway. By this point I was a familiar face, having met the twenty-one in the first few days after their release and weeks later traveled with them to Yola. I smiled and mumbled that I'd like to join them. She grinned back shyly and stepped aside. I could feel Mel following me. Having a burly male presence in such a small space might have made the girls uncomfortable, so I quickly explained my concern and asked him to get Tim, our self-effacing cameraman, instead.

All the girls were crammed into the midsize hotel room, arrayed in brightly colored blouses, ankle-length skirts, and head wraps. The jam-packed room was a canvas of bold reds, blues, and yellows. My arrival didn't interrupt their singing, though a few gave me small half smiles. Others looked as if they were far away, lost in reverie. I quickly realized they were singing Christian praise songs and many of them were holding Bibles: this was their daily evening worship—a time for exultation and prayer. Many of the girls sat on the bed, while others perched on the writing desk, and the remaining handful shared the few uncomfortable-looking chairs in the room. I spotted an unoccupied nightstand to the right of the bed and quickly made a beeline for it. From my corner, I found myself clapping along with the group while they sang. Though I quickly became swept up in the emotion of the room, I was struck by the serenity on the girls' faces. There was no sign of pain, anger, fear, or dark emotion in their expressions. How were these girls able to manifest such peace and joyfulness after being held captive for more than two years, after witnessing the worst of humanity? I struggled to make sense of it. Yet here they were, twenty-one girls with their spirits seemingly untainted, creating a sound so beautiful my own heart was buoyed beside theirs.

Tim soon arrived with his camera and positioned himself in a corner by the door to unobtrusively capture the singing and clapping. At first I worried that the girls would find his presence upsetting, but they were so focused on their singing that they remained oblivious to him. The girls took turns leading the songs. One would sing a few lines unaccompanied before the rest swooped in to carry the remaining verses higher and louder. It seemed to me that they'd developed a way of supporting and encouraging each other that was palpable in their singing. I felt cocooned by their voices and could have stayed there for as long as they had the breath to sing.

But after half an hour, their voices trailed off and the girls reached for their Bibles, ready to begin studying. I motioned to Tim for us to leave. My departure, like my arrival, was barely acknowledged. With heads bowed, the girls were immersed.

I stepped back into the corridor and looked around. Their voices had carried me far beyond the walls of that hotel room, and now I'd come back to earth—a little dazed, maybe even a little sad that it was over.

My thoughts turned to the long day ahead, and I felt a surge of anxiety kick in. Only one other CNN crew had made it to Chibok after the 2014 kidnapping. Our senior international correspondent Nima Elbagir, a dear friend and outstanding journalist, had led a team to the previously little-known town. On the way there, though, their car had been involved in a serious accident that left some in the crew injured. Road traffic accidents are one thing, clearly beyond anyone's control, but I also knew I was deliberately taking on a different kind of risk that involved militant forces with bloody intent. CNN had flown in Andrew Jones, a British security risk specialist (SRS) to oversee all the security assessments and preparations for the journey. I was going to have to wear an abaya, a headscarf, and a bulletproof vest the entire time I was on the move to protect myself. Andrew was also tasked with checking in with our CNN handlers back in Atlanta via satellite phone at preset times. And before receiving the final green light to set off on this assignment, I'd had to supply critical body identification and next-of-kin details in the event things went very wrong. A part of me simply wanted to shrug off the concerns of the executives far away in Atlanta and toss out the majority of the stifling security measures, but as Andrew made clear, that was impossible. This was Boko Haram we were facing, and the threat they posed was high. I'd be traveling in a convoy along a route that had seen several ambushes in the recent past. If Boko Haram caught wind that the stolen girls and an international journalist were making their way along open roads to Chibok, it would be easy to orchestrate a roadside attack or a kidnapping.

The sun was almost gone by the time I got back to my room. I tried to tamp down my anxieties, reminding myself that there were no other journalists traveling back to Chibok with the girls. My journey would be a world exclusive, the kind of assignment that journalists live for. Turning back to look at the contents of my bag strewn across the bed, I noted that the question reverberating at the back of my mind was far simpler: *But is it actually worth dying for?*

CHAPTER TWO

BEING HOLED UP IN A YOLA HOTEL WITH THE TWENTY-ONE CHIBOK girls felt quite surreal. Having covered their disappearance since the very beginning, I now found their physical presence a little jarring. Just as disconcerting was the sight of soldiers everywhere. The military had failed to protect the hundreds of girls back in 2014 on the night they were swept away by terrorists. Now at least, the Nigerian authorities seemed to be taking no chances with their security. The girls themselves showed no outward signs of fear or discomfort. They had eyes only for one another, constantly nudging, giggling, and whispering among themselves. And even though the reunion with their families was meant to be just for Christmas—at the end of the holiday season, they were supposed to return to the government-run rehabilitation center in Abuja, the nation's capital, where they'd been living—their excitement for this first visit home was plain for all to see.

But after more than two years in captivity, much had changed. These weren't the same girls returning to Chibok who had been stolen under the cover of darkness; they were older now and far removed from their sheltered, preabduction lives in their secluded Christian community. At the same time, Boko Haram was also different. In the intervening years, the terror group had morphed, in tandem with the shifting dynamics in the global war on terror.

As you read this, there may well be a part of you wondering why you should care about this story, about these twenty-one girls, after all this time. The world has moved on, you say. You're probably thinking I should do the same.

But pause and listen to me, just for a moment: I'm not asking you to care about the girls simply out of tenderhearted humanitarianism. I am also asking you to care about these girls out of pure self-interest. If you view what happened to these girls through the lens of national security, you'll see inherent in this tale the potential threat to you, your loved ones, and the global strategic interests of the United States.

Nigeria isn't some far-flung, insignificant, or forgettable nation. With Africa's largest economy and a population of more than 180 million people, it is arguably the most powerful country on the continent. "As Nigeria goes, so goes the rest of Africa" is the commonly held view among most political analysts. The country's president, Muhammadu Buhari, was one of only two African leaders known to have spoken by phone to President Trump in the early days of his new US administration; the other was South Africa's Jacob Zuma. Put simply, the United States and Nigeria enjoy a broad and deep strategic partnership dating all the way back to 1960, the year the latter gained independence from Great Britain. In spite of US concerns about governance, corruption, and human rights abuses, the relationship has survived through the decades and is largely held in place by a host of mutual interests, including trade and the global war on terror.

In fact, the United States is the largest foreign investor in Nigeria, primarily in the petroleum, mining, and wholesale trade sectors. It's worth noting that the nation was also the second largest US export destination in sub-Saharan Africa, to the value of $2.2 billion in 2017. Nigeria, for its part, is well known as a significant exporter of oil to the United States; less publicized is the West African nation's shipments of cocoa, cashew nuts, and animal feed to the States. The two-way trade in goods between the two countries topped $9 billion in 2017.

Meanwhile, Nigeria's leadership role in West Africa and the continent as a whole has made this young nation a critical ally in Washington's battle to beat back the global threat posed by jihadist forces. It took the events of September 11, 2001, to bring that threat into sharper focus. In the days that followed this national tragedy, many of us learned for the first time about the concept of "ungoverned spaces" and how these under- or poorly governed areas open up vacuums that, more often than not, go on to be filled by terrorists. In Afghanistan, for instance, decades of warfare throughout the 1990s reduced the central Asian nation to a failed state. Amid the broken infrastructure and shattered people, Osama bin Laden was able to take refuge. From this safe haven, the al-Qaeda mastermind plotted in staggering detail the events of 9/11, which claimed the lives of nearly three thousand people, the largest loss of life from a terror attack on US soil.

The availability of "ungoverned space" made that possible.

Turning to North Africa, we see how a local Islamist militant group borne out of the 1990s fight against Algeria's secular government aligned itself with al-Qaeda to become al-Qaeda in the Islamic Magreb (AQIM). In the years since 9/11, this Al Qaeda affiliate expanded to Mali, Mauritania, and Niger, entrenching itself in large tracts of land in the Sahara and the Sahel, that wide, ungoverned space in northern Mali and southern Algeria. From there, the group and its local affiliates launched attacks in Mali, Burkina Faso, Niger, Ivory Coast, and Senegal.

Fast forward to December 25, 2009, when the threat posed by "ungoverned spaces" once again stole the global spotlight. The 278 passengers and eleven crew members boarding Northwest Airlines Flight 253 in Amsterdam bound for Detroit had no idea Umar Farouk Abdulmutallab, a twenty-three-year-old Nigerian student, was in their midst with explosives tucked away in his underpants and a goal of bringing down the plane. As the Airbus A330 descended toward Detroit, its passengers described hearing what sounded like a firecracker and watched in horror as the young man went up in flames, a fire that quickly spread to the wall and the plane's carpet. Four quick-thinking passengers overwhelmed Abdulmutallab, put out the fire, and ensured he could be taken into custody by US authorities the moment the plane landed. In the days that followed, we learned that the "Underwear Bomber," as he became known, was a young man from a wealthy northern Nigerian family. He had attended posh boarding schools in England, grown up in luxury, and traveled the world. Initially, details of how and when Abdulmutallab became radicalized were unclear, but the role of the Yemen-based al-Qaeda in the Arabian Peninsula (AQAP) was quickly established. Al-Qaeda's links to Yemen go all the way back to the Afghan jihad against the Soviets in the 1980s. But it was Yemen's fractious civil war that cleared a path for the offshoot AQAP to flourish. Safely shielded within the borders of the poorest country in the Middle East, the group's senior leadership, including the US-born militant cleric Anwar al-Awlaki, hatched a plan to bring down a US-bound jetliner. Abdulmuttalab traveled to Yemen to receive his training, and by the time he said goodbye to al-Awlaki, he was convinced it was his religious obligation to carry out jihad. On the second day of his trial in Detroit, in October 2011, this attempted bomber suddenly pleaded guilty to all charges. At no point during the brief proceedings did he express remorse or regret. Instead he delivered this message to the court, from a pre-written statement:

> I attempted to use an explosive device which in the US law is a weapon of mass destruction, which I call a blessed weapon to save the lives of innocent Muslims, for US use of weapons of mass destruction on Muslim populations in Afghanistan, Iraq, Yemen, and beyond . . .

Abdulmutallab's failed bid to murder the 289 people aboard Flight 253 earned him an automatic life sentence with no chance of parole. It gave the rest of us traveling through the nation's airports the full body X-ray scanner, which allows officials to see through passengers' clothes and erodes yet more of travelers' sense of privacy. Before that Christmas Day attempt, only a small number of airports had deployed such machines on a trial basis. Thanks to what happened in the skies above Detroit, the US Transportation Security Administration decided in November 2010 to make the scanners, officially known as advanced imaging technology (AIT) machines, the primary screening method in many airports around the country.

This attempted attack was possible due to ungoverned spaces.

By all accounts, the young Nigerian felt confused, disgruntled, and lacked a sense of belonging to his social surroundings. Boko Haram has similarly been able to successfully exploit a sense of alienation among northern Nigeria's youth ever since the group burst into view in the early 2000s. At that time, the Nigerian terror group's grievances were decidedly local, its focus on the inequities and economic hardships facing the people of Maiduguri, the capital of the northeastern state of Borno. However, a series of increasingly violent clashes with security forces triggered a change in Boko Haram's agenda. It evolved from local to regional ambitions, before arriving at a national mission, of which establishing a caliphate, or an Islamic state, became the central goal.

Widely dismissed at the outset as no more than a band of murderous fanatics, Boko Haram declared such a caliphate in 2014 in the aftermath of its capture of Gwoza, a town with a population of 265,000 not far from Chibok. This state spanned the towns and villages under its control in Borno, as well as those in neighboring Yobe and Adamawa States. By some estimates at one point the group controlled an area of twenty thousand square miles—roughly the size of Belgium. By that time, theirs was a transnational agenda, with violence spilling across Nigeria's porous borders to disrupt life in Cameroon, Niger, and Chad. In 2015, a year after the girls disappeared, Boko Haram pledged allegiance to ISIS. In a released audio message posted on the Internet, the group's wild-eyed leader, Abubakar Shekau, purportedly declared, "We announce our allegiance to the caliph . . . and will hear and obey in times of difficulty and prosperity." The pledge was accepted in a separate audio recording, in which a supposed ISIS spokesman, Abu Mohammed al-Adnani, hailed the expansion of the caliphate to western Africa and congratulated his "jihadi brothers" there.

In 2016, ideological differences led to the splintering of Boko Haram into two distinct jihadist movements, with the longtime leader Shekau retaining control of one faction and the ISIS-endorsed Abu Musab al-Barnawi taking the helm of the other. At this stage the terror outfit also suffered a host of setbacks, thanks to hard-won military gains by the Nigerian military. This left the militants with ever-shrinking territorial control and their nascent caliphate in ruins. President Buhari has said over and over that Boko Haram is defeated. But it would be folly to declare victory and simply write it off. Let's not forget that between the two factions, the group still controls hundreds of miles of bushland that make up the vast Sambisa Forest in Borno State, and from this stronghold they still launch attacks in Nigeria's north and across the border in neighboring Cameroon, Chad, and Niger. According to BBC Monitoring, in 2017 the militant group targeted all four countries in 150 attacks, which ranged from armed assaults to suicide bombings. This is a significant step up from the 127 attacks Boko Haram reportedly mounted in 2016, and in both years the majority of the strikes occurred in northern Nigeria. On February 19, 2018, the ISIS-allied Barnawi faction, Islamic State West Africa Province (ISWAP), stormed the northeastern Nigerian town of Dapchi in Yobe State and abducted 110 schoolgirls, some as young as eleven, from their all-girls boarding school. A few weeks later, the group returned more than a hundred of them, but refused to release fifteen-year old Leah Sharibu, the lone Christian among them, because of her refusal to convert to Islam. At the time of this writing, Sharibu remains in captivity, despite the widespread pleas for her release. On March 1, 2018, Boko Haram attacked a military outpost in the remote town of Rann in Borno State. The site housed tens of thousands of people displaced by the group's unending rampage. Dozens were killed, including three UN staff members, and the attackers made off with three aid workers: Sifura Khorsa and Hauwa Mohammed Liman, who worked for the International Committee of the Red Cross (ICRC), and Alice Loksha, who'd been helping the needy in a center supported by UNICEF. The twenty-five-year old Khorsa was executed on September 16. At the time of her killing, ISWAP warned it would also execute Liman, Loksha, and Leah Sharibu if its demands—which have never been made public—weren't met within a month. On October 16, the ICRC received word that Liman had been executed. The group also threatened to keep Alice and Leah as "slaves for life."

The reality is that even though the militants have been pushed back in Nigeria, the world is now dealing with multiple entities, and the chaos and accompanying bloodshed continues. There is also no indication that the split means that these terrorists have abandoned hopes of establishing a caliphate in Nigeria. It's in this group's DNA to disappear from view, regroup, and bounce back with devastating effectiveness.

It remains to be seen what the alliance between Abu Musab al-Barnawi's Boko Haram faction and ISIS will become. Back in 2015, when Shekau orchestrated the initial union, a number of experts were quick to write it off, dismissing the move as no more than a propaganda coup for ISIS, and evidence of Boko Haram's weakened position in its fight against the Nigerian state. Today, the standing of ISIS is much different. Coalition forces in Iraq have driven ISIS militants from Mosul. Meanwhile, across the border, the Syrian Democratic Forces have routed them from their self-declared capital in Raqqa, liberating a civilian population long held hostage and the victims of unspeakable cruelty. ISIS is in disarray, and as it runs, the existence of ungoverned spaces and the threats they pose once again come into view. The group is now a death cult in search of new safe havens from which it can plot fresh murderous deeds.

Boko Haram's mass abduction of the Chibok girls in 2014 deserves to hold our attention. It highlights not only the group's audacity and tactical ability to pull off a spectacular act of terrorism, but also the precarious hold the Nigerian state has had on the northeastern part of the country, ever since the group rose up in the early 2000s. More than two million people have been displaced in the region and tens of thousands are eking out an existence in huge, overcrowded settlements. Food, water, and proper shelter are in short supply in these squalid camps, and there are numerous reports of women and girls being sexually assaulted and exploited by the very officials meant to protect them. Despite widespread longing to return to their homes, many of the displaced are too afraid to return to what's left of their communities because of the continuing unrest. Sadly, this conflict is far from over.

Many Americans are battle weary after years of fighting in Iraq and the seemingly unending war in Afghanistan. I understand why people in this country are more inclined than ever to want to stay focused on the domestic problems, which need to be tackled here in the US homeland. President Trump's shrieks of "America First," "Make America Great Again," and his withdrawal of the United States from multilateral agreements such as the Iran nuclear deal, the Paris climate accord, and the Trans-Pacific Partnership soothes nerves frayed by years of foreign intervention and international deals that at first glance, it could be argued, have done little to improve the lives of ordinary Americans. Yet these campaign slogans and diplomatic reversals belie a simple truth: America cannot afford to turn its back on its friends and allies, because globalization has made the world smaller. We are more interconnected than ever before.

It is a fact that remains front of mind for those working in the US State Department and the US Agency for International Development, many of whom balk at the Trump administration's repeated efforts to slash foreign aid budgets by up to 37 percent, though money sent abroad makes up a mere 1 percent of federal spending. If such a proposal were ever approved by the US Congress, the result would be even greater instability in the developing world, in places like northern Nigeria and a higher threat level for all of us living on US soil.

The interdependence of US national security and global security is a fact not lost on this country's counterterrorism apparatus. At the time of this writing, there are 7,200 US troops spread across Africa. Their missions are conducted under the radar and come to the surface only when things go horribly wrong—as was the case in Niger back in October 2017, when four US soldiers were killed and two others wounded alongside their Nigerien counterparts in an ambush by suspected ISIS militants. As demonstrated multiple times since 9/11, jihadist networks span the globe, and exporting terror is now easier than ever, thanks in part to the Internet, the low cost of travel, and myriad available routes. We can ill afford to ignore the actions of any terror group simply because its concerns appear to be entirely local, or its murderous activities are taking place far away. Terrorism in the twenty-first century has no borders. So with that in mind, I'm urging you to remove the boundaries on your thinking. What happened that harrowing night in Chibok wasn't just Boko Haram triggering a slow-moving nightmare for the people of that quiet community. It was also a flare illuminating the path of a transnational terror group with mutating ambitions.

One last thing: what happened in northeastern Nigeria in 2014 also offers a microcosm of the clash between opposing forces fighting to reshape our world. The mass abduction brought into focus a larger global narrative unfolding at this very moment. We are in the midst of an epic power struggle between militant Islam and the West, between progressivism and conservatism, between globalists and nativists, between a hoped-for open future benefitting many versus a set-in-stone, closed-off past rewarding the few. Boko Haram's actions in Chibok spotlight the efforts of regressive forces to deny an education and autonomy to huge swathes of people in an attempt to keep them underfoot and make them easier to control. The education advocate and Nobel Prize winner Malala Yousafzai, herself a survivor of the Pakistani Taliban's violent efforts to thwart her education, has repeatedly spoken of the fear felt by extremists, saying, "They are afraid of books and pens, the power of education frightens them. They are afraid of women, the power of the voice of women frightens them."

As individuals and as a country, to know the intention of groups like Boko Haram and to still look away from the Chibok girls is to betray our shared humanity. The horrors that these girls have endured do not belong in a Nigerian vacuum. The place for every single one of them is right at the heart of the conversation about the global threats America is facing, and the development of a more holistic counterterrorism response that might just make all of us a little safer.

CHAPTER THREE

A SEA OF PARCHED EARTH: THIS IS HOW CHIBOK LOOKS TO A VISITOR arriving here for the first time. The land, a patchwork of bald spots and swathes of straw-like savanna grass, lies flat for long stretches until bulging rock hills suddenly rise up and break the monotony. With the Sahara to the north, this is a forlorn-looking place of subdued yellows and hushed browns, bursts of green from gnarly trees. Straggly bushes haphazardly dot the desertlike terrain as nature's only concession in this muted landscape.

At every turn, the poverty that has long stalked this area and its population of just under seventy thousand is on display. The heart of Chibok, a dilapidated town center, sits bare except for a handful of half-empty stores and market stalls. Money is hard to come by in these parts, so business is often slow, leaving traders crouching in doorways or lounging outdoors in the shade with little to do other than swat flies and trade pleasantries with passersby. There are no paved roads, only uneven, dusty paths, which most locals navigate on foot or by some means of transportation with two wheels. You won't find indoor plumbing or electricity in the unpainted mud brick homes, and it's a rarity in the faded, crumbling cement ones. With only one mobile network and four telecom masts covering this area of approximately 840 square miles, cell phone service ranges from spotty to nonexistent. What you will find throughout this semiarid corner of the world are farms because, first and foremost, these are peaceful farming people. It's a way of life that goes back multiple generations in most families and runs deep in the blood of Chibok's Christians, who make up 90 percent of this community. According to their traditional beliefs, the land is the foundation of wealth, and farming must always be undertaken seriously. The earth is to be loved and revered, never bought or sold, only passed by inheritance from one family member to another. This long-held connection to the land is the main reason some Chibok residents have refused to move on from the area despite countless years without decent infrastructure or basic services and more recently, the ever-present threat of Boko Haram violence. Instead, they stay to work the hardscrabble earth, growing crops for personal use and as a source of income. This community's enduring relationship with farming isn't the product of chance, but rather a bond carefully, patiently fostered over time.

For the daughters of Chibok, the land carries an additional significance. They are typically given a small plot before they reach puberty—a pathway to developing an early sense of responsibility as well as financial independence. This nurturing of female autonomy in a part of the world where it is much more common to curb female independence stands out as remarkable—making this harmonious Christian-majority town, nestled deep within a Muslim-majority region, all the more noteworthy.

Yet for Priscilla, Mary, Saa, and Dorcas, four Chibok girls born in the late 1990s, the trials and traditions of life in this part of the world were nothing out of the ordinary. After all, their entire childhoods had been spent in northeastern Nigeria, and it was all they'd ever known. The young lives of these four very different girls had largely followed the same script, played out in simple homes and rudimentary primary schools, each act shaped by their hardworking parents. Before their personal bedrooms gave way to the bustling dormitories of their secondary school years, life as they knew it was a quintessentially undramatic affair.

As far back as Priscilla could remember, her parents had worked the land. It was never easy. They made their living from growing maize, beans, and groundnuts (peanuts). The latter is a highly profitable but time-consuming crop that more often than not is beset by weeds, disease, or pests—or sometimes all three at once. In keeping with local tradition, before she turned twelve, this tall, slender girl with doe-like eyes and a shy smile was given her very own piece of land, carved from the larger family plot and located a short ten-minute walk from their home. Priscilla had never experienced this kind of excitement before, and the thrill of ownership never faded. In contrast, the appeal of preparing the soil, planting the seeds, controlling the weeds, and harvesting her groundnuts disappeared almost immediately. Priscilla's lack of enthusiasm for farming never bothered her father, Mallum. He had eight children and Priscilla was his fifth-born and by far his favorite. So the fact that she didn't care for tilling or toiling wasn't a problem. Whenever she visited the patch, if her father was there working on the family plot, he always stopped and urged Priscilla to find a comfortable place to sit and rest. Then this elderly man with his reed-thin frame and wizened features would busy himself with the backbreaking work of tending to his daughter's crop of groundnuts. By the time she was a teenager, whenever she was back from boarding school for the holidays, whether it was on the farm or at home, Mallum wanted her close by. He loved these opportunities to regale his daughter with stories from his past and lessons for her future.

Rather than out with her father working the land, Priscilla was more likely to be found with Rachel, her mother, in the family's outdoor cooking area. Here she learned the intricacies of preparing local Nigerian dishes, with their many stages of grinding, chopping, peeling, boiling, frying, and always copiously seasoning. By her late teens, Priscilla confidently boasted about her cooking skills and how much her family enjoyed her signature dish made from kuka, the leaves of the Baobab tree, cooked with meat, beans, spices, and oil.

Priscilla's lifetime ambition, however, lay far beyond the kitchen. From the time she was a young girl at her local primary school she dreamed of becoming a doctor, and that dream was still firmly in place when she left home for the Government Girls Secondary School in Chibok. With her parents in tow, Priscilla traveled for just under an hour by car to her new boarding school, ready to start junior secondary one (JSS1), the first of six years of schooling on offer. Originally built in the 1940s by American missionaries from the Illinois-based Church of the Brethren, the Girls Secondary School didn't become a government institution, with the mission of educating the children of Chibok and nearby areas, until the 1970s.

Beyond the school's wrought iron gates stood a cluster of nearly two dozen single-story buildings. These boxy, utilitarian structures housed classrooms, dorms, staff quarters, and a kitchen and storage room. New students like Priscilla were greeted by unwelcoming metal doors and banks of large windows, many of which had lost their glass at some unknown point in the past. Almost all the buildings were painted the same dusky yellow, which matched the sandy soil they were built on. In the blinding light of the sun, you'd be forgiven for thinking that the school was actually folding into its surroundings, becoming less real in front of your eyes. The main classroom bloc was the exception to this color rule. It stood awkwardly apart with its blue-green walls, an ironic touch that brought to mind sea foam in this parched, semiarid landscape.

By the time twelve-year old Priscilla showed up on her first day, it had become routine in Chibok for most girls to complete primary school and then progress to secondary school. Compared with the rest of Borno State, in which Chibok is located, where more than 70 percent of primary-school-age girls are out of school, the percentage of girls progressing in their education in Chibok represents by far one of the highest rates in Nigeria. To move beyond the boundaries of this mainly Christian community is to find oneself in locales in northern Nigeria where more than 50 percent of girls will have already marked the defining milestone of marriage before they can turn their minds to celebrating their sixteenth birthday. In most towns and villages up and down this region, conservative Islam and restrictive social mores lay the groundwork for gender inequity. All the while in Chibok, education and opportunity are prized every bit as much for girls as for boys, further confirming this town's status as an anomaly in this problem-ridden part of the world.

Neither of Priscilla's parents was formally educated, but they worked hard to pay her secondary-school fees, which amounted to a little under ten US dollars a year. And they wholeheartedly championed their daughter's vison for the future. During school breaks, her parents ceaselessly prodded and reminded her to stay focused on her studies. As she made her way through secondary school, Priscilla increasingly understood her responsibilities, as well as the idea that whatever success she achieved was not simply to make *her* life better, it also had to usher in good things for those she loved most. It was this "benefit for all factor" that motivated Priscilla every bit as much as it spurred on her parents' support for her education.

They needed her to succeed because money was perennially tight in their family. Their day-to-day existence was shaped by the challenges of life in a mud brick house with no running water, no power or cooling, and having to rely on the land to feed, clothe, and cover every expense. Yet an overwhelming love shone through all the hardships and deprivation. Memories of her large family eating and playing together formed the foundation of Priscilla's young life and sense of self. And in times of trouble, it was to these memories that she returned again and again in search of comfort.

Mary's parents, Gaji and Felicie, were also full-time farmers without a formal education. But they grew a larger assortment of crops than Priscilla's family did—beans, groundnuts, guinea corn, and okra—which afforded them a relatively more comfortable life and the ability to buy their daughter frequent treats. They'd wanted siblings for her, but that wish remained unfulfilled. This meant their round-faced daughter, with her long, gangly limbs and warm, infectious giggle, was the center of their lives, and they took every opportunity to spoil her. When she was younger, before her departure for secondary school, Mary particularly looked forward to her father's homecomings every Wednesday, because most times he showed up with a small gift. Often it was fruit, but on occasion it was a new dress. In time, she'd amassed quite a collection of outfits. As the years passed and Mary returned home during the school breaks, the gift giving continued, but there was never any doubt as to which dress from her father was her favorite. The moment he had pulled the yellow gown out of the bag, she had fallen in love with it. Mary adored the brightness, its intricate beadwork around the neckline, and its length just above her knee. Years later, when the dress was lost in a blaze in her home, she'd wept bitterly.

Mary kept her ever-growing pile of gifts in her large bedroom, along with her books, a desk, and a small stereo. Her father had purchased the latter on one of his trips to Nigeria's commercial capital, Lagos.

The sound system was undoubtedly special to Mary, but it wasn't her most prized childhood possession. That title actually belonged to her bed, though not because it was exceptional looking. It was just a basic frame with a yellow foam mattress, but it facilitated her favorite pastime: sleeping. Whenever she wasn't at school, she retreated to her bedroom at every possible opportunity, kicked off her slippers, and gleefully dove into bed. Mary was at her happiest in this spot, stretched out beneath the covers, seemingly without a care in the world, even when she had a long list of chores to complete. Most days her parents turned a blind eye to the hours of lazing around. They even pretended to believe Mary when she lied about repeated headaches, which meant she couldn't possibly get out of bed to help her mother in the kitchen—yet again.

They let her get away with it most days, but not always. There were those mornings before the sun was blazing in the sky when her mother put her foot down and stormed into Mary's room. "Wake up! Up! Come and help me in the kitchen. Now!" Felicie's tone made it abundantly clear that there would be no game playing that day. Without delay, a sheepish-looking Mary rolled herself out of bed and followed her short, plump mother to the kitchen. Soon lying in bed was a distant memory, as task after task was assigned to her: washing dishes, drawing water from the well, sweeping the house, and on some days grinding maize into *semo*, a fine cornmeal. The cooking of *semo* itself is a grueling process that requires no small amount of patience and elbow strength. Ladles of water are scooped into a pot containing the cornmeal and continuously stirred until a gooey, spongy mass appears. The sight of women, doubled over pots with lips drawn, beads of sweat dotting creased brows as they stir, fold, twist, and whip their version of *semo* into a doughy, squishy blob is a common memory for many who've spent significant amounts of time in Nigeria, Sierra Leone, and Ghana. In Mary's household, while her mother's arm grew heavy and sore from turning over the *semo*, there'd always be a pot of gloopy soup or stewed vegetables cooking, to be eaten with the squishy balls of cornmeal.

For most Chibok families living off the land, barring Sundays, bad weather, a major family emergency, or the celebration of Christian holidays, part of every day is spent on the farm, for at least one if not both parents. Unlike Priscilla's family plot, which was barely a ten-minute walk from home, Mary's family farm was thirty to forty minutes away. Several times a week while she was still in primary school, once all the cooking was done, Felicie carefully would fill dishes with the piping-hot food and pack them into a basket before they set off for the farm. Often Mary's father had already been hard at work for several hours. But the food they brought would be his breakfast and provided a needed break, one of the few he allowed himself to take throughout the day. With stomachs rumbling, Mary, Felicie, and Gaji always settled under a tree to enjoy the tasty home-cooked meal. Mother and daughter ate together from the same dish, while her father had a plate all to himself. In those moments, sitting there flanked by her parents, Mary's stomach and heart were completely full.

Leaving for the Government Girls Secondary School, which was two hours away from her beloved home, had been terribly painful for Mary. The very first time her parents dropped her off, she wept uncontrollably. The mere thought of being separated from loved ones seemed life-ending to the then twelve-year-old Mary. She bemoaned the quality of the school's meals, which had to be eaten outside classrooms or in dormitories because there was no dining hall, and each time left her with a stomachache. Then there was the strict discipline, which essentially amounted to a whipping with a cane or being made to kneel down on the concrete floor whenever a school rule was broken. All of it triggered a steady stream of complaints from Mary. The constant upset became another excuse for her parents to spoil their only child even more, leading to a constant supply of edible treats, on-demand pocket money, and promises of weekly parental visits. But nothing could take away the homesickness she felt, so she cried throughout her six years at the school. Her tears fell even faster whenever a visit home ended and it was time to head back to the dorms. For all the emotional distress, there was never a conversation about her leaving the school. As far as Mary's parents were concerned, she had to get an education, and if that meant crying every day for years, then so be it.

Felicie dreamed of her Mary one day becoming a state governor or maybe even president of Nigeria. She never tired of reminding her daughter how such accomplishments would ease the family's financial burdens. So along with the treats and pocket money came the words "focus" and "study." In primary school, Mary had pictured herself becoming an airline pilot, but that began to seem less attractive as she made her way through secondary school. She ultimately settled on the idea of becoming an accountant, an odd choice given her weak math skills. But by her calculation, accountants were always in demand and commanded hefty salaries, which would be a boon to her and her doting parents.

For Chibok's Christians, devotion to the land is matched only by their passion for Jesus Christ; these are the twin tenets of life in this community. From birth to death, the focus is on God above and what comes from the earth beneath their feet. For these Christians, most of whom belong to the Church of the Brethren in Nigeria (Ekklesiyar Yan uwa a Nigeria, or EYN), faith isn't a hidden-away, occasional pursuit; it is a fervent, communal, all-consuming affair, the center of which is daily worship. Every morning in almost every single Christian home in Chibok, the same ritual has played out for decades, adults and children rising from beds and mattresses, wiping sleep from their eyes, readying themselves to worship and praise the Lord.

This identical scene also played out about an hour's drive from

Chibok in Askira, where Saa and her family lived. Saa can't remember a time when her Christian faith didn't frame her life. As the daughter of a onetime pastor turned Bible class teacher, she was introduced to the concept of God when she was still a baby. Some of her earliest memories include being with her parents and five brothers at five a.m. for morning devotion and then gathering again in the evenings. As soon as she was old enough, her parents sent her off to Sunday school. As the years went by, a host of church groups increasingly occupied her time, and this pretty girl with full cheeks and a quiet confidence fostered a deep faith.

Thanks to the teacher's salary her father received and income gained from selling the extra corn, beans, and peanuts they grew on their large plot of land, Saa enjoyed a comfortable upbringing. Her big house sat in a large compound with two mango trees and was separated from the neighbors by a fence. The family boasted their own well and generator. They also owned a couple of cows as well as sheep and goats; so if money was ever a problem, they could sell some of their livestock for extra cash.

But if there'd been money problems during her young years, Saa was never aware of them. She was a happy, though on occasion whiny child, especially when she wasn't getting her way. Being the only girl in the family definitely came with its perks, like having her own bedroom, as well as a television and DVD player, which made Saa a standout among friends in her corner of Askira.

Saa's love of school started back when she was a pupil in the neighborhood's Low Cost Primary School. Her older brother Peter, with whom she shared a birthday four years apart, was also enrolled there at the same time, which was an unending source of joy for his little sister. Saa enjoyed nothing more than trailing her brother all over the small compound, though how pleased he was with the situation remained unknown. Even in primary school she was an outstanding student. Finishing within the top three in her class brought gifts of money or clothes. When she finished top in primary 5, her father, Moses—whom she lovingly called "Baba," the Hausa word for father—bought her the bicycle Saa had been so eager to own. She'd already spent hours learning how to ride on her brothers' bikes, so by the time her beautiful pink two-wheeler arrived, she was ready to go fearlessly flying around the yard. The only person she readily allowed on her bike was her beloved brother Peter. The rest of her brothers were forbidden from even touching it. When it came to Saa's friends, once again she had to think long and hard about whether they deserved such a treat.

For all the perks that came with being the only girl in her family, there were also disadvantages. Being saddled with almost all the household chores was probably the most annoying of all. Throughout Chibok and the other towns and villages spread across Nigeria's north, most girls are expected to start their day washing dishes, collecting water, sweeping the floors, and helping their mothers in the kitchen, and only once those chores are done can they turn their thoughts to learning. After school, another to-do list waited: collect more water, clean the house, help prepare food, and wash more dishes. Like most girls in this region, Saa's mother, Rebecca, began preparing her for this path of servitude as soon as she could. But unlike most of her schoolmates, Saa wasn't even in her teens when her mother began traveling with the church choir, and she found herself with the responsibility of running the household and ensuring that her five brothers and father were fed and cared for. It was an enormous undertaking for an eleven-year-old girl, and though she asked for help from her siblings, she was quickly rebuffed—even by Ayuba, who was four years younger, but still felt empowered enough to reject her pleas. "Housework is for females," he said, before sauntering off proudly.

In her mother's absence, Saa knew there was no point turning to her father for help. Unlike her mother, who could talk and talk and talk, her baba said little. His preference was to lie under the mango tree in their yard and listen to the radio. The only time he could be relied on to intervene was if he actually saw one of his children engaged in a troubling act. In those moments he would call the entire family together to talk things through and pray. All of this meant Saa was left to juggle her schoolwork and the responsibility of running the household on her own.

While her parents had no qualms about loading all the domestic chores onto Saa's shoulders, they also strongly supported her passion for school. In fact, they were devoted advocates for education thanks to the time her father had spent in a pastors' training school, where he learned basic English, and in turn, had taught Saa's mother. The experience reshaped their appreciation of education, and when it came to their own six children they wholeheartedly encouraged them to work hard in school and aim to attend university. Surprisingly, there was little to no distinction in the level of expectation and encouragement doled out to Saa versus her five brothers. Saa was encouraged to be whatever she wanted in life—with one exception, becoming a teacher like her father. Baba was adamant that teaching would be a poor life choice because in his view there was no way to make a decent living within the profession. But he needn't have worried, because Saa had a very different idea of where her life was headed. She was going to be a doctor. Her decision wasn't predicated on how much money she stood to make, but rather the impact she could have. Before Saa left for boarding school, her mother had suddenly taken ill late one night in 2010. The nearby local government hospital was closed due to its striking workforce, and there was nowhere else in the vicinity to take her. With fear and despair rising, Saa watched as Rebecca's condition worsened rapidly and her mother slipped perilously close to death. Her survival was due to the lifesaving treatment she received from a family friend who'd been through medical school. It was in that moment Saa decided she would become a doctor, a profession that would allow her to make a difference in her community and to be on hand to save those she loved most.

She actually joined the Chibok school in its final year, senior secondary three (SS3), leaving behind her initial secondary school in Askira because her parents believed that in out-of-the-way Chibok, their daughter would be safe from Boko Haram's Islamic militancy. They told themselves that there Saa was beyond the group's widening tide of attacks on schools in major population centers—offensives intended to dismantle secular education across the three neighboring northern states of Borno, Yola, and Adamawa. Unlike Mary, who cried and complained without end, Saa bore her new school's cracked walls with broken windows, the crowded dormitories where most juniors slept on the floor, and the cramped classrooms of close to a hundred students, where she sat in groups of twos and threes to share benches attached to metal desks, without complaint. Her focus lay elsewhere—her life plan: secondary school, followed by university, then medical school, and returning home to help one and all. To Saa that was what really mattered.

When it came to their firstborn, Dorcas's parents believed their daughter could do no wrong. She was always well mannered and perfectly behaved, an all-around easy child. To her mother, Esther, this girl was the "messiah" of the family, the one with almond-shaped eyes and delicate features, the one who would help lift them all out of poverty. They made no secret of their belief that Dorcas was totally different from her four younger siblings: Happy, Marvellous, Ibrahim, and Missy.

The unusual story of how she got her name was a long-standing family favorite, told repeatedly and often. Long before their courtship and marriage, Esther's husband, Yakubu, would drive his Hilux pickup truck around town with a poster of a white baby girl plastered on the driver's side door. He'd grown up as an orphan and thought often about the parents he never knew. He'd bought the image in the market, and the cute, smiling infant somehow captured all his deep-seated yearning for a family. It also masked his secretly held fears that he would never find someone to love him or have a child of his own. So this unknown little one, to whom he had absolutely no real connection, became his "baby." Yakubu named her Dorcas, after the Hebrew woman found in the fifth book of the New Testament, Acts 9:36, "Now there was in Joppa a disciple named Tabitha, which translated, means Dorcas. She was full of good works and acts of charity" (ESV). According to the Bible, upon Dorcas's sudden death, as the entire community stood weeping and mourning her loss, she was brought back to life by Saint Peter. To Yakubu, the biblical Dorcas was a model Christian, with the perfect name for his model baby.

He also decided to have some fun with the situation and set about trying to convince his passengers that the white child plastered on his vehicle was actually his kid. This became a well-known joke in Chibok, producing a warm chuckle whenever it was shared. In due course, he met and married Esther, who soon gave birth to their first child, a girl. In keeping with their Chibok traditions, the day came when all their friends and relatives gathered in the local church for the naming ceremony. The pastor readied himself for the big reveal: "And the baby's name is—" he started. But before he could even get the words out, the entire church yelled in one voice, "Dorcas!" Though the baby was officially named Maida in honor of Esther's aunt, the name Dorcas had belonged to her long before she was conceived, and that would be the name that stuck.

Dorcas was a genteel child. Even as a toddler, while other young kids were busy rolling around in the dirt, she preferred to sit in her own special chair and play cook with a large empty tomato can that doubled as her cooking pot, using sand and water as her ingredients. She amused herself for hours and never got her clothes dirty. Simple things made her happy, including looking after her parents and siblings. As soon as she was old enough, Dorcas began shaving her father's head with a razor, and from that point onward, Yakubu left all his grooming needs squarely in the hands of his daughter.

Meanwhile, with Esther on the road buying and selling brilliantly hued fabrics for clothing, cushion covers, and bedsheets, Dorcas was caring for her siblings and running the household by her early teens. Before long, she was leading morning and evening devotion with her entire family, reading the Bible verses, singing the praises, and praying for them all.

She displayed a maturity far beyond her years, which may have been the result of living with her grandmother when she was seven or eight. It was during this time that Esther had returned to college to earn her Higher National Diploma. In the absence of her mother, Dorcas followed her grandmother everywhere: to the local government building where she worked as a cook, and to the family farm, where they planted groundnuts, maize, guinea corn, beans, and sesame. Just like the other girls, Dorcas was also given her own strip of land. But it was her grandmother who stepped up to do the majority of the work, gladly taking care of her groundnuts and beans while her granddaughter was away at school.

Esther proudly proclaimed her high expectations for Dorcas. Over the years she told anyone who would listen that her firstborn would be the one to head to university and come away with a bachelor's degree. She talked regularly with Dorcas about her future, asking about her dreams and ambitions. "Do you want to be a foolish housewife or a trader?" In time Dorcas decided she wanted to teach at a university and put all her energies into making that career choice a reality. Esther thought the plan was a good one and readily gave her blessing. As far as Dorcas was concerned, the Government Girls Secondary School in Chibok was neither the best of schools nor the worst in the region. Like Saa, Dorcas was a relative newcomer, having joined in SS3 after leaving a school in Maiduguri, the Borno State capital. Maiduguri, which was also the birthplace of Boko Haram, found itself in the terror group's crosshairs and the target of one attack after another, all of which led to Dorcas pleading with her parents to transfer her somewhere else where she'd feel safe. Once she was enrolled in Chibok, Dorcas did what she always did, working hard and keeping out of trouble.

Despite the ever-expanding trail of death and destruction caused by the insurgents in Borno, Yobe, and Adamawa, Boko Haram still remained a peripheral concern to the girls in Chibok, and they certainly didn't feel particularly vulnerable or believe they were facing a specific threat. The girls were just excited to be on the brink of finishing secondary school and had already cast their minds forward to new academic pursuits: different schools and exciting new adventures on the horizon. Likewise, their parents believed that their beloved daughters were safe in the Chibok boarding school. No significant conversations about fears for the girls' safety took place in the homes of Priscilla, Mary, Saa, and Dorcas. The Chibok school authorities and local government leaders never sent letters of warning to the parents or called a parent-teacher meeting, so the belief among these four families was that the situation in the Government Girls Secondary School in Chibok and the town itself was under control.

Plus, they had faith. Both the parents and the girls told themselves God would always watch over them and ensure no one came to any harm.

CHAPTER FOUR

EACH DAY AS THE SUN SET ON CHIBOK AND THE PACE OF LIFE SLOWED to a crawl, Priscilla, now eighteen, prepared for the approaching night across town in the girls' secondary school. The school had no electricity. So when the sun finally disappeared from the northern skies, all parts of the compound—the cramped classroom blocks, the sparse library, the bathrooms without running water, and the sprawling hostels—sat in near-complete, inky blackness. By that hour, only the beams of flashlights cut the impenetrable darkness, as Priscilla and the others wandered back and forth between each other's rooms, chuckling and exchanging bits of gossip, or finishing off their homework in a tucked-away corner.

The absence of basic amenities like electricity and indoor plumbing didn't bother this soft-spoken young girl—after all, these were the very same conditions Priscilla grappled with when she was back at home. In school, studying by flashlight every evening and then grabbing her bucket to collect water from the school's well the next morning was inconvenient, certainly, but her entire life had been fashioned by inconvenience. So when it came to expectations of comfort, Priscilla didn't have any. All she knew was that she was fortunate beyond measure to be receiving an education.

There were hundreds of girls, every one of them assigned to one of four dorm rooms in the four hostels. The hostels, in turn, were dubbed "Houses," each with its own unique name—Ganna, Mwoda, Jetau, and Likama. On some evenings, Priscilla spotted a couple of the female teachers moving among the girls, checking on how they were doing. Many of the school's teachers lived in the cluster of staff quarters within view of the hostels. So on the occasions when they suddenly appeared, neither Priscilla nor her friends gave it much thought; the girls simply carried on with whatever they were doing. Knowing there were adults nearby gave them a sense of comfort and safety.

The only people Priscilla expected to see on a nightly basis were the school's duo of nocturnal caretakers. First there was the graying Mr. Jida, somewhere in his seventies. He'd been there watching over the girls for as long as anyone could remember. Strikingly dark with tribal markings of a short vertical line on each cheek, he'd appear each evening on his bicycle. By then the day's classes were long done and the girls were back in their hostels. His concrete lookout post was a small shelter beside the hostel compound's gate that was so far away this wiry old man couldn't actually see the buildings or the girls he was supposed to keep safe through the night. Not that he was keeping a close watch. In fact, depending on whom you asked, some girls said you were more likely to find him curled up and fast asleep in that very spot with his trusty bicycle propped up against a nearby wall.

Meanwhile, closer to the hostels was an even older man. Pris-.

cilla and the others called him Kaka, which means "grandfather" in Hausa. Bony, with a head of white hair, he was tasked with constantly patrolling the area around the dorm rooms, but his energy had left him long ago. So when he arrived each evening, he plopped down on a stool by the hostels and remained in that corner for most of the night. Yet whatever he lacked in stamina, he replaced with geniality. He regularly soothed angry tempers and mediated arguments between the girls, which made Priscilla adore him.

When Monday, April 14, 2014, rolled around, all the Chibok schoolgirls were focused on one thing: exams. Their Senior School Certificate Examinations (SSCE) had been under way since the beginning of the month and would last till the end of June. Every single girl understood the necessity of a good showing in these critical end-of-secondary-school tests, which were meant to pave the way to university. If a girl didn't perform well, her career prospects would be hamstrung. And after years of sacrifice on the part of their families, the girls were all too aware of the weight of expectations resting on their shoulders. Still, with only 4 percent of girls in northern Nigeria completing secondary school, the mere fact that these girls had reached this point already made them success stories.

There are between 8.5 million and 10 million children out of school in Nigeria—the largest out-of-school numbers in the world for more than a decade. The country has faced a "multi-dimensional crisis" in education, according to a report by the UK's Department for International Development released in 2009. Sixty percent of the unenrolled live in the country's north—with girls accounting for more than half of those numbers. The report elaborated on the scale of the problem:

> Access is limited and quality is poor; Department for International Development (DFID) research found that learning outcomes in Nigerian schools were worse than in many

other countries in sub-Saharan Africa. There are insuffi-
cient qualified teachers, especially in rural areas. Quality of
teaching is often low. Many children leave primary school
and junior secondary school without adequate literacy, nu-
meracy and life skills. Teachers are often poorly supervised
and are described as having low motivation and inadequate
incentives.

The truth is, the situation in the northern states stands out as
particularly bleak. A 2012 review by the UK government high-
lighted that two-thirds of fifteen-to-eighteen-year-old girls in the
north couldn't read a sentence, a dramatic difference with the
southern part of the country, where that rate of illiteracy drops to
below 10 percent. In the eight northern states, more than 80 percent of women were unable to read, compared with 54 percent for
men. Between 2010 and 2015 only seventy-five females for every
one hundred males finished senior secondary school in the country's northeast. In 2014, with a state of emergency in place and Boko
Haram's accelerated efforts to disrupt education across the northern states of Borno, Yobe, and Adamawa, even fewer children had
the opportunity to take their seats in a classroom. This educational
crisis had forced local authorities to open up the girls' classrooms
in Chibok to boys a few years earlier. They were allowed to enroll
for the final three years of school—known as "senior secondary
school"—as day students. Thus, once classes were over, the several
dozen Chibok schoolboys who attended with the girls, wearing
uniforms of blue check shirts and matching pants, all headed home.

Less than a month before Priscilla, Mary, Saa, Dorcas, and 391
other girls and 135 boys were to gather to take their Senior School
Certificate Examinations, Borno State officials announced that all
state secondary schools would close due to stepped-up Boko Haram attacks. "They are to remain closed until the security situation
in the state improves," said the state's governor, Kashim Shettima,

to the BBC Hausa language service. But he decided that the secondary school in Chibok should stay open and serve as an exam center for the school's final-year students and those from places like Askira, Bama, and Konduga, nearby local districts where students had been unable to take their national and regional exams due to shuttered schools.

Despite being designated as an exam center, the school still didn't have a significant security presence. While the students pored over SSCE questions, you'd typically find only three armed men patrolling the grounds, a combination of soldiers and police officers in their respective uniforms. They stayed in place till nightfall, when the responsibility of securing the girls in their hostels reverted to Mr. Jida and Kaka, who were both very old and tired.

Earlier that Monday, the entire school had been bustling with activity. Some of the arts stream students had been tucked away in class taking a government exam, while those on the sciences side were exam-free for the day and spent the hours gleefully milling about the hostels.

In Mwoda House, Priscilla was at peace. As a science student, she had a chemistry exam the next day. She was feeling confident. This would be her sixth assessment. She'd already taken math, English, biology, agriculture, and physics. At this point, Priscilla couldn't wait for the whole trial to be over and to return home. She had a plan for what to do the minute she was through the door: spend as much time as possible by her mother's side, see friends, and generally just enjoy being with loved ones. Being home, though, wasn't the only reason this schoolgirl was excited about finishing. Completion also held the promise of a new chapter in Priscilla's journey and advancement to a new place of learning. Finishing these exams would move her one step closer to her long-cherished dream of becoming a doctor.

When Priscilla wasn't studying that Monday, she was hanging out with a group of girls from her neighborhood. In between studying and laughing, they paused to grab plates from their personal stash and make the short walk over to the school canteen. The group collected a serving of what was on offer and took their full plates back to eat in the hostel. Priscilla spent the latter part of the evening sitting outside, watching a handful of girls play games that occasionally drew loud cheers for the winners from some of the spectators. When she finally climbed into her top bunk it was close to eleven o'clock, and she fell asleep quickly. Priscilla had no concerns about what was happening at the gate, or whether Kaka was nodding off in a corner. Truthfully, she never even gave it a second thought. Concerns about her personal safety were the farthest thing from her mind.

Saa was also one of those enjoying a day off and feeling pretty good about the next day's chemistry test. So much so, this eighteen-year-old had had no reservations about heading into Chibok town to spend a long weekend with her father's sister, whom she hadn't seen in a long while. Saa then returned to her dorm room in Mwoda House that Monday around five o'clock with bags full of peanut oil, onions, and boiled nuts, all gifts from her aunt. She also brought back leftover ground yam and stew to share with her friends, Blessing and Glory. The three girls were in high spirits, excitedly tucking into the food and swapping tales from their short time apart. There was little out of the ordinary. They stayed together throughout the evening as they usually did. By ten thirty, Saa and Blessing lay on a mattress on the dorm floor, while Glory rested nearby on a bottom bunk. Before long, Saa had dozed off, and when Glory whispered her goodnight to Blessing before drifting off to sleep, Saa was none the wiser. She was already in deep sleep.

It was well after midnight when Saa opened her eyes. Blessing was tapping her frantically. "Get up, get up! Can't you hear what's happening?"

Saa made out the sounds of wild shooting in Chibok town, which was only a fifteen-minute walk from their school, and the sounds jolted her wide awake. The moment she heard *"Allahu Akbar,"* she knew Boko Haram had arrived in Chibok. This wasn't her first experience with the terror group. Several months earlier they'd attacked her family's village of Askira early one morning. The clamor of *"Allahu Akbar"* and guns going off were one and the same. Blessing immediately started searching through her own belongings, looking for money. Once she'd found it, Saa watched as her friend tore off her nightclothes and jammed the cash into the pair of socks she hurriedly slipped on. Saa now sprung up, ripping off the skimpy vest she'd been sleeping in and replacing it with a red blouse and a blue-and-white wrapper—a piece of fabric commonly draped around the waist by African women which fashions a skirt. She grabbed her cell phone—which the girls were usually forbidden from having in school, but the rule had been eased because it was exam time. At this point all the girls in her dorm room were awake. There was no shouting or screaming, just panicked faces, frantic movements, and hushed voices, each asking again and again, "What is happening? What should we do now?"

From their dormitory they could see flames. Something was burning in nearby Chibok town. The girls had no way of knowing that the mob of men had peeled off into different marauding bands. Some busied themselves with torching and ransacking the town center, as others made bullets fall like heavy raindrops from the night's sky. Meanwhile, there was another contingent moving determinedly through the dark toward the Government Girls Secondary School. Saa and the others pried open their room's door, peered outside, and stepped into the yard. Other dormitory doors were also opening, and soon the compound was full.

Seventeen-year-old Mary, likewise, had been bewildered when she woke. Still wearing her school uniform—a blue check blouse and matching wrapper—she'd fallen asleep outside on a mat with a bunch of friends, in an attempt to escape the stifling April heat in her dorm room. As soon as the shooting started up in the town, Grace, who was one of her best friends, rushed over to rouse her. Thanks to the big, fat moon shining brightly that night, Mary could immediately see panic-stricken girls dashing around the compound. Within minutes, she'd joined a gathering of fifty girls from her Christian fellowship group. All bowed their heads as a passionately devout girl called Monica Enoch led them in prayers. "We should believe in God and nothing will happen," she urged them. The group intoned the same four words, "God shall protect us."

Priscilla had been in a deep sleep when Hannah, a girl from the same area of Chibok, shook her awake. "Priscilla, Priscilla, wake up! Can't you hear what is going on?"

Almost as soon as she opened her eyes, the sound of sustained gunfire and explosions crowded out the thoughts in her head. There was something else.

"*Allahu Akbar* . . ."

"*Allahu Akbar* . . ."

"*Allahu Akbar* . . ."

Those words filled the eighteen-year-old with terror. There was a time when the melodious sound of "*Allahu Akbar*" had rung out across the towns and villages throughout Nigeria's northeast, and the first thought among those who heard it was that it was an invitation to prayer and quiet contemplation. But that was prior to 2009, before Boko Haram made the Arabic words its war cry and a harbinger of death and destruction. With the school being so close to town, Priscilla could distinctly hear the terrified screams of the townspeople echoing through the darkness along with the recurrent "*Allahu Akbar*." Unlike Saa, Priscilla was less certain about who had brought terror to her town that night. She suspected it was Boko Haram, but prayed she was wrong.

Priscilla quickly got out of bed. She was still wearing her brown check blouse and wrapper when she followed Hannah a few minutes later. She found the rest of her housemates standing right outside the dorm room. Several of them already had their belongings packed in bags. Beams from different flashlights illuminated girls with fear-filled eyes and small bundles balanced on their heads, while others had wrapped a few items in swathes of cloth and tied them around their waists.

"What is that noise?" Priscilla asked.

"We don't know," some of the stunned girls replied.

"Maybe terrible people have entered the town," another girl added.

They had all heard the horror stories of Boko Haram attacks, particularly those on schools.

As Priscilla was house captain of Mwoda House, the job of getting everyone in order fell to her. All the house captains were jointly responsible for keeping each other informed if there was an emergency at the school. She quickly ran to Ganna House next door. Its captain was a tall, fair-skinned girl with wary eyes called Bernice. She was fast asleep when Priscilla entered her dorm room and shook her awake.

"Bernice, wake up! You must gather your girls! There is some sort of attack happening in town!" Priscilla was gone before Bernice was even fully awake.

She returned to her housemates with an important reminder: "You all remember what the principal told us? We've been told that we should not run if we hear something." All the girls nodded quietly. "But this is a very different situation. So what should we do?" With furrowed brows and eyes wide with confusion, the girls scanned each other's faces.

"It is better for us to run!" one said.

"No—it's better for us to pray," another answered.

"We should run!" The girls continued to debate.

"Prayer can help. Let us wait and see what God will do for us."

"How are you going to run with all of this tied around you?" Priscilla asked those poised to sprint away, holding their most prized possessions.

"It's only our Bibles and a few other small things, so it won't be too heavy."

The girls struggled with their choices. Should they flee into the night, uncertain of what may be lying in wait beyond the school walls? Or simply stay put, right where they were, with the risk of being trapped if Boko Haram burst into their school?

"Let's pray, before we do anything," Priscilla said. At her instruction, the dozens of girls, Christian and Muslim, sat together on the ground and drew close to form one group. They bowed their heads in desperate prayer. The chaos from the town was spreading. The praying girls could hear doors opening and closing all around them, followed by quickened footsteps.

Priscilla thought back to a few months earlier. Three strange things had happened at the Chibok school. The first involved a letter found on its grounds warning of an attack if the school wasn't closed. Rumors had spread quickly among the students, and soon the entire school was gripped by fear. Within days a special assembly was called for the staff and students, and much to Priscilla's surprise, an imam and a pastor were also present. So many girls had been badly shaken. The two men of God were probably there to comfort them, she'd concluded. But in fact, the clergy had shown up to make fresh threats of their own.

The pastor kicked things off with his message. "Let the person who dropped the letter come out. If you don't, I will pray for the person who did it so something bad may follow the person." Next came the imam, who offered his own Islamic-tinged curses and prayers. The school's principal, Mrs. Asabe Kwambura, who was increasingly far more likely to be found in her house in the state capital of Maiduguri than in school, was present that day and offered advice to the dumbfounded girls. "What the imam and the pastor just did is a serious thing . . . don't joke with it. So if you are the one, you'd better come and explain yourself, so they will know what to do before something happens to you."

Priscilla and her friends seethed quietly, wondering among themselves why they were being intimidated and blamed when they knew nothing about the letter's origins. Several of them told their parents about their religious visitors' supernatural threats, including Priscilla, who admitted to her parents that she was afraid.

"Don't worry. Nothing will happen to you," they assured her, "if you're not the one who threw the letter."

And that was that.

A few weeks later, pandemonium broke out a second time.

It was early evening, around seven thirty, when a handful of girls in Jetau House saw a creature of some sort trying to enter their hostel building. Panicked, they took off, screaming as they ran and whipping the rest of the girls into a frenzy, who then zig-zagged through the compound in a state of complete confusion. A few days later the staff dismissed the entire episode as a case of childish misperception. They told the girls that a cat had tried to enter Jetau House, nothing more sinister. Priscilla was far from convinced, but like all the others had dared not challenge individuals who were older. Besides, the cat explanation was soon backed up with threats of punishment in yet another hastily called gathering.

This time, the vice-principal, Yerima Pudza, did the talking. His message was brief and to the point. "It was a cat that tried to enter Jetau House, so you shouldn't have run. In the future if you see something strange, do not run and repeat what just happened here, with all of you running about the place. If you do, I will punish everyone who is involved!"

Next he called Priscilla and the other house captains together.

"If something happens again and the girls are trying to run out of school, make sure you take down the names of all the girls." Everyone took in the vice-principal's stern warning and was fearful. Priscilla's father's advice this time around was also brief. "Pray and nothing will happen," he said.

But something else *did* happen. The third incident occurred less than a month later.

On this particular March evening, with dinner and evening prayers over, the girls were filling their time however they liked without any oversight from the staff living nearby. One girl had been absentmindedly looking out the window when she saw a figure—a man—perched on the wall surrounding their hostel. She motioned to the other girls in her dorm room to come over. Before long a horde of girls from the different houses were streaming in to stare at the individual. Priscilla couldn't make out his features, because he was too far away, but it was clear there was a man sitting on their hostel wall. The tense calm eventually gave way to outright panic. Soon screams could be heard as the girls once again ran wildly in every direction. Some girls whose families lived near the school scaled and leapt over the wall in the blink of an eye and headed home. A handful were hurt in that melee, including Saa, who injured her foot and wound up needing to take a week off to fully recover.

The girls never did find out who the man was or where he was from. On the other hand, there was no hiding the vice-principal's fury. "You must not run! If something happens in this school, you must stay in your hostels and wait for your teachers to arrive!"

So now on this hot April night, Priscilla and the rest of the girls from Mwoda House were doing exactly what they'd been told. The smell of smoke from Chibok town filled their nostrils, but they dutifully remained on the school grounds and waited for their teachers. Meanwhile, the attackers continued firing their guns wildly into the darkness.

A short distance away in Chibok town, a cell phone was ringing in Esther and Yakubu's house. It was late and everyone had been asleep for hours.

"Where's your baby?" asked Esther's brother-in-law, Bana.

The mother of five still wasn't fully awake, and she struggled to focus on what she was hearing. But right away she felt there was something very wrong. Why would he be asking about Dorcas, her fifteen-year-old daughter who was down the road at the Government Girls Secondary School?

"She's in school," Esther replied drowsily.

Bana told her Boko Haram was moving steadily across the sandy-dusty terrain, heading straight for sleeping Chibok town.

Her heart lurched and Esther was now fully awake. "What?" she screamed into the phone. Flustered, she felt her mind racing: What to do first? What next? *Dear God!*

She was alone in the dark bedroom. April's muggy heat had driven her husband, Yakubu, outdoors to sleep on a mat. The warm air hung heavily in their bedroom. She scrambled to find the blouse she'd tossed onto a pillow hours earlier. Bana was still on the line as she dressed hurriedly and rushed out to the veranda.

"Yakubu!" she called out, as she awoke him. "Your brother." She thrust the phone in his face. Esther stood completely still, trying to piece together the bits and pieces she could hear from their conversation. When he hung up, her husband confirmed her worst fears. "They may be heading to the school."

"Where is my baby? Where is my baby?" she muttered desperately as fearful thoughts rose up in her mind. Dorcas was her everything. Esther's heart pounded in her ears. She needed to find her. Nothing could happen to her precious firstborn. Bana's words kept echoing in her mind. *Those Boko boys are in town . . .*

Esther reached for the cellphone to dial her daughter when she remembered and felt sick. She'd confiscated Dorcas's phone just a few days earlier, when she'd been home prior to exams. Dorcas was wise beyond her years, diligent and responsible; she'd never caused them a moment's problem. But Esther had felt a motherly duty to do everything possible to make sure the teenager remained focused. For Esther, this meant eliminating all unnecessary distractions. Now her overzealousness had put Dorcas out of reach, and Esther was awash with anxiety. Should she run to the school? That would take too long. What could she do?

Her mind raced for a solution. She thought of Joyce, a distant cousin married to one of the teachers who lived in the staff quarters on the school grounds. Esther quickly scanned her contacts list searching for Joyce's number and hit Call. She would ask Joyce to warn her baby of the disaster that was coming. She waited for her relative to answer, but heard no reassuring click and no hello. Instead, the number just rang and rang. Esther's chest tightened. Why wasn't Joyce answering? Could it be that she was just asleep? Esther knew her cousin often put her phone on silent when she went to bed at night. Is that why she wasn't picking up? Neither she nor Yakubu knew what to think. They considered their limited options and struggled to stay calm as the minutes ticked by.

Then, out of the darkness came the echo of automatic weapons. Esther and Yakubu froze in terror. Less than two dozen Nigerian soldiers were stationed in Chibok to keep everyone safe. Could *they* be source of the raucous gunfire? They were both praying for this to be the case till the ominous chant of *"Allahu Akbar"* rose up amid the thunderous crackle of gunfire. Esther's faltering hope left her and they knew then that they were out of time. If they were going to do anything, it needed to happen—now.

They had no idea where their eldest daughter was, but they had to get her three sisters and brother, Happy, Marvellous, Missy, and Ibrahim, out of the house. From the sound of things, the fighters were closing in. Yakubu refused to hear Esther's pleas for him to take the children while she stayed home in case Dorcas appeared.

Soon twelve-year-old Happy and nine-year-old Marvellous were off with the neighbor. While Yakubu scooped into his arms their sleeping five-year-old son Ibrahim, Esther quickly tied three-year-old Missy, who was also fast asleep, to her back. Minutes later, they were running alongside thousands of people in the moonlight to a stone hill overlooking the school to hide.

Back at the school, the big, bright moon illuminated the faces of the hundreds of girls gathered on the hostel grounds. By now almost everyone was outside. Some sat, others stood in groups, and almost all of them were absorbed in prayer. The girls' fast-moving lips gave voice to ardent petitions for deliverance from the evil lurking nearby. For some it was too much to bear silently, and ever so often gasps of *"Jesus! Jesus! Jesus!"* were heard. Meanwhile, there were those who took comfort in telling themselves that even if Boko Haram turned up, they wouldn't be harmed, because the group was mainly known for targeting boys.

The sounds of chaos in town, though, were getting louder. Priscilla and some of her housemates sought out Kaka. She was relieved to find him sitting in his usual corner, looking the same as he always did. The girls could hardly wait for someone in authority to finally tell them what to do.

"Kaka, do you hear what is happening in town? Should we run?"

Kaka stared at them wearily, blinking slowly before he spoke. "Me, myself, I don't know what to do. You have gathered together in prayer. Let us just continue praying." That was all he had for them.

Disappointed, Priscilla and the group turned away to head back to the rest of their housemates. They'd taken only a few steps when she looked over her shoulder for one last glance at Kaka. He was gone! Priscilla gasped and the rest of the girls turned. Their beloved Kaka had fled without saying a word. Now they were more afraid than ever. Mr. Jida, also, was nowhere to be found.

Girls with cell phones dialed family members, their hearts racing. Saa found a spot to sit down, just in front of the hostel buildings, and dug out her phone. She dialed her father's number. No answer. She tried her brother next. The same. Saa tried her dad a second time and listened impatiently as the number rang, unanswered. A few minutes went by and then her screen lit up. It was her father.

"What is happening?" he asked. He'd been fast asleep and now his voice sounded tense. She'd never called him this late before.

"Boko Haram is shooting guns in Chibok town. We are at school and we don't know what to do."

There was a long pause. Then he advised his daughter to stay in school with the others and wait for their teachers. He also instructed her to pray for God's protection. Then the conversation was over.

Priscilla, meanwhile, was also trying desperately to reach her parents on her phone. She repeatedly dialed the number, but each time the call went nowhere. Frustration gave way to fresh panic, then a troubling new possibility. Maybe she wasn't getting them because they had run away once they heard all the gunshots. Could they really have left her?

The sound of a rumbling, sputtering motorcycle engine suddenly caught everyone's attention. Priscilla turned toward the gate and watched as a man in a Nigerian military uniform came through and drove toward the crowd of schoolgirls. He moved slowly and steadily. Soon he was close enough for her to see the lack of emotion in his eyes. Nobody said a word or dared make a move. Without warning he suddenly turned on his bike and sped off. Priscilla and all the other girls suspected they'd just received a visit from Boko Haram. She stared at the figure retreating in the moonlight. No one but Boko Haram would be bold enough to barge into their school without any kind of permission.

Within minutes she heard the clear sound of unfamiliar male voices just beyond the school's wall.

"Look, the school is empty. Come, let's go."

"No, we must at least go in to see what is inside."

"I have told you, there is nobody inside."

"We need to see the hostels for ourselves."

Startled, Priscilla looked around. What should they do? When the first handful of men entered the school grounds on foot, the girls were all still paralyzed by fear. As the men stepped out of the shadows into the light, they saw they were all dressed in the standard camouflage uniforms of Nigerian soldiers. Many were young, in their twenties and thirties. More and more walked through the gate, and at the sight of this endless stream of men, Bernice and several girls burst into tears. No one could believe what was happening. At least a hundred armed men marched toward them. The hostel grounds were completely overrun, and Priscilla, like all her schoolmates, was trapped.

"Don't be afraid. Come closer," the men instructed as they surrounded the trembling girls. "We are soldiers out on patrol. We're here to protect you and nothing bad will happen to you."

After so many hours alone and afraid, the relief among many of the girls was palpable. Soldiers had come to protect them! When the men gave instructions, the girls listened carefully, and without saying a word, quickly gathered together in front of their hostels as directed.

Priscilla did as she was told, but she couldn't shake the feeling that something was about to go terribly wrong. Once she'd been able to study the appearance of their intruders, she became convinced these weren't Nigerian soldiers at all. Yes, they were dressed in the same uniforms, but only a handful of the men wore shoes; most of them were in flip-flops, and a couple had nothing on their feet. Their water bottles also struck her as odd, filthy looking and haphazardly slung over their shoulders with lengths of rope. To Priscilla, these men were far more likely to be cattle herders than soldiers.

When Mary looked closely at the men, she wondered why Nigerian soldiers would be wearing black headdresses that covered their faces. By now the same feeling of alarm was spreading through the group. But any thought of trying to escape was pointless. The girls were hemmed in, and strange-looking men spread out across the compound. As more girls fought back tears, the group collectively prayed their worst nightmare wasn't about to come true. Then they heard it.

"*Allahu Akbar . . .*"

"*Allahu Akbar . . .*"

Boko Haram had arrived.

A wail rose up from the hundreds of girls, who now began to sob uncontrollably.

The men were unmoved.

"We are with you today!" one of them shouted. "If you don't do what we tell you, we will kill you! We can kill all of you here! We are Boko Haram!"

Were they all about to die? Priscilla wondered. The girls' wailing grew louder as they clung to each other with growing desperation.

Amid this burst of activity, a girl from Mary's house managed to peel away and make it to the hostel wall. Rahila quietly clambered up the wall and quickly dropped from view. Unbeknownst to her and the rest of her schoolmates, Boko Haram was not only *inside* the hostel compound, it was also *outside*. The entire school was completely surrounded. So within minutes of Rahila swinging herself over that wall, filled with thoughts of running to freedom, she was tossed right back into the compound, where she landed in a thud and a flood of tears. No one dared move. Her schoolmates could only watch as the sobbing girl writhed on the ground before she gingerly picked herself up, seemingly unhurt, and limped over to the rest of the group. The men merely snickered among themselves without saying a word to her. They had other things on their mind.

"Is this all of you?" the men asked roughly.

"Yes!" said the girls in unison.

The men remained unconvinced. "We don't believe you! There should be more of you than this! Where are the boys?"

"No, this is all of us. The boys are day students . . . they go home every day," the girls stuttered.

"You are lying!" the men growled.

One of the militants cleared his throat and spoke in a loud, clear voice. "If there is anyone hiding in any of the rooms, you'd better come out, right now! Or we are going to set these buildings on fire!"

Convinced the dorm rooms were completely empty, Priscilla was surprised when a group of agitated-looking girls suddenly came scurrying out of the various houses.

They were greeted with sneers and insults from Boko Haram. "You fools, did we not tell you to come outside immediately?" Unsatisfied, some of the men dispersed to search the hostels, only to return empty handed.

The men holding the group of girls continued their questions.

"Where's the cement block–making machine?"

"Where's the gasoline?"

Their queries produced confused looks and muttered responses of "We don't know," which only enraged the intruders.

"We will shoot you if you don't tell us where this machine is!" they threatened. But the girls didn't know. Some just wept where they stood.

"What about the store where the food is kept?" asked one of the men, as he pointed directly at a randomly chosen girl and motioned with his gun for her to show him the way. She remained rooted in place, tears streaming down her face, unable to move.

The other schoolgirls looked on, nervous about what might happen next.

"I will show you," offered one of the girl's friends, breaking the silence. The rest of them looked on while the two girls began a slow walk with the armed militant following close behind. The storage room was locked when the three arrived, but after several blows with his gun it was soon wide open and ready to be emptied. The men worked in two groups, the first carrying out the bags of rice, spaghetti, macaroni, milk, rice, yams, and onions, and leaving the others to load everything into the massive heavy-duty truck that pulled into the compound. The Mercedes-Benz LA 911, nicknamed "nine-eleven" by the locals, is a hulk of a vehicle with four tires at the back to accompany the two in front. The lumbering motorized wagon had a steel cage over the rear open cargo area and could carry well over a ton.

While the storage room was being looted, a separate group of men kept watch over the hundreds of girls who were now sitting quietly, too afraid to say or do anything that might anger their captors. As soon as the two friends returned it was time to get going.

"Move out!" shouted their captors. "Go over to the classroom area."

As Priscilla stood alongside the hundreds of girls, bands of fighters converged tightly around them, forcing them to proceed. She'd barely taken five steps when their hostels went up in raging flames. Priscilla looked back, transfixed by the inferno. Saa watched in horror as all her possessions and everything her classmates owned burned to ash, the flames leaping and twisting the whole time against the inky night sky. Up to this point, Priscilla had kept her emotions in check, even as most of the others fell apart all around her. Now she was distraught, and her mind was reeling: *Is this how my life will end? . . . Will they really burn me? Or will it just be my hostel? If I'm going to die, I think I'd rather be shot than burned.* Hot tears ran down her cheeks.

The men were propelling her forward out of the hostel compound toward the block of sandy-colored buildings that housed their classrooms. It was less than a five-minute walk, and she'd made this journey hundreds if not thousands of times during her six years at the secondary school. What Priscilla saw when she stepped beyond the walls of their hostel compound caused some of the girls to lose their footing. Others screamed, and loud gasps leapt from the throats of some. Close to three hundred more men stood there, sneering, with eyes flashing in the shadows. Upon seeing the girls, the waiting mob erupted in waves of *"Allahu Akbar."* Before Priscilla could even fully take in the spectacle of this flood of armed men, she heard the hiss and crackle of flames. Their classrooms were all now ablaze. So too were the hostels and the staff quarters.

"We will burn everything here."

"Nothing will remain!"

The declarations were met with more cries of *Allahu Akbar*, a riotous endorsement of the terror brought to bear on this small school.

Meanwhile, a spirited conversation suddenly broke out among several dozen of the men who were standing a short way off from Priscilla and the others.

"Let us carry them all with us," one suggested.

"No, no. Let us divide them into groups and burn them in the different rooms."

Burn us?

On the other side of Chibok, Esther squatted with the other members of her community on the stony mound on which they'd sought shelter, but her heart and soul were with her daughter, Dorcas. From the hill, she and everyone with her could see the outline of the school, the last building on the outskirts of town. *God, the girls are so quiet. Maybe they managed an escape of some type.* Esther lacked the presence of mind to worry about herself or the rest of her family, adrift in a town overrun by men with a hankering for chaos and death. All her mind was able to register were thoughts of Dorcas and the threat to her child's well-being.

She had good reason to be afraid. Two months earlier in neighboring Yobe State, Boko Haram had attacked the Federal Government College in Buni Yadi. Unlike the boarding school in Chibok, the college had housed both male and female students in their respective hostels. When the attackers appeared in the overnight hours, they swept through the chipped and faded arch at the school's entrance, moving among the school's twenty-four buildings and unleashing a hail of gunfire. Bullets whizzed through the air, cutting down terrified young men who died alone in pools of blood. When the sun rose the next day on this impoverished corner of Nigeria, every single school building on the site was in ruins and fifty-eight boys were dead, some burned beyond recognition.

There were girls in the school that night too, but they'd been handled differently. Before the murderous rampage began, the insurgents marched them out of their hostels and into the school's mosque, where, in a place of worship, the innocent stood face-to-face with terrorists and the girls feared the worst. No death sentence was handed down, though. Instead they received a stern lecture about the perils of Western education, along with the direct instruction to abandon their schooling at once and get married. Next they were ordered out of the school. With wrathful words of warning still ringing in their ears, the girls of the Federal Government College had bolted. Once the they were gone, Boko Haram gleefully shot and burned the male students till dawn.

Now the fact that no one could hear the Chibok girls troubled Esther deeply. In recent months, the school had become known for the hordes of teenage girls squealing and running around late into the night. *Why were they so quiet now that Boko Haram was in their midst?* Nobody on that rocky outcrop slept or spoke. They kept vigil and stared at the school in the distance. Esther's lips moved ceaselessly in prayer. *Father, please protect my baby. Let it be silent because the girls have found a place to hide. Father, protect Dorcas.*

In the quiet of the predawn hours, vaulting flames suddenly appeared, reaching high for the night's sky. No telltale sound of men yelling or panic-stricken schoolgirls screaming reached the Chibok residents gathered on their hill. Esther looked down at a growing inferno with mounting horror and frustration. Every single bone and sinew of her body was screaming—*Get up and run down the hill!* The last thing she wanted was to be so far away from Dorcas, but even in her altered state she knew that such a move meant almost-certain death.

When the boys from Boko Haram laid siege to Chibok on April 14, 2014, from eleven thirty on that Monday night till just before dawn the next day, hundreds of them terrorized this small tucked-away town. To the soundtrack of rapid gunfire and crescendoing cries of *"Allahu Akbar,"* the militants unleashed a shower of bullets, burned down the town's outdoor shopping complex, along with the homes of several prominent residents, and destroyed the girls' school.

Disturbing details from the raid on the girls' secondary school would later emerge. As those first shots rang out, every single one of the school's teachers had abandoned their students and crept out of the compound to save themselves. Meanwhile, the principal's home, which was on school grounds, also stood empty. Mrs. Asabe Kwambura was nowhere near Chibok; she was eighty miles away in her personal house in Maiduguri, the state capital, as had become her routine. As for old Mr. Jida, and even older Kaka, who'd urged the girls to stay in place and pray, they also melted away into the night.

For those hours that Boko Haram ransacked the town of Chibok, its residents remained out of sight, hiding up on hills above town or in nearby villages, praying for the night of terror to end. Up on the stone hill where she was keeping watch, Esther heard the rumbling of multiple engines on the move just after four thirty a.m. She gave her husband a questioning glance, but Yakubu simply stared back at her quizzically. He had no idea what was happening either. They concentrated on the sounds. One vehicle after another trundled along Chibok's sole dirt road and headed out of town. Eventually, the sounds of engines faded away and there was nothing else. Quietness settled around Esther and the assembled residents of Chibok town. Wherever they were, everyone hoped and prayed that the ordeal had finally come to an end.

The sun was just beginning to light the day when they all finally took off running down that hill. First, Esther dropped off Missy and Ibrahim at home. During the entire nightmare the youngsters had somehow stayed quiet. Happy and Marvellous were still gone with a neighbor, but she felt confident that they'd soon show up to care for their siblings. Next she stopped by her sister's home, and soon the two of them were half running, half walking to Dorcas's school. Almost everyone in the town was doing the same thing, rushing to the burning school to find out what had become of the girls.

CHAPTER FIVE

Similar to the way Priscilla, Mary, Saa, and Dorcas sat at the center of their parents' worlds, I knew my siblings and I were the sun, the moon, and the stars combined to Mamud and Kadi Sesay. A few years after my parents moved to London, my older sister, Jane, was born with cerebral palsy, a neurological disorder typically caused by a brain injury before or at birth, a condition that left her severely disabled. None of the doctors could provide a satisfactory explanation of what had happened to cause Jane's condition. But one English doctor said simply, "That's how evolution goes sometimes," before adding flippantly: "Don't have any more children."

As my mother enjoyed reminding me countless times over the years, she promptly tossed aside this advice, and I was born just over a year later in a north London hospital. Then came the surprise arrival of "the little prince," my baby brother, Mamud, named after our father, five years after me. By the time I was seven, I had been transplanted against my will from England to my parents' native country of Sierra Leone. The transition to Freetown, the capital city, wasn't easy, but my parents wisely ignored my grumbling and in time I grew to love my sun-drenched life.

I took great pleasure from my efforts to sway my father, Mamud Senior, into doing whatever I wanted, and he unashamedly spoiled me. He served as the in-house counsel for the Sierra Leone Produce Marketing Board (SLPMB), and I felt like Christmas and my birthday had teamed up and come early whenever my father took me with him to work. As an eight-year-old, in preparation for those visits, I would spend hours sorting through my books and toys, constructing a sort of emergency kit in the unlikely event that I got bored while I was with him. On the eve of each visit, my mother watched without interrupting as I carefully packed and unpacked several large bags. Looking back, I now know the strange look on her face was bemusement, that wry smile an acknowledgement of how much I was a daddy's girl. The night before these adventures, I could hardly sleep, nerve-tingling excitement keeping me awake. The next morning we would set off for SLPMB in the car as I gleefully mouthed the letters under my breath. One of the things I most looked forward to was a bowl of creamy chicken soup in the staff restaurant. Each time I'd eagerly grab my knife and reach for a bright yellow pat of butter to slather on my soft bread roll. Then, with grease-covered fingers, I carefully cut up the bread and slowly dragged it through the steaming-hot soup, savoring every mouthful of creamy, salty goodness. Afterward when we were in the corridors, my father would stop every couple of minutes to proudly introduce me to this "aunty" and that "uncle." I always stood perfectly still by his side, peering through my thick-rimmed glasses and channeling my best impression of meekness.

My father may have been my enabler, but my mother was the heartbeat and enforcer in our family. She set the rules and rhythm of our family life and kept every single one of us in line, including Mamud Senior—without fail.

Back in London when I was a toddler, she'd begun surrounding me with books. It wasn't long before I was reading voraciously. I read children's versions of most English-language literary classics—*Tom Sawyer, Robinson Crusoe, Great Expectations, Jane Eyre, Pride and Prejudice*—long before I reached primary school. By the time we were back in Sierra Leone, my mother was a senior lecturer, teaching English literature at the University of Sierra Leone. Unsurprisingly, reading widely, writing clearly, and speaking confidently were the cornerstone lessons of my childhood. For many years, in the run-up to major school exams, my mother would go through every one of my notebooks and create questions for each subject. She'd stay up late into the night, after her long days in the classroom, drawing up practice papers to ensure I aced my tests.

When I was about eight or nine, one of my teachers started bullying me. This plump, wrinkled old woman taught math and took great delight in humiliating and beating me whenever I got an answer wrong or simply when it suited her. The stress and fear began to make me physically ill. After days of listening to me complain of strange aches and pains in the mornings before school and the whole way over there, on one particular morning my mother slowed down her silver Peugeot 504 and gradually brought it to a stop on the side of the sloping road.

"What's going on, Isha?"

We were sitting a couple of yards away from my school, and I could hear the happy shrieks of the other pupils in the playground. I was miserable and afraid to tell her what was happening to me, so I just sat there, looking down at the green-and-white check of my school uniform.

"Tell me, what's wrong?" my mother pressed gently. "Please."

My resistance didn't last long; soon the words were tumbling out. Once the tears slowed after she'd managed to calm me, my mother was out of the car, marching into the school compound and headed straight for the head mistress' office. That old hairy math teacher left me alone after that.

At the time, we lived on the leafy, hilly University of Sierra Leone campus alongside dozens of other lecturers and their families. Our home was a modest bungalow surrounded by hot-pink bougainvillea bushes, as well as mango, plum, and black velvet tamarind trees, the latter known as "black tumbler" trees in Sierra Leone. I waited impatiently each year for the seeded fruits inside the black brittle shells to ripen and go from green to orange. At the first sighting of branches of black tumbler being sold around town, I'd beg my teenage cousin Fenthi to climb one of the two trees in our front yard to check the fruits' readiness. Hopping from one foot to the other, I'd yell up to him excitedly, "Are they ripe?" There was always a pause next, accompanied by the sound of cracking as Fenthi pulled a handful of black pods from nearby branches and broke them open. After what felt like a never-ending wait for his verdict, I inevitably shouted, "Fenthi!" in exasperation. All I wanted was to hear him say yes. And when he did, I squealed so loudly, half the neighborhood probably heard me. Over the next few hours I devoted myself to quickly cracking open as many of the small pods as possible to build a mountain of the round, spongy fruits. Once I was satisfied with the pile, I started stuffing large handfuls of the sweet-sour pulps into my mouth and rolling them around like marbles in my swollen cheeks.

During these years living on the campus grounds, my parents were in their thirties and working hard, but we weren't wealthy. Before we could afford a generator, I studied by lamplight on the frequent occasions we lost electricity thanks to the country's crippled energy sector. On the evenings when we were suddenly plunged into darkness, my father would break into song and I would eagerly follow along:

> Kookaburra sits in the old gum tree
> Merry, merry king of the bush is he
> Laugh, kookaburra! Laugh, kookaburra!
> Gay your life must be

I never did learn the rest of the song, but we sang this one verse over and over and over again. Whenever I pause to think about it, I can make out our voices singing softly, as if it were a lullaby. Memories of my father are in relatively short supply, though. He died unexpectedly at age forty, when I was twelve.

I'd been fast asleep when an aunt ran into the bedroom, and as soon as I opened my eyes, she breathlessly shouted, "I think your dad has died!" My mother wasn't home at the time, so in that moment it was just a heartbreaking rumor first delivered by a family friend. My father had been in London for many months receiving treatment for a kidney condition. Still, I'd told myself he'd be back home in time for Christmas and my birthday. I'd convinced myself that he'd return to live with us in that modest bungalow surrounded by all those fruit trees. Instead, I found myself trembling and desperately patting the sheets in search of my glasses, which had disappeared.

Within hours my mother was draped in the white linens of Islamic mourning and confined to the house. For those first forty days, she half sat, half lay on the bed and stared blankly at the procession of relatives, friends, acquaintances, and colleagues who formed an orderly line at the door. They entered, one by one, to offer condolences and to mumble words of support. For several hours each day, I squeezed myself into a corner next to her and watched her struggle to acknowledge the conveyor belt of mourners. Too shocked to cry, I remained dry eyed, running through an endless list of questions in my head. My mother was the person I turned to for everything, but in this moment she was beyond my reach. She mostly remained silent, till one day it all became too much and her stoic silence turned to uncontrollable weeping, sending tears down her cheeks so fast I couldn't catch them. All I could do was wrap my twelve-year-old arms around her and draw her close. I reached for one of her delicate hands.

"It's going to be okay," I whispered. "I'll look after you."

She smiled weakly.

After the funeral, I watched in awe as my mother negotiated life as a thirty-nine-year-old widow responsible for three children (one of whom was severely disabled), living in an African society riven by chauvinism. With her meager salary as an academic, she did all she could to maintain the comfortable childhood we'd had when my father was alive, while paying school fees and living allowances for a never-ending troupe of relatives and the occasional stranger. My mother believed education was the most prized possession a person could have and did everything in her power to share it with anyone eager to learn. From her I learned that while much in life is negotiable, gaining an education should never be, and a girl's right to be educated is always worth fighting for. My mother's strength molded me into the woman I am today, and with each passing year we've grown inseparable.

I was in the CNN newsroom in Atlanta on April 15, 2014, when I first heard that hundreds of girls had been taken from a boarding school in northern Nigeria. None of it made much sense. Details were muddled, numbers fluctuated, and the statements coming from various government officials only added to the confusion. I rang my mother quickly in Sierra Leone, in keeping with my habit of calling her to discuss everything of significance in my life and the wider world.

"Did you hear about the kidnapped girls?" I asked once she finally picked up.

"Yes! They're saying Boko Haram took them." She sounded incredulous.

"Uh-huh, unbelievable that this could be allowed to happen."

The overseas phone line hummed quietly as we both held silent for a moment, absorbing the injustice at the heart of it all.

The targeting of women and girls trapped in hot spots has long been an ugly characteristic of global conflicts. When men clash, the borders of their battlefields regularly extend to include the bodies of females. It barely raises eyebrows these days to hear that women caught up in hostilities have been abused, bought, swapped, or completely destroyed at will.

During World War II, some 200,000 women from countries that Japan occupied were forced to provide "comfort" to the invading Japanese soldiers. Hostilities in Rwanda and Bosnia, and the unending conflicts in the Democratic Republic of Congo, have produced tens of thousands of stories about wholesale female suffering. In Syria, ISIS established slave auctions to buy and sell women and girls from Iraq's minority Yazidi sect. Girls as young as nine were traded for rape and enslavement. In August 2017, world leaders watched Myanmar's security forces lay siege to the Rohingya community in the country's Rakhine State. Staggering brutality and destruction drove close to 700,000 Rohingya across the border into Bangladesh. Almost immediately, stories of systematic rape and sexual assault began to emerge, and those soon numbered in the thousands, all of them brushed aside by Myanmar's military, which continues to deny the widespread atrocities.

The perpetrators of this kind of wholesale violence against women and girls know that their chances of being held accountable are low to nonexistent. They are all too aware of the fact that provisions afforded to women to keep them safe during periods of armed conflict are weak, and actual enforcement of the law has been the exception rather than the rule. As Kelly D. Askin points out in her article "Prosecuting Wartime Rape and Other

Gender-Related Crimes under International Law," published in the *Berkeley Journal of International Law* in 2003:

> Women and girls have habitually been sexually violated during wartime, yet even in the twenty-first century, the documents regulating armed conflict either minimally incorporate, inappropriately characterize, or wholly fail to mention the crimes. . . .

The progress made globally in recognizing, prohibiting, and finally enforcing gender-related crimes has been painstakingly slow.

The root of the problem, Askin argues, is the centrality of men to the process of recognizing and prosecuting crimes of gender-based violence against women. The answer is the inclusion of more women.

> Until the 1990s, men did the drafting and enforcing of humanitarian law provisions; thus, it was primarily men who neglected to enumerate, condemn, and prosecute these crimes. While males remain the principal actors in international (and domestic) fora, in recent years, women have broken through the glass ceiling and are changing the traditional landscape by securing high-level positions in international legal institutions and on international adjudicative bodies.

Like Askin, I've always believed that more women must move from the sidelines to the center of efforts to bring about accountability for crimes against women and girls. In the meantime, the perpetrators of such violence know that striking at the females in a community creates a wound so deep within the heart of every family that it may never heal. The result is that communities and ultimately societies are changed forever, which is, of course, the intended outcome.

This was the first of many conversations my mother and I would have about crimes perpetrated against women and girls, and about Boko Haram and its objections to girls' being educated. By the time I hung up the phone, I was incensed. And I knew I would have to handle this story differently from all the others I'd covered. It was time to get to work.

From right there in Atlanta, I decided to make the story of the missing Chibok schoolgirls the primary focus of my daily news show, *CNN NewsCenter*. Our correspondent in Nigeria, Vladimir Duthiers, worked diligently to pin down what had happened in that faraway town the night the girls disappeared, but verifiable facts were hard to come by. A flurry of statements released by local and federal officials contradicted each other from one day to the next. It took more than a day to confirm that the number of girls missing was 276. On April 16, the director of defense information, Major General Chris Olukolade, announced the rescue of all "129 girls, except eight." He followed up with a retraction the very next day after enraged Chibok parents exposed his lie. Every day produced more questions about what happened before, during, and after the attack on the Chibok girls' school. And the biggest question of them all remained unanswered: Where were the girls?

After working for more than a decade in the broadcast news industry, I was aware of one of its most shameful secrets: Every day in Western newsrooms, news executives are making calculations, asking themselves consciously and subconsciously "Whose story matters?" and "How much screen time or how many column inches do they deserve?" In the United States, the travails and triumphs of white America tend to dominate the headlines, after which come stories of black and brown people. But they are still above black African women, who are arguably at the very bottom and consequently receive what most often amounts to "blink and you'll miss it" coverage. Of course, in the face of a catastrophic occurrence like the abduction of hundreds of schoolgirls, the story rundown is inverted, and those at the bottom rise to the top. But even here, there's a caveat: any increase in time and resources devoted to reporting on Africa is still predicated on whether anything else of perceived importance is happening on American soil at that particular moment.

The fact that not all lives are valued equally in the media was a painful lesson for me to learn on many levels, and it was a source of great disappointment to me as a journalist because I saw firsthand how these biases shape the way Western news organizations approach and cover stories about Africans and the continent itself.

In the immediate aftermath of the horrific Chibok kidnapping, CNN's coverage was limited. In this instance, it was hampered by a lack of information and by the swirl of misleading statements, which back then were simply dubbed "false narratives," but in the era of the Trump presidency would be called out as "fake news." But thanks to a handful of dedicated CNN journalists, the network remained committed to the Chibok story, which likely came as a surprise to the administration of then–Nigerian president Goodluck Jonathan. The government's strategy appeared to be one of withholding specifics of how things unfolded in Chibok and what was being done to reunite the girls with their families because, in the absence of details, this story would surely die. As they soon discovered, that was a grave miscalculation on their part.

Boko Haram's abduction of Priscilla, Saa, Mary, Dorcas, and more than two hundred other girls from their Chibok school dorms in 2014 earned the terrorist group global attention and scrutiny. Yet in actual fact, by the time that Boko Haram swarmed Chibok on that sweltering April night, they'd already kidnapped scores of other women and girls from across Nigeria's northeast. Reports date back to 2009 of women and girls being snatched from the streets of the group's stronghold, Maiduguri, the capital of Borno State, and likewise in Damaturu, the capital of neighboring Yobe State. Over the years, organizations like Amnesty International and Human Rights Watch have documented multiple accounts of forced marriage, rape, torture, domestic servitude, and indoctrination from those who made it to freedom. Fast-forward to February 2014, just a few short weeks before the raid on the Chibok school, when Boko Haram launched a deadly attack on the predominantly Christian community of Konduga and disappeared with dozens of women.

What made the Chibok attack so significant was the large number of girls taken at once, not the fact that Boko Haram had been engaged in the business of kidnapping. That much was known, even if broadly overlooked by large swathes of the Nigerian public. The events in Chibok were unique because they brought the group's expanding operational capabilities to light and, perhaps most critically, demonstrated the Nigerian military's struggle to fight successfully against this resilient homegrown insurgency, and the government's persistent inability to accurately assess the threat posed by the terror group. This ultimately meant that the Nigerian state continued to fail at its most fundamental duty: protecting its people.

From the very beginning of Boko Haram's rise to power, the federal government was slow to recognize the threat it posed. The group was founded in Maiduguri back in 2002 by a charismatic young preacher called Mohammed Yusuf. This band of insurgents, widely known today as Boko Haram—which in Hausa, the region's dominant language, means "Western education is forbidden"— had no name for years, and was simply referred to as *Yusufiyya*, or "Yusuf's ideology."

At the time of the group's inception, northeastern Nigeria was a region defined by vast disillusionment, particularly among its youth, due to economic stagnation, widespread unemployment, and the clear signs of government corruption. Yusuf was among those who fervently believed sharia law, or law based on the Qur'an, was the required remedy for all social ills. As such, he threw his support behind political aspirants running on sharia platforms in fiercely contested statewide elections, supporting candidates like

Ali Modu Sheriff, who won his race to become the governor of Borno state in 2003.

But what came next wasn't the sweeping overhaul Yusuf had expected. Instead, a moderate form of sharia law crept into place and failed to deliver the changes that many hankered for, leaving the chasm between the haves and the have-nots as wide as ever, and public discontent on the rise. The outcome of the political process led Mohammed Yusuf to conclude that politicians like Sheriff embraced religiosity simply for political gain. Yusuf, a lackluster theologian but captivating public speaker, now filled with a sense of grievance, began to preach against Western education, arguing it was incompatible with the teachings of the Qur'an. In addition, he declared working for the Nigerian government a sin, *haram*.

Yusuf's following grew in Maiduguri and beyond, primarily among the marginalized youth population of the northeast. These mostly poor young men, weary of government neglect, social inequities, and the lack of economic opportunity, clung to the Boko Haram leader's dissident antigovernment message. His denouncement of democracy, rejection of government corruption, and dissemination of powerful imagery depicting persecuted Muslims around the globe stoked their inherent disaffection for Nigerian society and those who governed it.

In a sermon delivered by Mohammed Yusuf in Maiduguri in 2006, he preached, "The infidels must be killed. They're not worthy of trust. Most of them are people who can't keep their word. They're sinners, they don't know the truth. A high-ranking officer will tell you: "We want peace and tranquility so we're going to protect you. We are Christians. They brought us here to protect you." But that's not true! In fact, he came to kill us, to hurt us."

The mosque where Yusuf preached—Ibn Taymiyyah, which sat by the Maiduguri railway station—became an increasingly critical lifeline for the town's poor, who flocked to the strategically located center to take advantage of its myriad community support programs, which included feeding orphans and providing free Islamic education. Meanwhile, Yusuf became increasingly emboldened. He took his sermons on the road, traveling across Nigeria's northeast and drawing large crowds, sometimes numbering in the hundreds. State politicians and local religious leaders, including Yusuf's former mentor, Sheikh Ja'afar Mahmoud Adam, took issue with his incendiary rhetoric and viewed his growing influence with dismay. As criticisms of his message and actions grew louder, local police began to harass Yusuf, arresting him multiple times. But Yusuf continued delivering his fiery public sermons, leading many to believe he had powerful patrons at the highest levels of the Borno state government protecting him. Regardless of who his political allies were, Mohammed Yusuf used his encounters with the police to stoke mistrust of government security forces among his followers and to entrench his favored narrative, that jihad may be required to end the persecution they and Muslims everywhere faced.

In February 2009 at Ibn Taymiyyah Mosque, Maiduguri, Yusef preached: "The lesson to be learned here is that if Allah tells you to do something, you must do it. If you ask for compromises, you're lost. . . . You see, here, in this town, they shout, they say we're idiots: they say a lot of things about us. They came looking for me. They arrested me. . . . They want to arrest me while people love me. I swear to you: We're not ashamed, neither afraid."

In turn, Boko Haram members increasingly responded to their critics with threats and low-level violence, which eventually morphed into general criminality and targeted assassinations; it has long been rumored that the killing of Sheikh Adam is an example of the group's handiwork. The famed Islamic scholar met the Boko Haram leader in the northwestern Nigerian city of Kano, just as the 1990s drew to a close. Back then a young Mohammed Yusuf was still striving to deepen his knowledge of the Qur'an and find a doctrinal home within Islam. The charismatic Adam drew him close and into the ranks of the Izala movement—a congregation of Sunni Muslims whose faith is shaped by Salafism—the belief in the literal reading and application of Islam's holy book to all of society's challenges, in concert with the Sunna, the traditions of the Prophet Muhammed and the examples of the first three generations of Muslims (the *Salaf*). Most notable is their vehement objection to other denominations of Islam, in particular, the Shia and Sufism (a mystical approach to the religion). The two men eventually fell out as Yusuf took off down a path of radicalization, which in turn gave rise to his rejection of Western-style education and denouncements of Nigeria's constitutionally mandated secular government. Sheikh Adam became increasingly alarmed by the words out of his mentee's mouth and by the aggressive actions of Yusuf's growing band of followers. He soon felt compelled to add his voice to the chorus of public criticism loudly condemning Yusuf and Boko Haram. On April 13, 2007, Sheikh Ja'afar Mahmoud Adam was gunned down while leading early-morning prayers in his Kano mosque. It is widely believed that his stance against Mohammed Yusuf cost him his life, though to this day there have been no claims of responsibility for the attack and no one has ever been prosecuted.

The escalating tensions between Boko Haram and the Nigerian authorities reached their climax on February 20, 2009, when a group of Mohammed Yusuf's followers, on their way to bury one of their own, clashed with local police during a routine traffic stop, leaving a number of Boko Haram members dead and others injured. As far as Yusuf was concerned, the episode was a game changer. He promptly escalated his attacks on the government, while calling for his followers to prepare for jihad.

The government requested that Yusuf travel to the capital, Abuja, for questioning. He refused and chose open conflict instead. Armed Boko Haram members took to the streets of Maiduguri and engaged in a pitched battle with Nigerian security forces. In response, the federal government launched a brutal crackdown on the group, going door-to-door in search of the dissidents. When it was all over, hundreds of people were dead and the Nigerian authorities faced widespread allegations of extrajudicial killings and collective punishment of innocent civilians.

On July 30, 2009, local police took a handcuffed and half-naked Mohammed Yusuf to the police station in Maiduguri for questioning, much of which his interrogators filmed on mobile phones. He was killed during a transfer involving the paramilitary branch of the Nigerian police. Much to the horror of his followers, gruesome images of their slain leader were widely circulated online. His bullet-ridden body, handcuffed, half-naked, and lying on the ground, was there for everyone to see. To Yusuf's followers, he'd been martyred, and his death was proof of the state violence he'd constantly talked about. The government, meanwhile, not satisfied with rounding up every follower of Mohammed Yusuf they could find, bulldozed his mosque. The remaining members of Boko Haram were driven underground. The federal government patted itself on the back for stamping Boko Haram out of existence—oblivious to the fact that its actions had set in motion something entirely different and more deadly.

Boko Haram remained out of sight for nearly a year, only to reemerge in June 2010 with a new leader, Abubakar Shekau, Mohammed Yusuf's former deputy. In an introductory video, Shekau announced the group's rebirth and new official name, Jama'atu Ahlis Sunna Lidda'awati wal-Jihad, which translates to "People Committed to the Propagation of the Prophet's Teachings and Jihad." One thing was immediately clear: Shekau understood the power of media and the impact of the words and images he put out. Rather than continue Yusuf's habit of sermonizing, Shekau focused on delivering messages loaded with threats of approaching violence, words delivered with all the zeal and theatricality of a madman, to an audience far broader than his predecessor ever contemplated. While Mohammed Yusuf had been focused on speaking to his fellow Muslims, Shekau was more interested in exporting a message of terror to the entire world. He often directly addressed the Nigerian president and other world leaders in his statements, as he did on January 11, 2012: "This is a message and an appeal to Goodluck Jonathan, the Christian leaders, and all the others. We are the Jama'atu Ahlis Sunna Lidda'awati wal-Jihad, those they call Boko Haram. Thanks to Allah, we have circulated information, and all we had to say has been said. . . . This my first appeal to you. Convert, Christians. This is my call to you. The work we do is not ours; it is Allah's work."

While under the direction of Mohammed Yusuf, Boko Haram's attacks had primarily focused on state and federal targets, but with Shekau at the helm this changed. Now the terror group expanded its scope of violence to include ordinary Nigerians, who suddenly found themselves targeted in churches, mosques, schools, bars, and markets. In time, the chaos extended beyond Nigeria's borders to disrupt the lives of civilians in Cameroon, Niger, and Chad. The group not only became exponentially more violent, its methods for delivering chaos to terrified local communities grew more sophisticated. Car bombs, improvised explosive devices (IEDS), and suicide bombers all became frightening new additions to Boko Haram's repertory of death.

"Know that for me," Shekau stated on March 25, 2014, "there are two categories of people in the world: those who are with us, and the rest. I'll be happy to kill those against us every time I encounter them. This is now the main goal of my mission, the mission of Shekau, who is talking to you. Now you'll know exactly who I am. Now you'll know my madness. You can imagine it, but you'll know more about it because, I swear, I'm going to slit your throats. I won't be content until I have cut your throats. I swear, I'm going to cut your throats."

The terror outfit unleashed a wave of deadly attacks on a near-daily basis across northeastern Nigeria, predominantly in the states of Borno, Yobe, and Adamawa. The death and destruction carried on largely unchecked till May 2013, when Nigerian president Goodluck Jonathan declared a state of emergency in those three states. Yet Human Rights Watch estimates that even with the massive deployment of troops and the imposition of a curfew, Boko Haram launched 192 attacks in northeastern Nigeria and Abuja from May 2013 to October 2014, and claimed the lives of over four thousand civilians. The government's response wasn't working.

The group then opened a new front in its war against modernity and progress, destroying the education system in the northeast. Shekau and his men systematically decimated and in many cases razed to the ground hundreds of schools, killed hundreds of teachers and students, and forced thousands of education workers to flee. At the time of the attack on the Government Girls Secondary School in Chibok in Borno State, schools at all levels had been closed for months in twenty-two out of twenty-seven local government areas due to the insecurity. On March 25, 2014, less than one month before Shekau's followers descended on Chibok, Shekau appeared on camera. During the course of his long and rambling remarks he repeated his opposition to learning: "Western education is a sin, university is a sin. Stop going to university, bastards! Women, go back to your homes!" Shekau's rant against Western education and his unerring belief that women should remain uneducated and instead committed to a life of marriage and domesticity was the continuation of a norm established by his predecessor, Mohammed Yusuf. However, Shekau's words should not be taken as a foreshadowing of the attack on the Chibok girls' school. That was not a preplanned action. Details about the sequence of events on the night of April 14 and the arguments among the men regarding what to do with the girls make it clear that their abduction was a crime of opportunity. The insurgents arrived at the school primarily looking for the male students and to steal supplies. When they found hundreds of girls alone and unprotected, the occasion to disappear with them presented itself, and the men took it. It was quite simply another example of the Nigerian government's failure to protect its own people.

To a man like Abubakar Shekau, who instinctually understood the value of images and the power of the media, the capture of the Chibok girls was a boon. The girls were not only priceless from a PR perspective, capable of transforming Boko Haram's erstwhile profile from national to global. They also gave Shekau and Boko Haram huge leverage over the Nigerian government as they negotiated for the release of Boko Haram members long holed up in prisons across the land. The Chibok girls were essentially a gift to Boko Haram, and in the months that followed their disappearance, Abubakar Shekau relied on sound and images of the girls to press home his newfound advantage.

CHAPTER SEVEN

"WE SHOULD BURN THESE GIRLS!"

"No, let's take them with us!"

"Why not leave them here?"

The men were still arguing, dozens of them trading verbal blows while Saa and the other horrified girls looked on. None of the men seemed particularly troubled by the fact that the lives of almost three hundred schoolgirls hung in the balance. Amid all the yelling, the girls had been divided into groups. Each batch would burn in a different room in the school buildings that were aflame just a few feet away. Tensions were escalating when a slim man with outsize eyes suddenly appeared. Saa had never seen him before. Like many of the insurgents, he too looked young and was just as scruffy. But when he spoke, tempers seemed to cool for a moment.

"Ah! What are you trying to do?"

"We wanted to burn them!"

"Why not take them with us, since we have an empty vehicle?"

His suggestion triggered a fresh round of quarreling. The same positions were expressed, and the newcomer continued to calmly repeat his idea of taking the girls with them, till he finally got his way. The girls later discovered his name was Mallam Abba. He was a commander.

"Follow us!" the men shouted.

None of it made any sense to Saa. *Why? To where?* As the insurgents shuffled her out of the compound, she felt as if her whole life were on fire. All Saa could see was the ominous orange glow of flames consuming every one of her school buildings. With every step, the fears within her grew. She struggled to make sense of the competing thoughts throbbing in her head. *This isn't supposed to be happening.* The insurgents had asked about the boys and the brick-making machine; they'd systematically emptied the school store, carrying bag after bag of foodstuffs and loading all of it into the huge waiting truck. With everything now packed away, Saa had thought the insurgents would simply let the girls go home. After all, that's what had happened during their previous attacks on schools—they'd always let the schoolgirls go, after handing out a warning to abandon their education and strict instructions to get married. Saa had simply expected the same thing to happen once more, not this.

She scanned the crowd of faces surrounding her; the creased brows and startled expressions of the others made it clear that everyone was equally confused. Whatever the turmoil they were feeling, they kept it to themselves. No one said a word. Saa fell into a sort of orderly scrum with the men corralling and motioning her forward with their guns, each weapon held high and pointed straight at the girls.

Saa and Blessing moved in unison, along with the hundreds of others, snaking along in the dark through the open compound gate, past the small guard post usually occupied by Mr. Jida, which now sat empty. Yelling came from nearby Chibok town. Saa could smell burning, then heard the sound of gunshots and people running. It was bedlam.

Just beyond the compound walls sat a crowd of bushes. As she and the men moved out into the open, Saa felt their thorns spring forward, eager to pull at her clothing and scratch and pierce her body. Careful not to yell out in pain, she tried to keep her clothes beyond the reach of the grasping thicket with no time to pause and examine what might be broken skin.

Saa retreated into herself and turned to the faith that had anchored her entire life. *Lord, am I going to die tonight, or will I survive?* Desperate to live, unspoken prayers filled her mind and she pleaded, repeatedly, *God save me.*

She was still praying as they walked down the dirt path away from the flaming school. The shabby-looking men with their wild eyes gave no explanation or directions. They simply motioned with their heads and the sweep of their rifles, making it clear to keep moving. As the reality began to sink in, Saa felt her chest tightening. Her heart was going to beat its way out of her body. But she couldn't allow herself to cry or make any sound. Any kind of display would make her a target, and who knew what these men might do?

The insurgents walked alongside, behind, and in front of her; they were everywhere. Every time Saa looked around, their menacing forms filled her view. Initially, all the girls were steered away from the main road and onto a rambling path overgrown with bushes; the detour was likely made in an attempt to avoid detection.

Saa had left the blazing school wearing a pair of flip-flops, but as she realized they were heading to some unknown destination on foot, she decided her footwear would make it difficult to keep up with everyone if the group suddenly had to run. So she grabbed the sandals, whipped off her headscarf, and wrapped everything in the fabric, tying the improvised pouch around her waist. She did her best to move quickly with the crowd along the uncleared trail and eventually onto the main road feeling the sting and burn of thorns piercing her feet and embedding themselves deep beneath the skin. All the while, the temperature was dropping, leaving the shaken teenage girl shivering and in growing pain as the trek continued in silence. Then without any warning—a new threat.

"If you have a phone you'd better throw it! If we catch anyone who has a phone, that person will be punished!"

Most of the girls did as they were told, but Saa refused to part with her one possible means of communication with her family. Tucked away in the pouch with her flip-flops, the cell phone pressed into her waist as she moved.

The girls walked for almost fifteen minutes before they reached the clearing. There, amid the bushes, sat the monster nine-eleven truck, the same one Saa had seen in her school compound being filled up with all their food supplies. Now it was parked alongside almost a dozen cars and pickup trucks.

"Sit down!" the men shouted, pointing to a large tree.

Saa and the others did as they were told and started to lower themselves without making a sound. The sight of the parked vehicles stirred up disturbing new questions. *What were these men planning to do next?* The insurgents were in deep conversation, but Saa could hear only fragments of what was being said. It was enough to know they weren't speaking Hausa, the dominant language spoken in northern Nigeria, nor Kibaku, the mother tongue of people from Chibok and the first language Saa, Priscilla, and all the other girls from this town had learned when they were growing up. The sounds she caught were the unfamiliar notes of Kanuri, the language of the ethnic group of the same name, from which significant numbers of Boko Haram members originated.

"Say your last prayers," the men ordered. At once the startled girls began to shake and whimper. For Saa, that command stirred up images of her beloved family. She pictured her adoring parents and the five brothers she'd fought and loved with such great intensity her whole short life. But she remained dry eyed and bowed her head to pray. Moments later, though, the group was told to get up and start entering the parked vehicles. Saa looked up and realized what was happening. They weren't to be killed. They were being kidnapped.

"If you refuse to get into the truck, stand and make yourself known! We will shoot you," said the men, glaring at the girls without any trace of pity. Saa had no doubt she should take them at their word. These men would easily kill any girl who showed the slightest sign of resisting.

The insurgents pointed them toward the waiting vehicles, but only the nine-eleven and a small sedan had space for passengers. The rest were already jammed full of food items they'd swiped from Chibok town. Saa watched as the majority of the girls were shepherded to the vast truck. Given its size and imposing bulk, it was impossible for any of them to actually climb in without assistance. One of the smaller cars started up its engine and slowly inched itself into position, allowing the girls to use its roof as a launching pad from which they could hurl themselves into the body of the vehicle. They moved in clusters. One by one the girls clambered onto the car and, while trying to stay upright, shakily scrambled inside the truck. When it was finally her turn, she stared at Blessing. With her friend's hand held tightly in her own, the two girls moved forward. It was hard to make her way onto the car and not slide off. Thankfully Blessing's outstretched hands helped steady her. Eventually Saa hoisted herself into the cavernous truck.

Once inside, she found the contents of their school store: bags of flour, potatoes, rice, pasta, onions, and containers of oil, all of it covering the floor of the nine-eleven and leaving barely any room for the nearly two hundred girls now crowding in. As best they could, Saa and her schoolmates settled down on top and in between the bags of food. Girls seated friends on their laps, limbs mounted on limbs, bodies squeezed in close, making it difficult to tell where one girl began and another one ended. Saa moved farther down in the long truck and wedged herself into a tiny space alongside Blessing and three other schoolgirls who were also from her hometown of Askira. She perched on the bags of food with her limbs twisted beneath her, her figure bent to take up the least amount of space possible. By the time the convoy pulled off, numbness and pain were rapidly spreading everywhere in her body. Dorcas was there too, buried deep in the throng of girls.

Now that the vehicle was packed with stolen children and food, the men were concerned about how fast the overladen truck might move. With that in mind, the driver of the nine-eleven was given a head start and ordered to set off before the rest of the convoy. Meanwhile, the only other available vehicle was crammed with twenty young bodies. Close to a hundred other girls were left without a mode of transportation and forced to travel on foot.

The open-air nine-eleven moved slowly, navigating the craters in the potholed road with great caution. It actually wasn't much of a road, more a dirt path eked from a landscape that became increasingly overrun by spiky bushes and sprawling trees the farther the convoy traveled. Saa stared long and hard into the darkness, but gave up after a while because she couldn't find any clues as to where they were headed. She had no way of knowing how long they'd actually been traveling in the truck, but it seemed like hours. Even so, Saa felt they were still somewhere in the vicinity of Chibok. Those suspicions were confirmed from time to time as an occasional girl in the truck suddenly perked up and pointed excitedly at her village as it retreated in the distance and the convoy rolled by. When they eventually left Chibok town and headed into Sambisa Forest, Saa was none the wiser. She had no idea they were entering a massive forest enclave that covers parts of four Nigerian states and borders the nations of Niger, Chad, and Cameroon—or that its harsh terrain of sand and low-lying savanna brush made it the most inhospitable of places.

The girls from Askira—Saa's hometown—were all squashed together in the truck and kept asking each other, "Where are we going? What should we do now?" As the minutes ticked by, their despair deepened. In the darkness, Saa heard a bloodcurdling scream cut through the night. She quickly turned. One of the girls was howling in pain and frantically clutching her thigh. While Saa and the others had squeezed themselves into body of the truck, this girl had preferred to sit above the others on the side of the vehicle with her legs outstretched. She never saw the large branch before it swooped down and slammed into her leg. As her screams grew louder and more desperate, Saa could tell from the way her leg was dangling that it was broken. Doubled over in pain, the wailing girl was brought down into the belly of the truck.

In time, Saa heard the sound of other engines trailing them. The convoy continued to move toward an unknown destination, and the girls in the nine-eleven found themselves ducking and cowering as the forest vegetation drew closer around them and thorny branches plucked scarves straight from their heads or found exposed arms to scratch and cut. When the truck came to an abrupt stop, Saa couldn't tell whether the crumbling shacks in the surrounding vicinity had occupants; she never saw anyone. The entire area seemed deserted. But within seconds the structures were on fire and the flames were greeted with cries of *"Allahu Akbar!"* and much rejoicing. As the smoke rose into the night sky, one of the girls alongside Saa whispered and forlornly pointed at the outline of her own home off in the distance. All they could do was stare. Both of them knew the girl's house might as well have been on another planet, as there was no chance of reaching it from where they sat in a convoy surrounded by lawless men.

When they finally got going again, the truck, laden down with girls and stolen provisions, continued at the same slow pace, as the talk among the girls in the truck turned to escape. Saa listened carefully as her fellow students encouraged each other to jump and make a run for it. She nervously contemplated the idea with the rest of the girls from Askira. They all knew there was no guarantee of success. If anything, there was probably a greater chance of winding up dead. Saa followed the back-and-forth conversation, thinking about the anguish her disappearance would cause her loved ones.

Two of the girls from Askira were sisters and the only Muslims in their group. They argued strenuously against the idea of jumping.

"No, don't jump!"

"What if you were to get injured?"

"If you jump and these Boko Haram boys see you, you could be killed."

"If any one of you jumps, we will tell the Boko boys what you have done."

The threat of exposing the others shocked Saa; why would they even think of blocking their schoolmates' bid for freedom? It was unclear how the sisters actually planned to tell the insurgents anything when the girls were alone in the back of the nine-eleven. The convoy was still edging forward, creeping deeper into the sprawling forest. At times Saa could make out what looked like farms and settlements between the trees, but never anyone moving about. *Where was everybody?*

The mere thought of jumping off the massive, high truck made Saa light-headed. She was still playing scenarios over in her mind when girls started leaping. Openmouthed, her heart pounding, Saa watched as girl after girl announced she was going to jump, got up, crawled to the side of the truck, then without warning threw herself over, to be swallowed up by the darkness of the forest. Each time, Saa waited for screams or the sound of gunshots, but each time she heard nothing. She was now trapped in a battle with her deepest fears.

I could break my legs or even my neck. I could even die from doing this.

If the other girls have jumped and we haven't heard anything, maybe they are making their way home. Why not at least try?

Let me sacrifice my life. I will either live or die.

Saa so badly wanted to go home. In the end, it was her family she was thinking of, the pain her abduction would cause. She leaned over and whispered to Blessing, "I am going to jump." She'd made up her mind. "I will follow you," Blessing whispered back.

Without saying a word Saa moved to the left side of the truck and paused. She felt the relentless motion of the vehicle and stared out at the bushes and trees passing by. The ground looked so far away. She had no idea how it would feel to land on it. But she came back to the one guiding thought: *I'd rather jump and die out in the forest where there is at least the chance of my body being recovered, than let Boko Haram take me and my parents never see me or my body again.* With that, she jumped.

Saa landed in the middle of the road, winded and disoriented. For the briefest of moments she just lay there, a little shocked she was still alive. Then she remembered that the other militants in cars and on motorbikes at the rear of the convoy were approaching. She mentally scanned her body to make sure she wasn't injured, then half slithered, half ran into the dense growth on the side of the road. She hid beneath a mass of thick bushes and waited. Saa lay absolutely frozen in the dirt until the rest of the insurgents swept past. Even then she didn't dare emerge from her hiding place. She waited till she could no longer see the lights of the convoy. Only then did she stand and try to make sense of her pitch-black surroundings. Looking around, she could distinguish only bushes and trees. There were also lots of weird noises she didn't recognize. She was overwhelmed. *I've jumped—now what?*

Saa stood in the dark wondering how she would get home and what lay in store for her deep in the forest. She was searching for answers and trying to solve the riddle of the strange sounds when she heard her name. She froze. It was Blessing! In the shadows of the forest, her only guide was the sound of the strained, barely audible voice of her friend. Saa nervously felt her way along in the dark and found Blessing lying in a crumpled heap near the road, injured and crying hysterically. She'd sprained both of her ankles. Still, a sense of relief flooded both girls now that they'd escaped the truck and found each other.

Blessing couldn't continue to lie out in the open. Saa bent down to help her friend to her feet, but the pressure made the girl groan in agony and her tears fell even faster. They moved farther into the forest, ultimately settling under a large tree surrounded by thick bushes. They sat there on the forest floor, terrified of snakes and the unidentifiable growls, screeches, and squawks coming from every direction. As the hours passed, the girls grew colder, and they held each other close. Saa spoke encouraging words to Blessing throughout the night, but there was nothing she could do to ease her friend's pain. By the time the sun rose high in the sky the next morning, neither girl had slept. Saa needed to get help for Blessing. The cell phone she'd flouted orders to keep with her turned out to be useless. She later discovered that Boko Haram had permanently damaged three of the four telecom masts that loomed over the Chibok town center before heading into the forest. So right then, her phone, the one thing Saa thought would save them, was about as useful as a rock.

Daybreak brought an instant smothering heat, and for the first time Saa could properly take in their surroundings. She and Blessing were completely alone amid clumps of savanna grass mixed with short, wiry bushes. Trees that ranged from scrawny to full bodied were scattered among the rest of the vegetation.

Saa would have to go in search of help by herself. She refused to sit there and die in the forest after summoning up the courage to leap from a moving truck. Besides, Blessing was still gripped by pain, unable to move. Saa was very afraid, but once again, she thought back to her family, who would be worrying, and she reminded herself that she would do whatever was necessary to get back to them. Saa was convinced that if she walked through the bushes, she would eventually find someone. She assured Blessing she would be back soon, then looked all around and listened. She could just about make out the sound of chickens clucking and decided to let that sound be her guide as she took off in search of help.

Saa had been walking only a short time when she came across a small, decrepit shack. The one-room lean-to was made from scraps that appeared to have been scavenged from the forest. Nomadic Fulani herdsmen have long roamed Sambisa Forest using the land to graze their cattle, and these traditionally fair-skinned people most times live in temporary dwellings spread throughout the trees and wild bushes. Inside the ramshackle shelter, Saa spotted a woman cooking while packing her belongings. From her complexion Saa readily assumed she was a Fulani and called out to get her attention. When the woman emerged, the schoolgirl immediately launched into a rapid-fire explanation of her situation, pleading for help.

The whole time, the woman, who looked to be somewhere in her forties, remained expressionless and just stared at the animated girl. When Saa finally paused, using a series of gestures and random words, the woman let Saa know that she didn't speak Hausa and hadn't understood a word Saa had said. At that moment the woman's husband emerged. Unlike his wife, he *did* understand Saa, who once again dove into her story, explaining to the equally baffled-looking herdsman what had happened, the condition Blessing was in, and how they needed to get home.

"Can you help show us the way home or even take us somewhere so we can find our way back?" she pleaded.

"No," he replied.

Saa was taken aback and stood there in shocked silence. The man explained that they never stayed in the same place for long and they were busy now, preparing to leave. The best he could do was to offer advice: "Do not to take the road that brought you into the forest. Rather, go through the bushes until you reach one village." Then he pointed the way they should go. As he spoke, gunshots exploded off in the distance and they all flinched. Saa felt the panic rising once more. *Boko Haram was still nearby!* Later she learned that a vehicle in the convoy had broken down, and while they tried to fix the mechanical problem, the men had started wildly firing off their guns.

Saa stared intently at the couple and decided she wasn't prepared to take no for an answer. Not after everything they'd been through. She started up again, explaining there was no way Blessing could walk anywhere with her injuries, let alone make it through the forest. Plus Saa wasn't strong enough to carry the other girl on her own.

"You're the only one who can help us," she told him and then stood there, refusing to budge. Much to her relief, something she had said got through to him, and he finally relented. The man grabbed his bicycle, which lay nearby, and the three of them headed off to rescue Blessing. She was exactly where Saa had left her, curled up under the tree. Together, they carefully lifted her onto the bicycle. The man and his wife pushed and steered while Saa followed along behind. Eventually they reached a village, where they found a man willing to make the journey back to Chibok with the girls on his motorbike. The long trek took them through dense bush. The whole time Saa was consumed by thoughts of her loved ones.

While she was fighting to get back to them, her family was likewise overcome with panic and grief. Hours earlier, as soon as Saa's father had ended the call with her, he'd called her back. Baba dialed and redialed her number, but she never answered, and suddenly the line went dead. That same night, Bitrus, one of Saa's elder brothers, had received a phone call from a friend living in Chibok who told him about the mass abduction. Early the next morning, he set off for Chibok. There, Bitrus found a devastated town of heartbroken parents.

When Saa finally returned to Chibok with an injured Blessing in tow, the town was still in a state of pandemonium. Residents were running about the place. The appearance of a handful of Nigerian soldiers had brought added chaos. The already traumatized locals mistook the actual military personnel for Boko Haram fighters, assuming the militants had returned to the town they'd ransacked just a few hours earlier. Eventually the situation calmed down and Saa found a man willing to take her and Blessing back to Askira on his motorbike for a fare. Luckily, Saa had the money they'd grabbed from their dorm just before the insurgents stormed their school. Due to Blessing's condition, Saa knew she needed to take the suffering girl home first. They made their way out of Chibok just as her sibling was anxiously wandering through town searching for news of his little sister.

The fear and tension that had taken hold of Blessing's family melted away the moment they saw her arriving on that bike. Within moments, they were rushing toward the girls and the air was filled with excited shrieks and words of thanks for their loved one's return. Amid their eagerness to sweep the girls off the bike, it took a few moments before anyone noticed that Blessing was injured. The joy in her mother's eyes gave way to a stream of tears.

She was still weeping when Saa and Blessing's older sister carefully carried the wincing girl into the house. But rather than take her to the hospital, the family decided to summon the neighborhood's "bone guy"—an old man known for tending to broken, sprained, and dislocated limbs. He showed up in due course and tended to Blessing's swollen ankles. In the midst of all of this, Saa heard her phone ring. Though the Chibok telecom towers had been targeted and damaged in the raid, now that she was back in town, Saa's cell phone spluttered back to life. The voice on the other end was her mother's. She was tense and stern.

"Where are you? Come home as soon as possible!"

For a moment, Saa felt a measure of irritation at being spoken to that way after everything she'd just been through. Then she paused and listened carefully. What she heard then was love, anxiety, and a mother's deep fears of losing her only daughter.

"I'm coming. I'm coming home."

Even with that assurance, her family continued to call incessantly, seeking continued reassurance that she was safe.

It was almost midday when Saa got to her house. The neighbors had spotted her as she approached on the motorbike, and now a crowd of people came rushing out and followed along as she traveled the last few yards home. Everyone in her neighborhood was overcome with emotion. When she finally walked through the door, seeing the pain and worry on her mother's face made Saa's heart ache. For Rebecca, it would take holding her daughter once more to convince her that Saa was real and not a ghost. As the entire family crowded around and cradled her in their arms, Saa felt as though she'd died and come back to life. The horrors of the night quickly receded, and soon there were no more thoughts. All that mattered were the surging feelings of love, joy, and gratitude that remained.

CHAPTER EIGHT

FEAR AND ADRENALINE POWERED EVERY FOOTSTEP ESTHER TOOK toward her daughter's school. She moved oblivious to the sweltering heat that had already drenched her in sweat. Nor did she notice the clouds of dust being kicked up as she shuffled down the rock-strewn path. All that existed was Dorcas.

Everything else faded into the background. Nothing but her perfect girl mattered. Not knowing the whereabouts of her child made her insides churn and her heart sit heavily in her chest. As she drew closer to the school, her head was pulsing. *Where is my baby?*

The same panic and confusion was also swirling in the minds and bodies of all the residents of Chibok town. The nighttime in-truders had come and gone, leaving most of the town physically intact. But more time was needed to fully assess the damage done to the heart and soul of this dusty place.

The badly shaken locals all asked the same question: "What has happened to our children?" At the center of everyone's thoughts were the girls. Concerns for them drew residents from their homes and hiding places, pulling them one by one to the school grounds to see for themselves.

As Esther made her way there, she heard desperate wailing and shouting. They were sounds of anguish that made her heart lurch.

"Our girls are no more."

"Our girls are no more o!"

A group of distraught men and women who'd been to the school were now heading back to Chibok town, stumbling and struggling to walk. Their pain reached out to smother Esther.

"Our girls are no more o!" they lamented while their bodies shook as they wept. The words threatened to shatter the hearts of all who heard them.

The group inched forward. Esther rushed toward them.

"What happened?"

The wracked sobbing suffocated their words, and those syllables that managed to break free threatened to destroy Esther.

"Our girls are no more o!"

"Nobody is in the school. The girls are no more!"

The statements made her tremble. Esther stared at their tear-streaked faces. *It's not possible.* She searched for her faith, her lifeline. She'd sat on the cold rock of that hill all night long, praying without end for God to shield her child from the killers in their midst. Her whole life, she'd been told to trust God, to hone her faith for life's difficult moments. And she'd done so. She refused to now abandon what she'd learned and practiced all these years. She couldn't accept the words of these distressed locals about the fate of her child.

She needed to get to the school to see for herself. She was convinced her baby was likely hiding somewhere out of sight from everyone, unseen by these broken souls who now wrongly proclaimed all the girls were gone.

At five thirty a.m. Esther finally stood in the school compound and faced the burning buildings where her fifteen-year-old had happily slept, studied, and played, and she felt as though she were being sucked into the charred structures. Unable to turn away, she watched as the flames lingered and clung to the hostels, the storage room, the staff quarters, and the principal's house, burning with an intensity that seemed almost impossible given the fact that the blaze had been lit many hours before. The fire burned with ferocity, occasionally spitting and hissing when it absorbed something that gave it more fuel.

In that moment, Esther felt hopeless, but she willed herself to remain calm. She struggled to piece together what had happened during the overnight hours in the school.

Looking around the compound, she knew there was no way her daughter could be in hiding amid the rubble. *My Dorcas is not here.* Her child, along with all the other girls, had simply disappeared. All that remained were mementos: an open notebook filled with swirly handwriting facedown in the dirt, a solitary shoe dropped midflight, a worn-looking school uniform quickly tossed aside. Proof that just hours earlier this was a place of learning, where hundreds of hopeful girls once filled its classrooms and dreamed about bigger, bolder lives, until Boko Haram appeared.

What have these Boko boys done with my Dorcas? Esther was still struggling to contain her mounting panic when a fair-skinned girl wearing a disheveled school uniform walked into the compound around eight o'clock. The reaction to her sudden appearance was one of shock, rather than celebration.

Esther rushed to her. "Do you know Dorcas?"

The girl nodded. "We are in the same class."

"Have you seen her?"

"She went home." The girl looked utterly confused by the question, but nonetheless nodded her head to emphasize her point.

Eventually Esther realized the girl was in shock and had no idea what had happened to her schoolmates. She had undergone her own ordeal that night, different from the others. Esther learned that the girl had been unwell and curled up fast asleep in the hostel when Boko Haram arrived. Somehow she'd remained asleep while the men raised their voices and filled the nighttime air with endless cries of *"Allahu Akbar."* She'd been overlooked when the men searched the hostels for hiding girls until the smell of the burning school finally woke her. By the time she made it out into the compound, not a single girl was in sight. Everyone she knew was gone.

But she hadn't been completely alone. She could hear voices nearby. Panicked, she climbed a tree and from there watched as strange-looking men strutted through the compound and torched the various buildings. Soon the heat of the growing inferno made her hiding place unbearable and she clambered down quickly. As her surroundings burned, the girl made the split-second decision to scale the school wall, and once on the other side, she took off running in search of safety. Hours later she had come back to see for herself what had happened to her cherished schoolmates and her school. Before long, hordes of other fearful parents had surrounded the girl, besieging her with queries about their own missing kin. Esther never got around to finding out her name, and the two never spoke again.

By eleven o'clock, other dazed-looking girls started to appear. They arrived tired and bedraggled, some in groups of twos, some alone, while others showed up in clusters of five or eight, and they would continue to arrive over the course of the next two days. Every one of them had escaped from the convoy and hidden in the bushes of Sambisa Forest until it felt safe enough to attempt the journey home. On that first day, Esther scanned every face, desperate to spot her beautiful daughter among them, each time praying for a moment of instant recognition. Esther peppered the girls with questions about Dorcas. A handful confirmed her worst fear: Boko Haram had carried her daughter away.

Some of the escapees said they'd been sitting with her child inside the nine-eleven truck. Dorcas' slightly older cousin Lydia told Esther she'd been by her side and had asked Dorcas to jump to freedom with her. Initially she'd said yes, but when the moment to escape presented itself, the younger girl had a change of heart.

Esther easily understood her daughter's behavior. Dorcas's closest friends were still in the vehicle, and they were her only source of comfort and support. Plus the prospect of jumping from a moving truck several feet off the ground in the pitch dark would have been too harrowing for a fifteen-year old. As Lydia told her story, Yakubu, Dorcas's father, stood by his wife's side. The words of the traumatized girl drove both parents to a new low.

Esther could see for herself that her daughter was gone, but she couldn't bring herself to accept it. She started to sway. "It's not true, it's not true," she bawled. "Lord, why did you allow me to see this day?"

The compound was full of townspeople, and a small group gathered around Esther and did their best to urge her to accept what had happened. Their words made no sense to her. How could she accept? As with most families in Chibok, this mother had poured everything into her daughter with the understanding that Dorcas would surpass her parents' achievements. She would go off to college, excel, and become a professional. In Esther's case, Dorcas was going to be their family's success story.

Lord, how will my dreams for my baby come true, if she is nowhere to be found? Why would you keep me in this world without my baby?

Esther couldn't imagine a life without her child. With each passing moment her heart broke further, and eventually the despair sent Esther crashing to the ground. Her knees sank deep into the dust, and a wail from the depths of her soul broke free from her lips and filled the compound with her unbearable grief.

It seemed as if the entire population of Chibok town was there, packed into that schoolyard. As the minutes ticked by, the sense of mourning deepened. Soon the collective sorrow was so great, it was nearly impossible to distinguish the anguish of parents whose daughters had been taken from the misery of the rest of the supportive community. Distraught parents, distressed family members, concerned locals, all of them stood together weeping and shouting in mounting confusion and anger.

As the hours passed and the day's heat intensified, rather than go home and rest, the grief-stricken locals remained on the school grounds, and their frustrations mounted. "Where are our girls?" they demanded. "Where have these boys taken them? Who has seen them?"

But there were no figures of authority present to hear their pleas or to provide answers. The state's governor, Kashim Shettima, was based in the state capital of Maiduguri, a little over two hours by road away from Chibok. For reasons never satisfactorily explained to this disconsolate community, he wouldn't arrive for several more days. The handful of soldiers assigned to protect the people of Chibok had scattered into the night the moment the boys had arrived. Esther had seen several up on the hill among the rest of the townspeople. In the aftermath of the attack, they'd been spotted briefly before disappearing once more and remaining stubbornly out of sight. The people of Chibok had only each other to turn to for solace.

All morning long, girls continued to emerge from the bush, bruised and wide eyed with terror. Some wandered first to nearby villages because they got lost on their way back; concerned villagers from those respective places brought them back to Chibok.

For hours, Esther stood out in the sun, her eyes raw with grief, listening, staring, and holding out for anything that would revive her hopes. All the while her lips were never still, in perpetual motion, reciting an endless loop of prayers. "Please God, perform a miracle."

After many hours in the heat, dust, and smoke, families began to leave. The punishing grief had left people weary, and there was a need to return home for respite and to consider what should happen next.

Despite the pleas of her husband and his brother, Esther refused to leave. "I have a right to be here, to welcome her home when she returns," she snapped at them. As two thirty approached, she'd already spent more than eight hours in the school compound, and now her family feared they'd never be able to make her leave. Yakubu and his brother were growing increasingly concerned about Esther's physical and emotional well-being. They approached her slowly.

"Dorcas has made it back! She's at home, now, waiting for us."

"Is it true?" Her mind was whirling. *God, you have answered my prayers and brought my baby back to me!*

With words of praise falling from her lips, Esther took off running for home, without any thought of waiting for her husband. The only thing that mattered to her was holding her child in her arms. She had to see her child. *I must hold my baby and make sure she is unharmed.*

By three o'clock Esther was home. "Dorcas!" she shouted as she came running through the front door. Her heart pounded. Her face wore a wide smile as she stood waiting for her daughter to respond.

But there was only silence.

"Dorcas!" she called out.

Nothing moved and the house remained quiet. Esther headed quickly to her daughter's room. Surely Dorcas was in there and had simply not heard her. But when she opened the door, she saw the room just as she'd left it hours before, full of Dorcas's clothes, her bed, books, and table. There was no sign of her beloved girl.

Panic stirred within her. Esther was moving faster now through the house—searching each room, pushing past furniture, yelling Dorcas's name. In each room she found only more stillness and silence. Esther scanned every inch of the house. She muttered to herself. If her child wasn't inside, maybe she was outdoors. She rushed through the front door, heading straight to the outdoor toilets and washing area. "Dorcas!" She was screaming now.

Neighbors peering from their own homes watched with growing sorrow as Esther ran about her compound, calling her daughter's name over and over, her face and blouse soaked with tears. By the time Yakubu and his brother reached her, Esther was overwrought. She was still searching for Dorcas, crying so hard she could hardly breathe. Her voice was hoarse by now and still she cried out, "Dorcas!"

Yakubu gently led Esther back into their house. "I'm sorry," he said. "Dorcas remains lost to us." He'd lied to her, he explained. He could think of no other way to bring Esther home.

Through her tears, Esther nodded. She stared at her beloved husband and felt only compassion for him. There was no anger; she understood why he'd done it.

All she knew for certain in that moment were two things.

Her child was gone.

And life had lost all meaning.

CHAPTER NINE

As with much of the world, most Nigerians had never heard of the town called Chibok before April 14, 2014. Far from places like Abuja, the nation's capital and nexus of political power, and Lagos, a commercial megacity, this small corner off the beaten track in the country's northeast had never been the sort of place that crept into the conversations of the nation's rich and powerful. In fact, with little of importance ever taking place there, it was just as unlikely to be a topic of discussion among the nation's poor. Chibok was so far off the radar that in the minds of most, it simply didn't exist.

As news of the Chibok kidnappings emerged, Nigerians began to build a faint picture of the place. Details from domestic news outlets were sketchy and often contradictory, which made it difficult for most people to grasp what had happened. Unanswered questions multiplied rapidly. How could hundreds of schoolgirls have been stolen from a school in Borno, which was under a state of emergency? Where were their teachers? What were they doing in school anyway? Weren't all schools there supposed to be closed? How were the terrorists able to round up hundreds of girls and carry them off in the middle of the night so easily?

A day after the girls' abduction, the Nigerian authorities claimed the number of girls taken was just over a hundred and most had been rescued, a lie intended to lessen the gravity of the situation. Almost three weeks went by before President Goodluck Jonathan made his first public statement about the tragedy. In a country where most of the citizenry take their cues from leaders when it comes to formulating an opinion on issues of note, the government's relative silence spoke volumes. It also created a vacuum, one that was readily filled by skeptical Nigerians who'd come to the conclusion that the events in Chibok read like a fantastical tale, set in a place they had never heard of, with sketchy details that didn't add up. Soon Nigerians from various walks of life, up and down the country, began to publicly muse that the mass abduction was a hoax.

To understand how Nigerians could respond to a mass outrage of this nature by calling it a "fake news" story requires the unpacking of a confluence of factors. First, the fact that the kidnapping occurred in the north touched on the historic tensions that beset the relationship between Nigeria's largely Muslim north and its predominantly Yoruba and Igbo Christian south. The union of these two regions, which created Nigeria in 1914, came about unnaturally, courtesy of Britain. Spurred on by imperialist ideas, its arrogant colonialists made the decision wholly for the economic gain of the British empire, paying little attention to the religious, ethnic, and social strife such a move would trigger.

In the decades since, a significant number of northerners felt increasingly sidelined by the nation's Christian leaders, who they believe continue to deny the region its rightful share of resources for economic development, which in turn has led to higher levels of poverty, illiteracy, and unemployment in the north than in the south. Over the years, this resentment has burst into view in the form of one military coup after another, each of which severely rocked the nation. In an effort to contain this discontent, the nation's power brokers reached a critical agreement: every two terms the presidency would rotate between an individual from the north and the south of the country. Yet even with this deal in place, the political animus remained and factored into support that grew for the ideology of Mohamed Yusuf, who founded Boko Haram in the early 2000s.

Emotions were already running high at the start of 2014. With every month that rolled by, the political discourse became increasingly charged as the following year's presidential election drew closer. The incumbent president Jonathan, a Christian from the Niger delta in the south, had already served out two terms but was still signaling his intention to mount another run for the presidency, in open defiance of the power-sharing agreement. The mere idea of it incensed northerners, and almost immediately the question taken up by the president's critics became that of what it would take to oust Jonathan from office. This was the backdrop when hundreds of girls from the north seemingly disappeared into thin air. To the administration and the president's supporters, the timing of the mass abduction was proof: this was the work of northern conspirators who had devised the ploy to disrupt Jonathan's reelection chances, and without delay they quickly cried foul. Even when they realized that the majority of the missing girls weren't Muslim but were Christians like the president himself, it did nothing to lessen the belief that this was a plot to energize northern Muslim voters and to depict the president as weak and unable to keep the country safe from Boko Haram. The Nigerian public found itself divided when it came to the veracity of what happened in Chibok, and this in turn created a feedback loop that benefited the administration of Goodluck Jonathan. Most in his government believed enemies had orchestrated the events in Chibok, so they were in no rush to mount a robust response and as there wasn't the public pressure to do so, the administration defaulted to its do-nothing position.

What happened in Nigeria had many similarities to events that would play out in the 2016 US election, where we saw candidate Trump, and eventually President Trump, weaponize information and stoke a climate of confusion in a divided country. In the case of Nigeria, the suggestion that events in Chibok were somehow un-real, or had been set into motion by people with a political agenda, sowed just enough doubt to limit what should have been wholesale outrage and widespread calls to hold the government accountable for its obvious inaction.

Those pushing the narrative of a northern Nigeria political hoax had a host of factors on their side. Chibok was practically beyond the reach of the entire world, except for the Nigerian military, hid-den behind a cordon put in place by the state of emergency. Jour-nalists were forbidden from traveling to Chibok, and even those with the inclination to do so faced a logistical and security night-mare to reach this town, which lay in the Boko Haram heartland. In addition to the physical challenges of reaching Chibok, there was also the problem of poor cell phone coverage. This meant getting information out of Chibok was an ordeal, and by extension, it made it difficult to counter the narrative of "nothing happened here" when it sprung up in the early days of the abduction.

Meanwhile, the lack of visibility for the missing girls' parents also factored into how everything played out. The president's sup-porters routinely argued that the absence of TV and newspaper images featuring distraught Chibok parents was yet more proof that no girls had been taken. The truth was that the majority of the missing girls were from families so poor, they simply couldn't afford to travel to places like Lagos and Abuja, where, at least for a time, hordes of journalists were eagerly waiting to hear their stories of what had happened on that hot night in April. These heartbroken parents were held back by not only their inability to afford the hefty transportation costs, but perhaps just as much by their limited education. Chibok isn't some media-savvy community whose locals would grasp the critical importance of getting the stories of their missing daughters out to Nigeria and the wider world. As a result, there was a gap created by their lack of visibility and silence. Unfortunately, many inside and outside the government would step up to fill it with spin.

Finally, if you look closely enough, you'll also spot something else at play, buried deep in the hoax narrative that took hold of so many: Nigerian society's implicit bias against its poor. Even before the Chibok girls disappeared from their communities, they had been rendered invisible by their poverty in Nigeria's class-conscious society. Their status informed the government's response at the most fundamental level, long before the religious, regional, and political tensions set in. You'd be hard pressed to find anyone in Nigeria who could honestly say that the disappearance of hundreds of schoolgirls from wealthy Nigerian families would have been met with the muted yet taciturn response from the Jonathan government. Instead, we'd have most likely witnessed a marshaling of the full assets of the state. Similarly, attempts to establish a hoax narrative would have been challenged at every turn by educated parents and loved ones, who would have then flooded the media and eliminated the government's ability to use their daughters as pawns in the long-running political battle between Nigeria's north and south.

The truth is, had the Chibok girls been rich, they would have been seen as more valuable, their parents' stories would have been listened to more attentively, and the Chibok community's anguish would have been felt more collectively by their country. Quite simply, the girls would have mattered to many more people.

CHAPTER TEN

FOR ALL THE NIGERIANS WHO DISMISSED THE REPORTS OF THE Chibok girls being abducted from their school in the middle of the night and turned away from their brokenhearted parents, there were many others, also in Nigeria, who quickly recognized that a grave injustice had occurred.

To people like Obiageli "Oby" Ezekwesili, the country's former minister of education, onetime vice-president of the World Bank for Africa, and Nigerian presidential candidate, what happened in Chibok was a painful wrong and the Nigerian government bore the responsibility to make things right. The girls' disappearance shocked Oby to her core, and on April 23, 2014, nine days after the girls were taken, a sense of duty compelled this mother of three sons to seize the moment when she addressed an audience gathered to honor

UNESCO's selection of the Nigerian city of Port Harcourt as the World Book Capital.

Tall and imposing, Oby possessed a deep voice, which was thick with emotion, and her piercing eyes flashed with intensity as she called on everyone present to take a stand "and make a collective demand for our daughters to be released, for our daughters to be rescued. Join us in declaring that Port Harcourt as the book capital of the world makes a collective demand for the rescue of our schoolgirls . . . So today, we call together, bring back all our daughters." Her words struck a chord with the event's organizer, who underscored Oby's plea. "We take it home, bring back our daughters."

The impassioned remarks also struck Ibrahim M. Abdullahi, a Nigerian corporate lawyer who watched Oby's speech on TV from Port Harcourt and immediately posted a message on Twitter amplifying her call to action: "Yes #BringBackOurDaughters #BringBackOurGirls declared by @obyezeks and all people at Port Harcourt World Book Capital 2014." This was the very first use of the hashtag #BringBackOurGirls. Once Oby retweeted Abdullahi's message a few hours later and then followed up with her own—"Lend your Voice to the Cause of our Girls. Please All, use the hashtag to keep the momentum UNTIL they are RESCUED"—the hashtag was turbocharged. According to the now-shuttered social media analytics firm Topsy, close to eight thousand tweets used that hashtag by the end of that same day, ostensibly making it the official rallying cry for those campaigning on behalf of the missing girls. The next day saw the number of tweets almost double to 14,700. By the following week, the hashtag was being used thousands of times a day.

It's worth noting that much of the online traffic around the hashtag was centered in Nigeria, driven by concerned citizens who were demanding answers and action from the government of President Jonathan, an administration that alternated between giving false information and saying nothing at all. As the days went by, Oby grew increasingly frustrated by the president's refusal to engage with the grieving families or to publicly address the issue of the missing girls. So in this patriarchal society prone to minimizing female agency, four women—Oby, the activist and politician; Hadiza Bala Usman, a lawyer and child rights advocate; Dr. Maryam Uwais; and the women's rights activist Saudatu Mahdi—united and called for "a million-woman march" to the national assembly on April 30 using the #BringBackOurGirls hashtag to promote it. All protestors were asked to wear red in a show of solidarity, the color chosen to signify the danger the missing girls faced and the passionate love felt by all advocating for their release.

Aisha Yesufu was an unknown Nigerian citizen when the girls first disappeared. This fortysomething Muslim woman had been busy running her successful real estate business and caring for her husband and two teenagers when the news of the abductions emerged. The few details she heard affected her deeply, and she couldn't shake her feelings of upset. Despair turned to short-lived joy when the Nigerian military initially announced that all but eight of the girls had been rescued. That joy quickly became bitter disappointment, though, when it emerged that the statement had been a lie.

At the gym one day, a friend told Aisha about a planned April 30 protest.

"I'll be there!" she'd replied, without even pausing to think about it. Immediately, she turned to finding a red hijab to replace the dark one she wore every day in public.

At the time of the abductions, her twelve-year-old daughter, Aliyyah, attended one of Abuja's most elite private schools, where she rubbed shoulders with the children of the rich and powerful, a Nigerian who's who. Meanwhile, her son, Amir, attended a private boarding school in England. Married to an accountant and with business success of her own, Aisha considered her life to be good. But it hadn't always been that way.

Aisha had grown up in staggering poverty, so deprived she often went to school without breakfast and came home without having any lunch. She always understood how poverty in a place like Nigeria casts people as faceless, nameless, and voiceless. If she'd have fallen victim to the same misfortune that swept away the Chibok girls, she knew that no one would have spoken up for her, no one would have listened to her poor parents. Her personal history triggered an enormous sense of responsibility to fight for the Chibok girls, because it was clear their own government wanted to see the story squashed.

On the day of the planned march, April 30, a crowd of a few hundred gathered at Abuja's Unity Fountain. The skies were dark and angry, threatening to open and deliver rain at a moment's notice. Draped from head to toe in her new scarlet-red hijab, Aisha was an unforgettable sight among the masses of men and women, all wearing a collection of red skirts, blouses, dresses, and trousers. An assortment of hand-written signs spoke for some of the protestors.

WHERE ARE MY SISTERS?

PLEASE PROTECT US.

RESCUE OUR CHIBOK GIRLS

THE GIRLS DON'T DESERVE THIS.

These demands, scribbled on large pieces of white paper and carried by a relatively small number of people, spoke to the deep-seated frustrations felt toward the government by millions across the country. When the time arrived for the marchers to set off for the National Assembly, big, fat droplets began to fall. Groans rose up from the protestors. Some shuddered. The will to continue with the march began to falter.

Oby, the former minister of education and person who initially called on the Nigerian government to "bring back our daughters," stepped forward as the rain fell harder, her closely cropped hair glistening in the downpour.

"Are we going to melt if the rain touches us?" She was defiant, glaring through her narrow glasses. "Do we know what our daughters are going through? Is it the rain that will stop us?"

For a moment the crowd was silent. But then it roared back to life, shouting, "No!"

The rain now came down fast and heavy, while dark storm clouds did their best to snuff out the day's light. A contingent of police officers, on hand to provide protection, accompanied the protestors as they began their slow walk to the federal building. As they walked, they chanted: "All we are saying is, 'Bring Back Our Girls'!"

Aisha walked in her red hijab with thoughts of her daughter on her mind. She knew that if her child's school were ever attacked, she wouldn't need to be out beating a path through a gloomy Abuja, because the entire machinery of the state would be deployed to find children with famous last names. The steps Aisha took along Abuja's wide streets weren't primarily for her own twelve-year-old, they were just as much for the poor, hungry, gap-toothed little girl she herself had once been, invisible to almost everyone, and constantly at risk of permanently fading away on the margins of society.

The whole time they walked, Hadiza Bala Usman, the lawyer and child rights advocate who'd been one of the four to organize the march, cautiously hoped that a tentatively promised meeting between the protestors and the Nigerian president might, in fact, become a reality. By the time they arrived at the National Assembly, though, every one of the marchers was drenched, and Goodluck Jonathan was nowhere to be found. The marchers met with the Senate president and the Speaker of the House, both of whom promised to seek out more information about what the government was actually doing to find the girls. The crowd listened patiently and respectfully, but Oby made sure the politicians understood they were on a deadline.

"We will come back. We are giving twenty-four hours. Tomorrow we will gather here at the same time, three p.m., if there is no clear message as to the effect that our daughters have been found," she said.

On Twitter, meanwhile, the #BringBackOurGirls campaign gained a significant breakthrough that same day: more than 100,000 tweets with the #BringBackOurGirls hashtag were posted.

There are two likely reasons for this increase. One, false news reports emerged that day, courtesy of the missing girls' families and local villagers, that some of the schoolgirls had been sold off as child brides for a sum of approximately twelve dollars each, which enraged people, particularly in Nigeria. And two, a host of celebrities began using the hashtag, including the American R&B singers Chris Brown and Mary J. Blige, the British journalist Piers Morgan, and Malala Yousafzai, the Pakistani advocate for girls' education and a former target of the Taliban. Their advocacy brought the movement to a global level of heightened attention.

Back in Abuja, the protestors returned to Unity Fountain once the demonstration at the National Assembly was over. Aisha watched openmouthed as a member of the Chibok Parents' Association fell to his knees in the fading light and pleaded with all of those assembled. "Please don't abandon us with this issue. If you do, the government will forget about us and we just do not have the strength of voice to be heard."

No one knew what to say initially. But then different voices weighed in.

"Are we going to wait for the Senate to come back to us? Or are we going to keep coming back every day?" someone asked.

"We're going to keep coming back!" a chorus shouted.

"But wait!" cautioned Oby. "Let me remind you of what coming back every day means." She spoke slowly and seriously. "It means no matter how long it takes."

A unanimous "Yes" rang out.

For Aisha Yesufu, it seemed the time had come to finally stand up and use the voice she had fought so hard to gain. Still, she didn't really know what she'd agreed to beneath the trees at the Unity Fountain. Like the others gathered, she had no idea how long the kidnapping might take to resolve.

By May 7, a little more than a week since the march, the #BringBackOurGirls hashtag had been tweeted a total of one million times. Shortly afterward, then–first lady Michelle Obama added her voice with her own tweet. She also shared during her husband's weekly radio address that she was "outraged and heartbroken" by the crime in Nigeria. The list of celebrities throwing their weight behind the movement grew. Beyoncé, Alicia Keys, Sean Combs, Kim Kardashian, Ellen DeGeneres, Justin Timberlake, Jamie Foxx, Salma Hayek, and Ricky Martin all went online to show their support for #BringBackOurGirls.

Not everyone welcomed the surge in hashtag activism, though. Some critics labeled it self-serving and questioned what it would ultimately achieve.

But Aisha Yesufu was pleased with the attention. The social media community that formed around the Chibok girls made it impossible for the Nigerian government to ignore a truth she held near to her heart. These girls were valuable. They were missed and they mattered.

CHAPTER ELEVEN

LONG BEFORE BOKO HARAM EVER APPEARED, SAMBISA FOREST, HID-
den away in Borno state in Nigeria's northeast, was a part of
Chibok's collective consciousness, a place shaped by fear and fan-
tasy. Once upon a time, it had been home to lions, leopards, and
camels; they'd strode across this sweeping landscape of nearly forty
thousand square miles while majestic elephants made their way
to Sambisa from central Africa along corridors crisscrossing the
sprawling enclave. Until 1960, when Nigeria was still under British colonial rule, Sambisa had been designated a game reserve. For
years, up until the 1970s, excited tourists flocked to see the wildlife
and admire the vistas, spilling out across five northern Nigerian
states.

But in the decades since, most of the large game animals disappeared, their populations decimated by mismanagement and poaching. They live only as memories now, grandiose stories from another time when the forest was buoyed by the wonder and joy of those venturing along its overgrown paths. Today, Sambisa is the preserve of smaller fare—different types of monkeys, antelopes, gazelles, and myriad poisonous snakes.

It is also home to Boko Haram.

In early 2013, the terror group chose the harsh terrain as a base for its camps. The men suddenly emerged from the forest's dense bushes, spreading out among its array of trees and winding through its caves and into the mountains—taking advantage of the tree cover and hidden spaces in their war against the Nigerian military. Since then, Sambisa has become a place where dangerous men perform wicked deeds, and the forest nights are the stuff of terrifying dreams. In this place, time has a different quality, shifting and buckling to create its own frightening, fragile reality.

These men slid into Sambisa with the stolen girls, though their captives were most likely unaware they'd crossed its threshold. There aren't any signs or billboards to warn or welcome newcomers to Sambisa Forest—no announcements of arrival at ground zero for one of the deadliest terror groups in the world.

While almost two hundred girls were carried off in the vehicles that formed the slow-moving motorized procession, Mary was among the nearly one hundred girls who formed a convoy following on foot. She shuffled along while wearing just one blue-black flip-flop, urged forward by a phalanx of grim-faced men with their fingers resting on the triggers of long-barreled guns, which they seemed ready to use at a moment's notice.

Sweat ran freely down her back as she tried to stay alert and avoid potholes that might send her tumbling. Mary walked with her mind wrapped up in thoughts of her parents, picturing them totally distraught at the news that their only child had been taken.

She feared the loss would destroy them. Mixed in with that fear was a sense of foreboding that Mary couldn't shake off, a distinct feeling that her life still hung in the balance. Every time this idea rose to the surface of her consciousness, it came with the question, *What will I tell God if I am killed?* She felt unprepared for death, uncertain she'd done enough in her short lifetime to give a successful accounting.

The day's heat grew more intense as a fierce sun appeared in the sky and sapped her energy. Brutal vegetation spilled onto the path, scratching and threatening to block the way. One by one, the girls Mary was walking with began to tire. Then came a wave of despondency. She saw it touch each one and push them all down into an emotional spiral. But Mary looked deep inside herself for the strength to resist.

"The Lord is with us and for that reason we should not fear anything," she reminded her schoolmates. There was no reaction from their captors as she spoke her words of faith. They barely acknowledged the girls, choosing instead to stay silent.

Mary had been walking for several hours when the cluster of bushes and savanna grass thinned out to reveal nearly two dozen crumbling structures. They were little more than shacks, with rough walls made from forest grass and roofs fashioned out of bits of plastic weighted down by heavy rocks. The settlement appeared abandoned, and as far as she could tell, there was no one around. The silence triggered questions that there was no one to answer: *What had happened here? Who once lived in this place? What did they see that caused them to disappear?*

Now the entire convoy was slowing, and Mary heard loud voices. None of the men surrounding the girls offered an explanation for why they were stopping. Not that she even cared. For her and the others who'd been walking, it was a welcome moment of relief, a chance to rest their bruised and aching feet a short while. The girls were finally offered something to eat and drink, and Mary glared at the men through narrowed eyes as they held out water and cookies. A low-grade rage burned within her. She accepted the water from their filthy-looking bottles out of sheer desperation. Mary was parched and longing for a sip of anything to ease the discomfort of her burning throat, but that's where she drew the line. The cookies she would not accept, rejecting them firmly, without any hesitation.

The insurgents quietly chatted among themselves while Mary huddled with the other girls and nervously looked on, unsure of what was about to happen.

Then a loud voice.

Mary learned there was still a large distance to be covered; those on foot would never make it. "You must find space in these vehicles. If you fail, we will shoot you." The threat left her more confused and afraid than ever. How were they all expected to suddenly find space in the same vehicles that had been unable to accommodate them just a few hours earlier?

Without warning, plumes of smoke suddenly rose into the skies above Sambisa. Desperate for space to accommodate the leftover girls, the militants had decided to burn the contents of three vehicles, food that had been stolen from Chibok town. As the bags of rice lay engulfed in flames on the side of the road, a terrified Mary looked on as the other girls were shooed into the waiting pickup trucks. When it was her turn, she dared not resist, dutifully moving in the direction of a pointing gun and solemnly climbing into the back of an already crowded vehicle. She wedged herself among the frightened-looking girls. There were close to twenty of them packed in the small space, leaving Mary folded in on herself and barely able to breathe. Only the tiniest movement was possible; anything more would make her wince out of discomfort.

Priscilla had also been walking and now watched as Mary and others were crammed into the three waiting trucks. Until that moment, the group she'd been trekking with had successfully hung back and evaded being loaded into any of the vehicles. Once more, to her relief, the cars were packed, too full to take anyone else. Priscilla stared at their kidnappers, whose eyes burned with anger at the sight of a dozen girls still standing amid the bushes. But there were no pronouncements of execution or punishment. Instead, the men talked among themselves before shouting, "Let's go!" Engines started up and the cars edged forward, while Priscilla took a deep breath and followed on foot once more.

Less than half an hour later, Priscilla and the remaining girls still on foot heard the sound of a vehicle approaching. The pickup that came into view was largely empty. As the convoy slowed to a stop, the truck parked nearby. Now the men turned to Priscilla and the dozen walking holdouts.

"Get in the truck immediately! Anyone who refuses, we will just shoot you and go. You can't just keep on walking. What if people are trying to follow us? Get in now!"

Priscilla didn't move. Neither did the others. She struggled to gather her thoughts as her pulse quickened and she fought to catch her breath. *Am I really going to enter this car?* Priscilla feared that climbing into the vehicle would set her on a course from which she might never turn back. It felt like giving up on the possibility of freedom. She imagined the pain of those who would grieve for her.

"We will not go!"

"Get in the truck or we will shoot you!"

"We will not get in!"

"We will kill you!"

She pulled close to the girls as they argued with their kidnappers. Priscilla didn't see one of the men break away from the group till he returned with a reed cane high above his head.

Whack! Whack! Whack!

The long cane made a whistling sound as he swung it through the air and she shrieked in pain as it made contact with her back and legs. With tears blinding her, Priscilla twisted and flailed, then scrambled into the back of the truck with the other girls, where they were promptly joined by five militants. She was still crying when the rumble of engines filled the air and the convoy of trapped girls took off.

Every available inch of the truck bed Priscilla sat in was occupied. The weight of the girl in her lap pressed her legs into the bag of rice and other food items beneath her. She was slowly losing sensation in her limbs, but the discomfort barely registered. Priscilla's eyelids were swollen from crying and tears rushed to fill her bloodshot eyes. They came not simply because she was being carried away from all she'd ever loved. She also knew the devastation that would befall her family the minute they realized she was missing. She thought especially of her gentle, loving father, who doted on her every chance he got. Her abduction would break his heart.

From beneath the crush of tangled limbs, she watched her schoolmates struggle with the weight of their own fearful thoughts. As the truck bounced and swayed along the barely existent forest path, the girls' heads hung low, their lips quivered, and the unstoppable flow of tears glistened their cheeks and lashes.

Priscilla and the other girls in the truck moved for hours toward an unknown destination with three men perched on the roof of the driver's cabin and another two hanging off the back. The whole time the five pairs of glaring eyes remained fixed on her and the others. The legs of the young men seated up high hung loose, and their arms casually cradled AK-47s aimed directly at them. To her, the militants seemed to be without a care in the world. All five of them sported the same camouflage uniform worn by the Nigerian military, but each showed dusty, calloused feet in tattered flip-flops. Priscilla scanned their faces, taking note of the soft features. They looked more like boys than fully-grown men. But they displayed no traces of youthful warmth and ease, only sneers and defiant stares. They guarded Priscilla and the others without saying much. At times, she got the distinct impression that the young men cared not one bit if the girls lived or died.

There were other moments, though. For instance, when a spasm of grief took hold of the group and their guards' eyes softened a little for a brief time and they tenderly urged the girls to stop weeping. "Come now, stop crying . . . crying will not solve anything." Though once they were out of patience they quickly added, "Keep crying if you want, there is one day that you will stop."

Priscilla was making this terrible journey alongside friends from school. Side by side in the lurching vehicle, they tried to comfort each other, though under the watchful eyes of the men they could do no more than smuggle whispered assurances past barely moving lips. Whenever words failed them, they pressed their bodies closer and clasped each other's hands more tightly.

The convoy of girls moved through dense, thorny bushes and wild-growing trees so thick in places that the vegetation threatened to overwhelm the slow-moving procession. All the while, Priscilla's contorted limbs shot sparks of pain through her body. No one in their vehicle wore a watch, so their relationship with time quickly unraveled. Hours, minutes, and seconds ceased to have meaning. Priscilla felt as if she were floating in a dreamscape. The further she traveled, the more lost and disoriented she became. The same whispered questions ricocheted among the girls.

"Where are we going?"

"Where can they be taking us?"

"What place is this?"

From the confines of the pickup, Priscilla stared at the shifting terrain. Her hopes had surged when she first noticed a number of crumbling shelters scattered throughout the bush, but she never made out another human being and those structures became less frequent before eventually disappearing altogether, giving way to an increasingly desolate-looking landscape.

The surroundings grew bleaker, and unidentifiable howls and

screeches now signaled wild animals were nearby. As long as the sun was out, the beasts remained out of sight. But when darkness provided cover, a host of creatures appeared in the moonlight and stalked the convoy. Monkeys and antelopes suddenly emerged from the bush. Priscilla let out a startled scream. With the rest of the girls she lunged backward, praying for a gap to open up among the web of bodies crowding her so she might disappear. Fear, grief, and shock refused to allow her eyes to close for the first twenty-four hours she was in the truck.

A growing undercurrent of anxiety, meanwhile, ran among them. When the captors offered them something to drink, Priscilla's eyes darted from their faces and the foul-looking water bottles they held in grimy outstretched hands. She quietly but firmly refused, even though her mouth and throat were agonizingly dry and the hunger pangs in her belly were sharpening.

The schoolgirls began to ask, "What is going to happen to us?" with increasing alarm. They passed this question back and forth quietly at first, but eventually it spilled out into the open with raised voices. Maybe the boldness came from hunger, or perhaps weariness had worn away their fears. Now Priscilla and the other girls peppered the men with the same questions that were tormenting them.

"Where are we going?"

"What is going to happen to us?"

The band of militants didn't reply; instead, they stared back dispassionately. Met with silence, Priscilla returned to whispering with her friends. Before long, their questioning started up again and the reaction they received remained the same. When the men finally chose to speak, their words triggered instant dread in Priscilla.

"As long as you accept our religion, you will be fine."

For girls like her, whose parents had nurtured in their offspring the irrevocable belief they were indivisible from their Christianity, these words brought into focus a threat much greater than simply losing one's life. As much as Priscilla most definitely did not want to die, her fear of death wasn't strong enough to overcome what she considered to be a fundamental truth: that living without Christianity was no life at all. There was no way of separating this teenager's faith from her existence.

So in unison with the other girls, she shouted "No!" to the idea of conversion. If their outright rejection offended their minders, they didn't let on. The men merely sneered and shrugged.

But Priscilla wasn't about to give up on her search for answers just yet. After a brief pause, she joined the others in lobbing the same questions at their captors.

"If we get to our destination, will you accept our religion?" the men asked again. "Nothing will happen to you. Will you accept?"

This time the no from Priscilla's lips was louder and firmer than everyone else's in the truck. She felt her heartbeat quicken as she waited to see if her boldness would land her in trouble, not that it stopped her from looking up and glaring at her abductors in open defiance. Undoubtedly sweet and gentle, Priscilla also possessed a resolute strength at her core that oftentimes shocked those trying to bully or take advantage of her, and on more than one occasion was as much of a surprise to Priscilla as to those she was challenging.

Now the men held her gaze for what seemed like an eternity. Meanwhile, the watching girls all held their breath, as Priscilla continued to stare them down. When the pack finally looked away, the captors collapsed with laughter.

At points, the thought of escape weighed heavily on the minds of the girls in Priscilla's truck. They had no idea that dozens of their schoolmates who'd been loaded into the nine-eleven had already leapt to freedom. All Priscilla knew was that five armed men surrounded her and there was no chance of escaping her present situation. Even if her minders were somehow distracted, following close behind their truck were hundreds more militants riding a cavalcade of motorbikes. Now Priscilla cast her mind back to the trek she'd made from the school into the bushes before they started loading the girls into the vehicles. *Could she have escaped then?* She had to accept that the odds for success even then hadn't been any better. She'd been completely surrounded by militants. Even a cursory attempt to inspect her footwear had drawn bellowing warnings against any attempt to escape from their watchful minders. Fast-forward, and now all she could do was stare at the forest they were passing through and mourn the gap opening up between her and her family, growing wider by the minute.

The convoy pushed deeper into Sambisa. For Priscilla, everything became a blur. The only marker of the passing hours was when they stopped to allow the men the opportunity to pray. Five times a day, as required by Islam, the procession paused. No announcement was made, but she learned to read the slowing of the vehicles as a way to judge the passing of time. The girls stayed put, while some of the men got out and knelt in the dirt right in front of the vehicles. The others kept watch, trading places when the first group was done. Priscilla never saw prayer mats unfurled and put down; the conditions of the path never seemed to be an issue for the men. Wherever they stopped was where they prayed. With the religious devotions completed, the militants rose to their feet and calmly reentered the trucks filled with stolen girls and continued the journey through the seemingly unending forest.

For Priscilla, the truck became her entire world. The girls in the convoy were allowed out only for bathroom breaks, always accompanied by an escort. For the girls in Priscilla's vehicle, they weren't even permitted those moments of relief, because this clique of girls refused to accept chaperones. Trapped in their respective vehicles, the girls were victims to a host of emotions, from an overwhelming sense of helplessness to overpowering grief for all they were losing, and a debilitating fear of what lay ahead.

On the second day of their journey, when the sun was high in the sky, the vehicles suddenly ground to a halt. The girls were ordered out. Priscilla's entire body ached, and the chance to move and stretch brought gratitude and sensation flooding into her bones. As she took in her surroundings, she noticed the tall grass thickly grown and blanketing the clearing. Their captors had chosen to stop where the thicket of vegetation did the work of a shield. This prevented the girls from seeing much of anything apart from their immediate surroundings, and likewise made it difficult for anyone beyond the clearing to spot the hundreds of schoolgirls.

Once feeling returned to her body, Priscilla and the hundreds of captives now took in the fact that they were filthy—covered from head to toe in layers of sandy brown dust. It was in their eyes, caked on their faces, and blanketing their clothes. Priscilla quickly pulled off the swath of fabric covering her head and used it, as best she could, to clean herself up before she joined the rest of the girls sitting on the ground. Now that the trucks and cars were empty, groups of friends reunited and everyone spread out across the clearing with as many girls as possible seeking protection from the sun under a large tree. Mary was completely exhausted and the moment she eked out a spot in the shade, she fell asleep. Many of the girls wondered whether the convoy had reached its destination.

But this was not a camp. There were no dwellings of any description to be seen, though it appeared the insurgents knew the spot well. This suspicion was all but confirmed by some of the girls' discovery of a couple of plates and a small pot under the tree. The militants fanned out in the enclosure and carefully surrounded the group, closing off every opening that might present itself as a chance to make a run for freedom.

A short time later, a couple of men approached with macaroni, spaghetti, onions, oil, and a very large pot, all taken from their school store. They also brought firewood and a large bright yellow plastic container filled with water. They placed the items on the ground in front of them. The girls eyed the men suspiciously.

"You should come and cook," the men told them.

The group remained silent. Priscilla saw the mounting irritation in the men's eyes. When it became clear the girls had no intention of responding, the militants randomly selected three girls and instructed them to prepare food. Without saying a word, the trio set about the process of cooking for their schoolmates.

Soon a pot of pasta and seasonings was cooking away. Eventually the hastily chosen cooks ladled piles of steaming food onto the several large platters for the famished girls. Groups formed quickly—everyone tucking in with their hands; no one was put off by the lack of silverware. But not all gathered round.

Priscilla refused to touch the platters. Overwhelmed by a fresh wave of despair, through her tears she watched dozens of girls eat.

Mary, meanwhile, had been asleep for about an hour before the sound of cooking woke her. When the time came to eat, she too refused, preferring to repeat to herself, "God shall pull me away." She chose to depend on those words to calm and sustain her.

"No! Do not move. Remain exactly where you are seated."

A handful of girls wanted to head into the bushes to relieve themselves, but the no was unequivocal. No one was allowed to move away from the group. Any bathroom needs would have to be dealt with in front of everyone, right there in the open clearing. The girls stared at the men in revulsion.

The time for midafternoon prayers was approaching. The men quickly counted the hostages, chose a Boko Haram member who looked to be in his teens to act as their caretaker, and then headed off to a quiet corner in the clearing to pray.

Among the schoolgirls there were at least a dozen from Mary's home village of Thilaimakalama. Seated together under the tree and now being watched over by an adolescent guard who couldn't understand Kibaku, the conversation among them shifted to crafting an escape plan. While the tender-featured young man looked on, groups of girls soon felt emboldened enough to wander into the bushes by themselves—and he never said a word. The girls from Thilaimakalama quickly agreed on their plan. The dozen would divide into groups of two, and each pair would head into the bushes. Then, hidden from view, they would take off running. Mary watched the first couple of girls stand and saunter over to the bushes. They never returned, and the young man failed to notice.

It was soon her turn. Mary turned to her preselected partner, a girl called Reba, and motioned that it was nearly time to leave. Much to her astonishment, Reba shook her head, muttering that she wasn't ready yet. She wanted more time to rest. Mary stared at her escape partner incredulously. With her frustration growing, she looked around at the horde of Thilaimakalama girls and spotted Deborah. Within minutes they'd agreed to team up. Filled with fear and desperation, the pair leapt up and began to make their way over to the nearby bushes. They'd barely taken a dozen steps when someone shouted in their direction.

"Where are you going?"

They stared at each other nervously before slowly turning around to face the militant who'd suddenly appeared. The girls responded in unison: "We want to go and ease ourselves." Their need meant nothing to him. Instead, a Boko Haram member thrust a small plastic kettle into Deborah's hands and ordered her to fetch him water to drink. With her mind set on escaping, the girl made sure the expression on her face was one of calm as she took hold of the vessel and headed over to the yellow water container. She carefully filled the man's kettle and steadily walked back. The whole time he'd been eyeing every move she made, but he seemed satisfied and took the water from her without further comment.

Now they were free to head to the bushes unaccompanied. The girls moved briskly without saying a word to each other. Within minutes Mary and Deborah were out of sight and quickly pushing through the vegetation. When they broke into a run seconds later, neither girl dared stop and look back till they'd moved well beyond the reach of their captors. It was about three in the afternoon when they broke free, and they had no idea where they were headed—their only guide was the sun. *If you're ever lost, just follow the sun* . . . It was advice given years earlier by Mary's grandfather. Now the frightened schoolgirl clung to those words as she wandered through the forest wearing just one flip-flop, with Deborah by her side. The pair was still walking when the sun dipped and eventually traded places with a bright moon.

For more than three hours they moved through the shadows and tall grass, sweeping aside low-hanging branches and swatting away swarms of insects. Their bodies remained tense the whole time. Mary couldn't help but wonder about the creatures that had made the surrounding bushes their home; even so, such thoughts weren't enough to slow her down. She just kept on running—through her fears, her hunger, and her indescribable thirst. When they suddenly heard the low purr of motorbikes in the distance, Mary and Deborah flung themselves to the ground, too afraid to even breathe as they lay there. Eventually the sound faded into the background and the two girls were moving once more. All Mary had were the clothes on her back and the prayers on her lips. The little bit of money in their possession—5,000 naira, a little less than $14, belonged to Deborah.

The sudden appearance of a Fulani man in the bushes brought Mary unbridled relief. He gave the girls directions to a village far in the distance. It would take the kindness of a second stranger to get them to that destination by seven that evening—the young Fulani man wheeled them along on his bicycle in exchange for 1,500 naira, about $4.

Amid the falling-down shacks that made up this small village the girls discovered a chief, who listened sympathetically to all they'd been through. He made sure they were given a meal and then found a man willing to take the girls on his motorbike back to Chibok for 2,500 naira, roughly $7. Fearful of running out of money, the girls haggled over the fare and begged him to take a little less—they settled on 2,000 naira, in the presence of the chief. When Mary climbed onto that motorbike, her heart was doing somersaults. *At last I'm on my way home!* Over and over again she repeated the comforting words to herself and pictured the look of joy that would spread across her parents' face when she reappeared. Lost in her thoughts, Mary didn't immediately notice that the bike was slowing down. When it came to a complete stop and the driver told them to get off, she froze, openmouthed. It was close to midnight.

"I cannot take you any farther."

"But why?" spluttered Mary. "You agreed to take us home for two thousand naira!"

"I cannot go on."

"Why won't you take us?"

"Because I am afraid. You should walk."

Before Mary and Deborah could even collect their thoughts, the man was gone—with his bike and their money.

Mary stood in the darkness with fear and anger coursing through her body. *How could he just leave us here? What are we to do now?* Too afraid to stay where they were, Mary and Deborah chose to continue walking in the direction they'd been going with the man who'd pretended to be taking them home. Suddenly they heard something moving in the bushes nearby. Every thought that came to mind was terrifying. But thankfully what actually came into view moments later was another forest-dwelling Fulani. Startled by the sight of two distressed young girls, he led them to his home. Mary was too tired to think or feel much of anything when they finally stumbled into his small, dilapidated house. She eagerly laid her head down on the ground and closed her eyes, but

she managed only a fitful sleep. The sound of forest animals passing close by and growling softly kept both girls on edge and praying through the night.

Mary and Deborah gratefully welcomed the sun the next
morning. They quickly discovered that the couple who owned the
dwelling spoke no Hausa. But luckily their daughter, who was visiting from Yola, was on hand and able to translate. These cattle-
herding nomads had barely enough to get by, and yet they still
shared their small amount of food with the two strange-looking
girls who'd suddenly appeared in their home in the middle of the
night. Mary was ravenous and grateful for the gift of masa, a northern Nigeria breakfast treat traditionally made from ground rice,
sugar, and yeast, then fried till a puffy cake takes shape. The girls
were overwhelmed by the family's generosity and thanked them
profusely for both the masa and the instructions for how to get
back to Chibok. It was midafternoon by the time they departed,
and Mary began the two-and-a-half-hour trek till they reached a
second settlement. Unlike the others, in this encampment there
were actually people present milling about, completing chores,
getting on with day-to-day life.

Amid all the settlement activity a Fulani man sat quietly in the
sun. Mary nervously asked for help. The old man listened intently,
before leading them to a shack that belonged to a kind-looking
woman. Her eyes filled with concern when she looked over the
girls. Within minutes she'd brought them water to drink and was
busy making them a meal, before washing the dirty clothes she
stripped from their backs. Mary and Deborah would spend the
night here with this woman and her husband, who showed up before long.

The next morning he agreed to take the girls back to Chibok.
Mary squeezed onto the bike with Deborah and held on tightly
to the small grips on each side of the seat. Hours later, when they
pulled up in front of her uncle's house in Chibok's town center, all

she could do was cry. Deborah's father arrived first and scooped his daughter into his arms. When Mary's dad arrived a short time later shouting, "God has answered my prayers!" Mary's tears temporarily blinded her. She was still crying when she arrived home and laid her head on the bosom of her mother, Felicie. "Don't cry," she cooed. At the sound of her mother's voice, Mary broke open and relief poured out. It had taken her two days to get back, and now it was finally over.

Mary and Deborah, like Saa and Blessing hours before them, were among the fifty-seven girls who fled the clutches of Boko Haram in the immediate aftermath of the raid on their school. For two whole years they were the only ones able to reveal what had happened behind the walls of their school that night. But long after news organizations had moved on and much of the world had forgotten about the events in Chibok, these girls remained just as mired in the past, haunted by their memories of what they witnessed.

I ARRIVED IN LAGOS ALMOST THREE WEEKS AFTER THE CHIBOK girls had gone missing, though my presence actually had nothing to do with the girls' abductions. I was there to cover the World Economic Forum (WEF Africa), a regional showing of the annual international economic event traditionally held atop a mountain in Davos, Switzerland. Now, for the first time, Nigeria had been chosen to host this Africa-specific WEF conference in the nation's capital, Abuja, giving Nigeria the distinction of welcoming global leaders across politics and business, as well as change makers and celebrities. The conference was an acknowledgement of the country's growing economy, as well as the burgeoning investment opportunities that existed in Africa's most populous nation and in many other places in sub-Saharan Africa. The news network had been planning its coverage of the high-profile gathering for weeks.

But almost immediately upon landing, news of my arrival began to trend locally on Twitter. The message I'd posted from my sun-filled hotel room was innocuous enough: "I'm here in Nigeria." Seated on the edge of the hotel bed, I tried to figure out why my presence was causing such a stir. Why all the retweeting?

From the moment I'd learned of the girls' disappearance, I'd been covering the government's lackluster efforts to find them from our CNN headquarters in Atlanta. So when I'd boarded my flight to Nigeria on May 1, 2014, I thought I had a pretty good grasp of the facts on the ground. Sure, I knew the Nigerian officials' public statements about the abductions were muddled and left a lot to be desired. But finding the girls was a priority for President Jonathan, and everything possible was being done to bring them safely back to their loved ones. Those were the "facts," as I knew them.

But now I could hardly keep up with the stream of messages pouring in via Twitter, all essentially asking the same key questions.

What is the government actually doing to find these girls?

What really happened that night in Chibok?

Why isn't the government sharing information about its actual efforts to recover the girls?

As I sifted through my Twitter feed, I realized I'd misjudged the situation. Badly. On my phone, a completely different picture was taking shape, and it involved an information blackout on the part of the Nigerian government, which had refused to categorically lay out what its response to this mass abduction entailed.

Sitting there in my hotel room, I wondered how I could have been so misinformed. I cast my mind back to the moment the story first broke. I ran through the numerous interviews I'd done with my close friend and CNN's Nigeria correspondent, Vladimir Duthiers. I could see it clearly now. Vladimir had done the best job possible under the circumstances. But I'd failed to realize that the slow drip of information from the authorities represented their attempt to kill the story. Only now that I was *in* Nigeria, engaging with Nigerians on social media and reading the local newspapers, did I fully understand the full scope of the story, and recognize how much I (and all the other Western journalists like me) didn't know. Suddenly, the cascade of messages made sense. People were desperate for answers. They hoped my presence and CNN's involvement would provide them. "We've got the story all wrong!" I said breathlessly down the phone to Atlanta. My bosses listened as I explained the apparent information blackout in Nigeria and lack of any discernible effort on the government's part to find the missing girls. "Trust me," I urged. "Something's not right here."

CNN had spent countless hours planning my coverage of WEF, and now here I was trying to convince them to scrap it all. Nonetheless, I asked the network to shift its focus away from tales of Nigeria's burgeoning wealth to the mass abduction of these girls. Thankfully, they agreed and the network recalibrated. Reporting teams received new assignments, and CNN did what it does better than just about any other network in the world: we kicked into high gear. I was ready and primed for my new mission. More than anything else, I felt I needed to speak to more Nigerians for their insight to the situation. Luckily, I'd been invited to a cocktail party that evening for some of Nigeria's wealthiest and most well-known women. I'd get answers there.

By the time I arrived at the upscale gathering, the room was hot and abuzz with chatter, clinking glasses, and the sound of cameras flashing as photographers eagerly captured some of Nigeria's most recognized women gathered in one crowded room. Before long, I was in deep conversation with multiple guests. There were moments when I couldn't believe what I was hearing. The women I spoke with expressed a mix of skepticism, derision, and low-grade resentment for the Chibok girls story.

"Are you sure there were girls actually taken?" one woman asked.

"I don't believe any girls are actually missing," another mused.

"Let CNN not come here again to show Nigeria in a negative light o!"

I watched and listened while one woman after another rolled her expertly made-up eyes and waved a well-manicured hand to emphasize her personal doubt in the story of the missing school-girls. I did my best not to stand with my mouth open and eyes bulging out of my head. Repeatedly, one particular point was ex-pressed. "These northerners most likely had a hand in the kidnap-ping of their own children to make Goodluck look bad."

I realized there was a significant section of Nigerian society that strongly believed the Chibok abduction was no more than an elaborate hoax with political objectives. These "Chibok deniers" saw a direct connection between Boko Haram and politicians from the north, many of whom strongly opposed the plan of the current Nigerian president to take part in the upcoming presidential elec-tions scheduled for the following March, ten months hence.

More than anything, I was struck by the complete lack of sym-pathy for the missing girls, and I wondered whether that hard-heartedness stemmed from the fact that the girls were poor and from Nigeria's Muslim north. Most of the women I spoke to in that room were well-to-do Christians from other parts of the country. I was reminded again of the stark fault lines that divide Nigerians into disparate, self-interested groups.

As I made my way back to the hotel at the end of the evening, my car wound its way through Lagos's congested streets, with their endless motion of cars and bodies on foot. All I could think about was the narrative of denial I'd encountered. It weighed heavily on my thoughts and torpedoed my original theory that all of Nigeria was united in the face of this national tragedy. The cocktail party had also revealed something else: not everyone was thrilled to see CNN back in Nigeria and taking an interest in the Chibok story.

There has long been consternation in some quarters in Nigeria about CNN's coverage of Africa's most populous nation. Some staunchly believe the network has an agenda to portray their country as corrupt, politically unstable, or blighted by terrorism. After being in Nigeria for less than a full day, I already saw clearly that tensions were running high over what had happened in Chibok. Covering this story was going to be far from easy; it would be fraught with challenges every step of the way. Knowing that a difficult path lay ahead didn't scare me. In fact, quite the opposite—it focused my mind and made me more determined than ever to stand my ground on behalf of the missing girls and their loved ones.

For the next two weeks I hosted my nightly show, *CNN News-Center*, from a cramped hotel balcony in Abuja. Under a flood of lights, I battled heat, an army of flying insects, and countless technical difficulties, as well as a fleet of combative Nigerian officials. I felt like I was climbing into a wrestling ring at the start of each show. I matched the Nigerian government's belligerence with my own aggression, going after every lie, every half-truth and evasion. These fiery confrontations drew national and international attention, along with no shortage of condemnation of me from some of the rich and powerful in Nigeria. I continued to push for answers all the same, clashing most famously with the Nigerian minister of information, Labaran Maku.

"When did you learn of this attack?" I asked him repeatedly. The minister, attired in flowing lilac robes and matching hat, stuttered, trying to pivot the conversation back to his several-minutes-long argument in which he blamed the local Borno State government for opening the Chibok school in defiance of the federal government's mandate to keep all schools in Borno closed. Impatiently I pushed, "We have been through this, so let's move forward to share information with our viewers. When did you learn of this attack?"

From the look on Mr. Maku's face, his annoyance was peaking; he shuffled and stuttered with discomfort. "As a government it was the following day. . . . As a government at least for a decision to be made it was the following day and this thing was in the middle of the night. And even when this information came, it was very, very hazy. Because the principal was not on ground. She came back the next day and said some eight students were unaccounted for." He added this last bit while waving his arm to emphasize his frustration.

"Okay," I replied.

"You know we went through this with you before."

"Okay," I repeated.

"And the moment we confirmed this was the case we went into action."

My head titled to one side and my eyes narrowed. "Not what we heard from people on the ground—" I shot back.

He interrupted me now. "No, we did. No, no, no, no, come on," he repeated in rapid fire. He refused to pause for breath. "Excuse me! Excuse me!" He held his hand high to stop me midsentence.

I carried on regardless, speaking over him, challenging his version of events with statements I had gathered from people there in Chibok that night, who, I told him, continued to contradict his statements, who said that is not what happened.

He pushed back. "No. No, no."

I raised my voice. "All we are asking for is the Nigerian government to be transparent with us."

"No, no, no, no," Maku continued. "We shouldn't turn this into a trial of the Nigerian government."

My eyes flashed and my jaw tightened. I tried to speak slowly and maintain my composure as I searched for the right words. "It is *scrutiny* of your response," I replied, with my own hand movements stressing my every word.

"No, no, no," he practically shouted.

"It is not a trial. It is scrutiny," I said coldly.

With a producer in Atlanta counting down in my ear to the end of the show, I was forced to bring the interview to a close, which meant further talking over the minister and effectively shutting him down.

When we were finally off the air, I made a halfhearted attempt at small talk with Labaran Maku. He would have nothing to do with my pleasantries. Before I could get a word out, he ripped off his microphone and exited our makeshift studio like a whirling dervish, declaring his fury for me as he hurried toward the hotel elevators.

Tensions rose further when Amnesty International released a report on May 9, claiming the Nigerian military had failed to act on multiple advance warnings about the Boko Haram raid on Chibok's state-run boarding school. My interviews with other government officials grew increasingly contentious. The senior special assistant on public affairs to the president, Doyin Okupe, started a response to one of my questions with a patronizing, "Listen, sweetheart."

The comment, made during a live broadcast, placed me in a split-second debate with myself. Should I acknowledge the condescending remark and tackle it head on? I settled on a cold, disdainful glare and the satisfaction of knowing he had exposed himself to everyone around the world.

My choice was confirmed when I checked social media hours later and saw the outraged reaction to his words. His remark spoke to the warped gender dynamic at play in Nigeria. On the one hand, fanatical groups like Boko Haram were doing all they could to prevent girls from being educated, advocating for marriage and domesticity. On another, a senior aide to the president had called an international journalist "sweetheart" on live television. Both positions, I would argue, are part of the same problematic continuum in which females are treated as secondary sexual objects that are subservient to men.

An added dynamic fueled the animosity on display during these encounters. I'd generated a great deal of controversy and ill will during an exclusive CNN sit-down interview I'd done with President Jonathan in the presidential villa back in 2010:

> **Isha Sesay:** There are many who believe that with your decision to compete in the election you are going against the zoning agreement which states that the presidency will rotate between the north and the south every eight years. The late president Yar'Adua was a northerner. He died in his first term. There are those who feel that you are putting personal ambition ahead of the stability and peace of Nigeria. Is that what you are doing?
>
> **President Jonathan:** Definitely not. The argument about zoning and the presidency of Nigeria is like the philosophical argument of the egg or the hen. Who is older through the evolutionary process, who came first? In the first place if this country has agreed the presidency rotates between north and south I would not be the president today. I couldn't have been if there is an agreement in this country that it rotates between north and south. I couldn't have been the president the day Yar'Adua died—another northerner would have taken over and I could have continued as the vice-president.

We clashed throughout the conversation.

Before this point, President Jonathan had rejected practically every single in-depth interview request from local Nigerian media. He'd agreed to sit down with me only because it was billed as part of "Eye on Nigeria"—CNN's special week-long coverage of his country. But when the time finally came, as we sat under the lights, surrounded by cameras and handlers in his home, Jonathan was ill prepared for my pointed and unflinching questioning, and he became increasingly flustered.

The interview had damaged his credibility.

Afterward the president and his supporters exploded in a fit of pique—and labeled me rude, aggressive, and disrespectful to a head of state. The affair established my reputation as a thorn in the side of his administration. So now I was back in the country, challenging Jonathan's government for its inadequate response to Chibok. I was racking up personal enemies faster than I could keep track.

It was midmorning when I walked into our workspace, and I immediately knew something was very wrong. The CNN production team, now close to a dozen people, looked worried. The tension in the room was unmistakable.

"What's wrong?"

I discovered that our "fixer"—the local journalist CNN had hired to help with background research and logistics—had quit out of the blue. He'd overheard a conversation among a group of powerful Nigerians discussing the possibility of harming the CNN team, and me in particular. He believed the threats were serious, and working with CNN had just become too dangerous for this young man.

Days before, a close friend had called to warn me of possible attempts by certain unnamed forces to doctor video footage that would show me in a compromising sexual situation. He'd learned of the mischievous musings during a conversation with a fellow Nigerian—a well-connected man who was always in the know. Dutifully, I passed on the unconfirmed story to my CNN bosses. Hours later, I found myself paired with Mel, a bodyguard. That had been bad enough. But now, having our fixer drop us out of fear took things to a whole new level. The Atlanta bosses and our security coordinators decided to change our hotel rooms and moved me into one adjoining our workspace. Mel, meanwhile, would sleep in the other room also connected to the working area.

By this point, I'd been in Nigeria for more than a week, and I was beginning to feel under siege. My movements were severely restricted, and I was essentially confined to the workspace and my hotel room. At the end of each workday, while the others on the team wandered down to the hotel bar, I retreated to my room. I locked the door and then checked and double-checked it before eventually climbing into bed and staying awake for most of the night.

I was frightened, but not about to back down from my tough line of questioning.

Then Boko Haram released a video, twenty-seven minutes of footage showing 136 of the missing 219 girls, their first appearance. The girls all sat on the ground, concealed in hijabs and looking distraught. Three members of the group spoke directly to the camera, declaring that they had become Muslims, two of them having converted from Christianity. In the same video, Boko Haram's leader confirmed the religious conversions of the entire group of 136 girls with great satisfaction. "These girls, these girls you occupy yourselves with. . . . We have indeed liberated them. These girls have become Muslims," Shekau spoke to the camera.

Seeing the girls' frightened faces and knowing of the distress these images were causing their loved ones, I hounded government officials for details of the search-and-rescue operations said to be under way. Meanwhile, Chibok parents scanned the faces of the girls who appeared on camera, desperate and praying the whole time for a sighting of their missing children. As for their location, the world believed the girls had been taken to neighboring Cameroon and were no longer in Nigeria at all.

Then another personal safety warning arrived for me, this time from a relative who was in the US diplomatic corps. The advice was straightforward: back off from the aggressive questioning of Nigerian officials—you're upsetting too many powerful people and Nigeria is a dangerous place.

As the warnings mounted, the Nigerian government continued to clamp down on the flow of information to the media. The continued lack of details inevitably meant public interest would begin to wane. Sure enough, by the middle of the second week, in the absence of fresh, compelling images, interest on the part of my stateside bosses was also on the decline. I was frustrated, but in the absence of new developments, there was little I could do to counter the situation. I was hardly surprised when the bosses began to pull my colleagues out and redeploy them to other stories.

My mother called. Her voice was strained. "You've upset too many people and a Nigerian friend just called and told me you'd better leave."

I muttered under my breath.

"Isha, it's enough. You've done enough. It's time to go home." Her tone was stern and unyielding. I sighed from fatigue and frustration. But there wasn't any point in fighting with her. I was already booked to head back to the United States that weekend. Her mood lightened when I told her.

"It's good you're leaving," she said. "These are bad people you are dealing with and they would not think twice to hurt you."

Amid all the outrage and threats of violence, I reflected on how much of the rancor was driven by my gender, Africanness, and relative youth. These powerful figures certainly wouldn't have felt as insulted by the harsh questioning had it come from any of my male colleagues—white or black, regardless of age. If the questioner had been a white woman, age would again have been put to the side, and these Nigerian men would have found it in themselves to bear the sting of her questioning, albeit reluctantly. But a younger, African woman publicly challenging them with temerity and dismissing Nigeria's enduring cultural norms of male unassailability? Now, that was simply too much to bear. Though my mother agreed with my position wholeheartedly, all she really cared about was the fact that I was leaving.

A few days later, when I finally boarded my flight home, I felt a sweep of different emotions: Relief—I was exiting a high pressure atmosphere and could finally stop looking over my shoulder. But I also felt a tremendous amount of sadness for the girls who were still lost to their loved ones. For all my efforts, we were really no closer to knowing where they were or providing their families with any comfort. I felt like I'd failed.

To make matters worse, in the pit of my stomach I felt the number of people who cared about these hundreds of girls just one month after they disappeared was dwindling rapidly. Though the #BBOG hashtag continued to trend to a degree, its prevalence was waning. A dark mood settled over me while I confronted an ugly truth. I realized the world had a far greater attention span for the disappeared Malaysian airliner MH370, which all signs sadly pointed to being lost forever with 239 people on board, than for nearly 300 black schoolgirls, who were missing but still alive.

CHAPTER THIRTEEN

P<small>RISCILLA</small> <small>WATCHED AS CONFUSION SLOWLY SPREAD ACROSS THE</small> faces of her captors. The men were counting the girls again, convinced a mistake had been made the first time they'd counted, which would explain the sudden discrepancy in the numbers. They looked increasingly perplexed and asked each other, "How can there be fewer girls now than when we left for prayers?"

As they painstakingly added up the total once more, Priscilla had already guessed at the truth. Some of her schoolmates had slipped away while they'd been under the supervision of the boy militant. She hadn't actually seen them leave, but now as she looked about the clearing, it was obvious girls were missing. With the recount done, no one could ignore the truth any longer. In an instant, the men's tempers were flaring.

"Where are the rest of the girls?" they screamed furiously.

The looks on their faces made it clear—this time they would not accept the groups' customary silence.

Looking nervously at each other, the teenagers spoke slowly. "Maybe they have gone to ease themselves."

The men looked unconvinced. Yet to Priscilla's surprise, they replied, "Okay, let us wait."

An uneasy quiet took hold as the militants and their captives shifted attention to the surrounding bushes, all of them eager to see if any girls actually emerged. As each minute ticked by, the sense of dread and agitation in the clearing grew. Priscilla had lost track of how long they'd been waiting when the men exploded.

"Where are they?"

"We don't know where they've gone."

"You must know something! Tell us!"

"We have no idea what happened!"

The girls pleaded with the men to believe them, but the situation quickly spiraled out of control and soon the men's guns were aimed directly at them. By this point there was little Priscilla and the others could do but pray.

Suddenly the men announced, "Let us go after the missing girls! If not, they will bring us trouble." And with that, dozens of militants abruptly swung their guns away from the trembling captives and dove into the nearby bushes.

They'd been gone for less than thirty minutes when the bushes all around the clearing started to stir and Priscilla heard the sound of rapidly approaching footsteps. She looked up in panic, only to see the search party burst through the tall grass moments later.

"Quickly, pack up!" the men shouted. "Take the girls and leave immediately, or they will find us here!" The militants were gasping for air. As they spoke, the girls looked around, trying to figure out the source of their alarm.

Hours earlier, when the kidnapped girls had first walked into the clearing, they'd sought relief from the cramped conditions in the vehicles by spreading out across the entire area. Now bands of men moved quickly to gather the scattered clusters into one large group, while other militants loaded up the vehicles with the pot, platters, firewood, and other items used to make lunch. All of them moved with the speed and focus of individuals being pursued. The girls were bewildered. *What had the men seen in the bushes? Who was coming?* Those questions were swirling in their heads when militants stunned the group with a proposition.

"If you are willing to accept our religion, then go ahead and stand to the side."

Priscilla felt as if she'd been struck at this first formal attempt to convert the girls to Islam. Her heart beat faster as each girl stood. One . . . two . . . three . . . four . . . five . . . She counted as girls rose and said yes softly to their captors before stepping away from their schoolmates. Priscilla felt their desperation to cling to life, and she felt deep sadness for these wide-eyed girls. In the end, nearly a dozen stood, ready to embrace Islam. The men were far from pleased. "What of the rest of you?" they asked roughly. Then they added, "We are taking the willing converts and we are going to kill the rest of you!"

The girls who remained seated on the forest floor were very afraid, but there was no trace of that fear when they gave the men their answer. "No, we will not." For Priscilla, whose life had been shaped by the personal tenet "Born a Christian, die a Christian" her no was final. Suddenly, she felt compelled to speak out, and the words were as shocking to Priscilla as they were to her captors. "No one can kill us if God doesn't want us dead." Her boldness stunned them all, and for a moment, the men stood around staring at each other and Priscilla—marveling at her audacity. She waited for an outburst of words or bullets in response, but nothing came. Words seemed to fail the insurgents, but eventually their shock became chuckles, before dissolving into full-blown laughter.

As far as she was concerned, nothing more needed to be said.

"Maybe when you reach where we are going, you will agree," the men retorted.

The focus turned back to the dozen girls who had stepped away from the group. Priscilla stared at them, standing there dry eyed, with heads bent, silent. Those eyes suddenly filled with terror when it emerged that the converted girls would no longer be allowed to travel alongside their schoolmates. Instead, for the rest of the journey, they'd be transported in a separate vehicle. The twelve girls shuddered, and Priscilla felt a rush of pity for them.

Just then one of the men shouted abruptly, "Everyone into the cars! Hurry! Let's go! Let's go!" Priscilla and the others were dragged and pushed in the direction of the parked convoy. Men sprinted and hurled themselves into the assortment of vehicles, whose engines started up immediately, and they were on the move. The men never let on what had sent them scurrying, and none of the girls had seen anything unusual. In the absence of details, Priscilla was simply left to wonder as they trundled deeper into the forest. *Could the men have spotted their parents approaching?*

Armed with only a long stick, Dorcas's father, Yakubu, had trekked for hours alongside hundreds of other men, many of them also parents wrestling with the same heartache and fears for their own lost daughters. There were others present whose families remained intact, untouched by this tragedy, and yet they felt compelled to help, part of a community-led effort to find and rescue their missing girls. The rest were from the Civilian Joint Task Force (JTF), a collective of local vigilantes formed in 2013 with a clear mission—to protect their local communities and to support the Nigerian security forces in their fight against Boko Haram. The massive search party wielded sticks, makeshift bows, arrows, and rusty machetes. When they finally entered the fabled Sambisa Forest, Yakubu found the wild undergrowth and imposing trees completely overwhelming, unlike anything he'd ever seen before. But he continued to move forward, fueled by his personal tragedy. He brushed aside all that nature had put in his way and listened carefully for any sound of the stolen girls, all the while scanning the surroundings for visual clues.

At one point, the rescue group noticed movement in the near distance. Yakubu saw a long line of moving vehicles pulling away. He didn't know what to think. *Was Dorcas among them? Had he found his beautiful child?* Spurred on, the search party moved faster, determined to follow the procession deeper into Sambisa. They'd taken only a few steps when a handful of men emerged from the bushes and blocked their path.

"These boys have weapons," the strangers told the Chibok townspeople. While they spoke, Yakubu stood quietly and simply stared at them. He noticed they were of various ages, a few looked to be teenagers—all of them spoke in Fulani, with the certainty of those who knew the forest intimately. He suspected they were in fact Fulani, part of the sprawling horde of herdsmen who have long called the forest home.

The unknown men added, "They can kill you."

From the very moment they'd left Chibok at the crack of dawn armed with only rudimentary weapons and determination, every one of them had known what they were up against. But these words of warning from the Sambisa men were a new reality check. Yakubu and the others paused to fully assess the challenge ahead. The weaponry they carried consisted of sticks, machetes, and bows and arrows, while their opponents were armed with AK-47s and who knew what else. The townspeople were simply no match for the heavily armed militants.

"If you reach them, both *you* and your girls will be no more," the men from the bushes pressed home.

The search party's confidence took flight, leaving the Chibok men with only heavy hearts. Minutes later, with heads hung low and eyes stinging, they slowly retraced their steps out of the forest.

Back in Priscilla's truck, the captives were sobbing. They'd become increasingly convinced that their parents had been close by and might have been able to rescue them. Now the girls were more desperate than ever to know where they were headed. "Where are we going?" they asked their five minders. Though met with only silence and blank stares, the group remained undeterred, repeating the same question loudly and often.

When the men finally spoke, it was sharp and brief. "There is no need to ask that," they snapped, before returning to their surly silence.

Priscilla saw the sun rise and set two more times before the convoy came to a standstill. When it did, the girls cowered in the back of the cramped truck and stared at each other in confusion.

Moments later the men yelled, "Come down!"

Priscilla had no idea what was about to happen to them. But they all knew it couldn't be stopped, so one by one they warily climbed out of the vehicles.

She was in shock. Now outside the truck in the blinding sunlight, the young girl could see only small structures dotted across a landscape of brownish yellow, reedlike grass. The dwellings sat off in the distance, but they were close enough for her to notice that the ramshackle houses were also made of the same reeds, and the vast area was surrounded by a parade of trees. Strewn about the place were piles of discarded motorbikes and battered-looking vehicles. Priscilla could also make out women and children moving about. The women all wore hijabs of black, brown, and gray that fluttered gently as they walked. Their faces were veiled.

They'd arrived at a Boko Haram camp.

"Go under that tree!" demanded the militants.

Startled by their words, Priscilla noticed for the first time the colossal tamarind tree standing a few feet away. Her eyes widened in disbelief, taking in its mammoth trunk and its most striking feature, a sprawling mass of bowed limbs. Every branch was weighed down so heavily by leaves and fruit that its end almost touched the forest floor. Mother Nature had created a hooped skirt around the tree, and inadvertently a hiding place from the world.

The hundreds of girls moved en masse for protection and stood weeping at the foot of the tree. Priscilla wanted to scream at what was happening to them. Instead, like all the others, she parted the branches and disappeared out of the sunlight. Initially she struggled to see. For those first few minutes, they all simply stood in the shadows of the tree and wept. Priscilla's eyes gradually adjusted to the darkness of the leafy labyrinth, which was punctuated by a few stubborn streams of light. *What kind of place is this?* She gasped as she looked around. The space was larger than a soccer field and easily held the hundreds of girls, with room still left over. Overwhelmed, she sank down into the mossy grass next to dozens of other girls. Lost in her grief, she didn't immediately feel the multitude of tiny movements beneath her body until the stinging sensations jolted Priscilla back to her senses. *"Ayyyyyyyyyeee!"* She was being bitten on her feet, legs, and thighs all at once. Priscilla leapt up and saw that the soil was alive. In the dim light she made out the source of her pain, a swarm of moths delicately fluttering at her feet. Everywhere she looked their translucent wings glimmered. Other girls were shrieking now as they too realized they were not alone in this secret place. Eventually all the girls sat down once more. They had no choice. They willed themselves to ignore the nipping earth. They were prisoners.

The overburdened branches of the tamarind tree didn't uniformly touch the ground. In some spots they hovered just above and created an opening that allowed the girls a narrow, ground-level view of whoever was close to the tree. Priscilla strained her eyes but saw no trace of their captors. More and more of her school-mates were struggling to remain calm in the oppressive heat of their enclosure. A mantra started up, whispered from one girl to the next, transforming the dank enclosure into an echo chamber.

"Stay calm and pray," they urged one another.

Before long, Priscilla heard the sounds of people approaching. The girls slowly crept forward in the murky light and peered out to see several pairs of dirty feet. Priscilla and the others fell quiet and listened.

"We have brought this old man to live with you."

The girls exchanged puzzled looks: *Live with us?*

The disembodied voice continued, "You must do everything he tells you to do."

An old man with a turban suddenly appeared in their midst.

That was it. No more information. No name, or details of where he was from or why he'd been chosen. Unlike the militants who had seized the girls, this small figure wasn't in a Nigerian military uniform. He wore a pair of shabby pants, a threadbare T-shirt, and on his shriveled feet, a pair of tattered slippers. He eyed the girls silently with an inscrutable look. Meanwhile, as Priscilla continued to assess him, she noticed the tribal marks on his face, one soli-tary line on each cheek. They were the same as the ones borne by Mr. Jida, the Chibok school watchman. As both men were elderly and similarly marked, the girls gave their new guardian an old, fa-miliar name: Jida.

The same ghostly voice delivered another announcement: "We have also brought you food to cook, firewood, and water."

But rather than providing a feeling of relief, the statement trig-gered an outburst among the girls. "Ah! Are we going to live here?" they shouted in dismay.

"No. You will only stay in this place for three days and then we will take you back home."

Priscilla heard the words "take you back home" and felt such a deep sense of longing, tears instantly filled her eyes. A ripple of excitement ran through the group. *Home in three days.*

She was still in a state of reverie when Jida was told by the men to choose four of the girls to cook the food waiting outside. Without delay he quickly made his picks, pointing and saying "You, you, you, you," in a low voice. He motioned to the four to follow him, and once more the tree branches parted, shafts of sunlight pouring in as the old man and the quartet shuffled out.

The four girls carried bags of rice and beans, along with oil, seasonings, onions, cooking utensils, pots, and platters over to another tree a few feet away from the giant one housing the schoolgirls. Once again, everything they had been given was cooked together in one pot. The girls improvised and made a type of "jollof rice," a spicy tomato-based dish enjoyed throughout Africa. When the cooking girls finally carried the trays of steaming-hot food to their waiting schoolmates, the hungry girls had already divided themselves into groups of ten for each platter.

As daylight ebbed away and the sun set over Sambisa, Priscilla sat in almost pitch blackness under the tamarind tree. By this point the ravenous group cared little about how much they could see. All that mattered was that everyone could gather and eat. At first Priscilla tried to hold out, but her nagging hunger won, and soon she too sat among her friends from home and gratefully filled her stomach.

When the food and the light were all gone, they sat in the darkness. No lamps or torches, just hundreds of stolen girls tormented by fearful thoughts deep in the forest. Unbeknownst to them, Jida had managed to sidle up to the tree. Now his voice floated through the gaps between the webbed leaves and branches. "If you are feeling sleepy, then you should sleep."

Sleep? Priscilla snorted with derision. *Do these people really want us to sleep here?*

A sudden succession of loud pops rang out nearby. *Gunshots?*

Priscilla's breath caught in her throat. She listened to the sounds going off like a cascade of firecrackers. The already frightened girls pulled even closer together. "What is happening?"

In the days that followed, Priscilla learned that shots fired by Boko Haram in the dark were a regular affair. The shots were supposed to frighten off the animals that made strange sounds in the bushes all around. On that first night in the camp, the girls fretted constantly about what was lurking in those bushes and, more important, wondered if it came out in the dark. Sleep was the farthest thing from everybody's mind. Even without the fear of unseen animals, no comfort was to be found in this place. There were no blankets or ground coverings of any kind, only a roof of leaves overhead. As a bone-chilling cold settled in their bodies, they could no longer feel the sting of the writhing soil. The girls were exposed to the elements from above, below, and all around.

Priscilla's eyes searched the darkness, but all she could see were her loved ones back home. They were fraught and inconsolable because she was lost to them; nothing could stop their weeping. Hot tears sprang from her eyes in the darkness of the tamarind tree. She felt as lost and alone as ever.

CHAPTER FOURTEEN

ALLAHU AKBAR, ALLAHU AKBAR,
   Allahu Akbar, Allahu Akbar,
   Ashhadu alla Ilaha Illallah.

The strains of the Muslim call to dawn prayers signaled to Priscilla that day two in the Boko Haram camp was beginning. Late into the night she'd listened to the sound of the girls' sobbing in the darkness. As the morning arrived, she could begin to make out her schoolmates' distressed faces. It was clear hardly any of them had slept.

Someone was walking toward the tree.

"If you are a Muslim, get up. Take your hijab and pray where you are." The shuffling footsteps belonged to Jida. His feeble voice wormed its way through the leafy curtain that shielded him from his charges. Priscilla watched as the twenty Muslim-born girls in their midst dutifully obeyed and slowly rose to begin their supplication in the shadows of the tamarind tree.

As the day wore on it grew punishingly hot. The girls shared what was left of the water in a yellow five-gallon plastic container. Priscilla tipped it into her palms, grateful for the feel of the cool liquid as it ran down her parched throat. As with the day before, men eventually delivered bags of food, and the same four girls disappeared to do the cooking. Those they left behind remained on edge. They were deeply fearful of what the second day would bring, and it left many of them weeping uncontrollably for hours at a time. In fact, nothing happened that day. The militants all but ignored their captives, leaving it up to old Jida to watch over them.

Come nightfall, turbulent thoughts about the forest wildlife took over and paralyzed the girls wherever they were beneath the tree. For a second night in a row, Priscilla's body remained upright in the dark. Her mind was racing once more, outpacing the pull of sleep. From the deepening silence around her she could tell more school friends were succumbing to exhaustion on this evening. Eventually, all the girls fell silent and sleep triumphed over Priscilla's mental resolve. She slowly lowered herself onto the cold, hard earth and told herself to ignore the stones digging into her weary body. Groups of girls clumped close to one another as the temperature dropped, hoping physical proximity would bring warmth. In time Priscilla closed her eyes, but sleep was short lived. She'd barely begun to dream when panic stirred and sprung her upward once more.

On the fateful night Boko Haram had spirited away the girls in Chibok, the men had warned of serious consequences if their captives left the school with any personal belongings. In a panic, Priscilla had quickly tossed aside the cell phone she'd been hiding. But there were others who'd steeled their minds and cradled Bibles, notebooks, and pens in the folds of their clothing. In the dim light of the tamarind tree these items were revealed. The Bibles were now totems of their former lives and connections to faraway loved ones. They provided comfort in a harsh and cruel place. Yet they also had the potential to be a source of pain and suffering. If the Muslim fanatics discovered the holy books, the girls were guaranteed a whipping, if not much worse. Meanwhile, lined notebooks that were once used to scribble down facts and worldly knowledge acquired in their Chibok classrooms now became diaries in which girls recorded the date they were stolen—April 14, 2014—and thereafter, details of life in their now closed-off world deep within the forest. Weeks later Priscilla would seek out this same comfort, as she tore scraps of paper from the boxes that delivered their food supplies and borrowed pens to capture her tumultuous emotions.

Before sunrise on the third day, when the Muslim girls stood to perform their prayers, the Christians answered a personal call of their own. Wherever they sat or lay, they too prayed quietly. In due course, the quartet of girls who handled the food disappeared, and the day appeared to be unfolding exactly like the previous two. Priscilla sat listlessly under the tree for much of the afternoon till the men arrived.

"All of you come out," said an unknown voice.

Eager to escape the stifling conditions of their dwelling, the girls rushed out. In the open Priscilla joyfully sucked the fresh air into her lungs and relished the unfiltered sunlight.

Standing in front of them were several men she'd never seen before.

"Do you know why we're here?" asked one of them.

"No," the group of girls said together.

"We've come to tell you that there is no need to waste your time sitting around like this. Those of you who want to convert, stand up and come over on this side," the man said pointing. "And if you know you will not, then come over here," he added, now stern faced, motioning to the other side.

Priscilla scanned her schoolmates' faces, anxious to see where they would stand on this second attempt to convert them to Islam. A few minutes later, fewer than twenty girls had taken the momentous step and agreed to conversion. More than 150 others took the opposite position.

The man who'd done all the talking looked confounded. Turning to those in the "no" camp, he demanded an explanation. "What is your reason for refusing to convert?" he asked.

The answer Priscilla and the other objectors gave was short and to the point. "We don't feel like converting."

The man pressed his case for Islam with passion and the requisite reverence. "It is in your interests to choose our religion," he stressed. Still he failed to win over any more girls. Defeated but undaunted, he signaled that Boko Haram's efforts to turn them away from Christianity were far from over. "Okay, I may be back again," he warned.

In return for saying yes and agreeing to convert, each one of the willing girls was handed a hijab from a pile lying on the forest floor and was allowed to leave the towering tree for a new open-air spot, under a different tree a few feet away—in clear view of the enclosure holding Priscilla and the others. Once the handful of girls had been moved, the men left.

For the converts, their days now revolved around deepening their newly acquired faith by attending Qur'anic classes. As it turned out, Old Man Jida was determined to make Islam the focal point of life for the holdouts as well, filling the hours with lectures about the righteousness of the religion. But his efforts to coax Priscilla's lot were quickly rebuffed with forceful nos. For these girls, overcoming the acute inconveniences and discomfort of being hidden away was what mattered.

Each morning after dawn prayers, the group was split up, and the converts were instructed to move to their dayside perch. Though physically separated for parts of the day, the holdouts and converts remained bound to each other. They were together again at mealtimes, when the converts came over to collect platefuls of whatever the chosen quartet had cooked, before retreating to eat under their own tree. And in the fading light of evening they returned once more to huddle with all the other girls through the night. From day to day, there was little discernible difference in the way the girls were treated by their captors. Things stayed that way until Priscilla and the rest of the holdouts received a second visit from the man who had earlier tried to convert them. This time, his easygoing manner was gone, replaced by a new aggressively impatient one. Within minutes he delivered a stark message to the girls.

"Those of you who convert will be allowed to go home. And those who do not convert, you will remain here." The tone was menacing. Once more he told the willing to make themselves known by standing apart from the group. But now the girls had questions of their own. "Didn't you tell us when we arrived that we'd only spend three days in this place and then you'd return us?" they asked defiantly.

The question caught the men off guard, and when they finally spoke, they sounded nervous. "No, no, we were not the ones who told you that. We will return you to your families in two weeks. But first, all of you must take the hijab," they said.

Unimpressed, the girls remained silent.

The pressure to convert felt greater to Priscilla. The girls' longing to be reunited with loved ones was overpowering, and it proved strong enough to pry large numbers of girls away from their religion. And with that, dozens and dozens of them chose the promise of reunion with their families over their faith. These decisions also stemmed from the increasingly desperate need to end their nightmare after dark days and nights spent behind a veil of leaves and branches.

Trapped deep in Sambisa Forest, Priscilla wanted nothing more than to go home. But forgoing her faith was simply too high a price to pay. So she stayed sitting on the forest floor and didn't make a move.

For those who had sacrificed their belief for freedom, there would be no return after all. All the new converts got was a hijab and a seat alongside the earlier converts in the shade of a different tree.

The holdouts were asked once more about changing their minds. Their response was instant: "We will never give up our faith." Then came the warning—"We shall see." The words signaled a shift.

After that second visit, the girls who wore hijabs were given preferential treatment over the holdouts. From laundry detergent to food and clothing—no matter the item, the militants made sure the converts received their share before the others. If there wasn't enough to go around, Priscilla's group did without. Their captors couldn't have cared less about the misery that caused.

By the third visit, the men had given up on the idea that Priscilla and the nearly two-dozen staunch holdouts could be convinced to renounce their Christianity. They now understood the depth of their devotion. These girls would never willingly choose Islam. Knowing that, the militant group recalibrated its demands. It emerged that on Boko Haram's list of priorities, obscuring the female form in loose, flowing hijabs ranked higher than the specific God to whom the girls prayed. So though the holdouts were ultimately allowed to reject Islam, there was no debate about shielding their bodies from the eyes of men in the camp. That was mandatory. Priscilla was appalled by the order to put on the hijab.

"Even if you refuse to accept our religion, you must wear the hijab," the men told the girls. The militants applied extra pressure to ensure they submitted: "Once you have all put on the hijab, we will take you home, in two weeks." Priscilla knew the girls had been cornered. In the absence of free will, the small group of rebel girls put on the shabby garments.

Days later, Priscila was awoken by loud male voices pacing and shouting around the tree. "Wake up! It is time for all of you to get up and pray!" Without warning a new routine had come into being. From that day forward, each morning, both bleary-eyed Muslims and devout Christians got up from the cold, unyielding earth. The Christian girls emerged from beneath the tamarind tree cloaked in their hijabs to take part in the prayer rituals of a religion they continued to reject—though in reality, they mostly just stood there silently, with lips unmoving because they didn't really know what to do while the others alternated between kneeling and standing all around them as they prayed.

Later in the day when they were sitting in their hour-long Islamic lessons, they remained hidden in the flowing gowns. This forced immersion in Islamic doctrine left Priscilla and the other Christians feeling under siege, and they wept bitterly while the imam taught the group. Though Jida was the one dedicated to hovering over the girls, bands of militants also monitored them from a distance. They were armed and ready at all times. Whenever Priscilla turned her head, the men would be staring at them, on the lookout for even the smallest action that hinted at the contemplation of escape. The girls were permanently on edge, unsure of what was about to happen. For hours, Priscilla was tormented by a single thought: *Is it my time to die?*

While they did their best to keep track of time, at some point during the suffocating heat of the day and the crushing despair that took hold at night, the girls lost count of the exact number of days they'd been in captivity. Occasionally one of the schoolgirls wondered out loud, "What day is it? Do you think it is Monday or Tuesday?" At that point the entire group paused to think long and hard before eventually giving up and admitting they had no idea. The pall of sorrow that hung over the girls rarely waned. Sometimes they wept till they ran out of breath. During these moments they willed each other to be strong. "Trust in God," they murmured. Then at others, the grief they wrestled with was so great, it drew to them a number of compassionate militants who felt compelled to coax the girls to stop crying. "Don't worry, everything is going to be fine. We will take you back," they promised softly.

Long after the pledged two-week deadline for their release had passed, the girls confronted their captors. Jida had summoned the men to face the increasingly restless girls, having grown weary of ducking questions he couldn't answer.

"You promised us that if everyone takes hijab then after two weeks you will release us, and you haven't. Why?"

The men had no real answer for the girls. "Our *oga*, the boss man, is not here. You must be patient," they pleaded.

"We want to go home to our parents!"

The girls were in no mood to be patient or to believe they were still being held because the "boss" wasn't present. The men tried to reassure the increasingly frenzied group with vague statements: They would be released "soon," they promised. Without skipping a beat, the girls pounced on the possibility.

"Swear to God!" they demanded. They wanted a sacred oath to bind these zealots to their words. The girls relished the discomfort it caused in their kidnappers, men who considered themselves to be pious. Now that they'd been backed into a corner, the militants shuffled and stuttered as they vowed to release the girls in the coming days. With these promises extracted, the teenagers were filled with hope.

Ironically, the same men holding the distressed girls captive were also blaming them—the victims—for their own abduction and current plight.

"We told all of you that no girl should be in school. As we found you there in school, that is why we took you," the men repeated to the girls often and with no apology.

Girls should not be in school? Priscilla repeatedly turned those words over in her mind. She was confused. Prior to her abduction she'd been unaware of the Boko Haram edict. Her parents, she knew, had been similarly oblivious.

"That is a lie. That is not the reason you took us!" Priscilla spat back at her captors one day, after they'd trotted out this explanation for the umpteenth time.

"Sit down!" the militants shouted at her. By now, the men had grown accustomed to Priscilla's outbursts and bold challenges to their authority. With a wry smile they stared at her, as they often did in these moments, and then burst into laughter.

She refused to accept her abductors' logic, that she was in captivity because of her own choices. And yet Priscilla remained remarkably clearheaded. If her seeking an education was in fact the *real* reason they'd taken away her freedom, she would still never regret being in the classroom or abandon her future dreams and ambitions.

The girls' hopes of quickly returning home floundered as the weeks piled up. Nothing changed; they remained prisoners in the forest. Until that point the men had brought them water in plastic containers, plus bars of soap and told them they were free to bathe. In reality, there was never enough water for a full dousing. But at night, groups of girls crept out from under the tree and in the bright moonlight used small quantities of water to ensure their bodies didn't start to smell. They'd also turned to the tree that imprisoned them and broken off twigs to use as toothbrushes. But now that promises of reuniting the girls with their loved ones had been made and broken, the captives concluded that a change in behavior was necessary. They felt that if they continued to follow their captors' instructions and remain agreeable, it would erode their chances of being released quickly. So rebellion became the order of the day. The girls decided to transform the realm of personal hygiene into a battleground. Uncleanliness was now an act of resistance and the girls abandoned cleaning themselves altogether.

As they grew increasingly unkempt, some of the militants gently suggested certain moments as opportunities to bathe. Every offer was unanimously spurned. "Why should we bathe when you came and took us away from our parents?" they asked.

Not knowing what to say, the men backed away in embarrassment. Priscilla was fully committed to the group's collective action and embraced the revolt with glee.

While the girls drew their own battle lines in Sambisa, unbeknownst to them, their disappearance had escalated the war between Boko Haram and the Nigerian government. It had also triggered an increasingly rare show of true global diplomacy and an international search operation. It was this kind of large-scale global attention that Boko Haram's deranged-looking leader, Abubakar Shekau, craved. Within a few weeks of their abduction, he made his first public statement about their disappearance, in a nearly hour-long video released on May 5, 2014. Speaking in a rambling mix of Hausa and English, he gleefully claimed responsibility for the girls' abduction and warned of further heartbreak.

"I abducted your girls. I will sell them in the market by Allah. There is a market for selling humans. Allah says I should sell. He commands me to sell. I will sell women. I sell women."

The video sparked even greater global outrage and accelerated the spread of the #BringBackOurGirls hashtag. Countries like the United States, France, Canada, Israel, and China quickly stepped up with offers of support to find and rescue the girls. Shekau's on-camera bluster also heightened criticism of the Nigerian government's slow response to the kidnapping.

Almost a month after the girls' abduction, on May 12, 2014, Boko Haram released a twenty-seven-minute video. This was the world's first opportunity to lay eyes on the missing girls since they'd vanished. At the same time, it showcased the results of the militants' pressure campaign to convert the girls to Islam, presenting

136 converts. Priscilla and her gang of holdouts did not make an appearance. The militants told those girls who appeared on camera that the video would be sent to their parents as proof they were still alive. The majority of them huddled together on the forest floor, while some stood at the rear, two of them diligently holding up the black flag of Boko Haram. They were clothed in Boko Haram's standard-issue drab head-to-toe hijabs of black or gray, which hid the school clothing they were all still wearing. The filming was done a short distance from the tamarind tree, out in the open in a clearing surrounded by trees and semiarid earth, with no distinctive natural features to give away their exact location. All the girls stared forlornly into space as they loudly and solemnly recited Muslim prayers, their captors' proof of their conversion to Islam. An interviewer who remained off-camera queried three girls. One explained her new faith by declaring, "Jesus is not the son of God."

Shekau, the terror outfit's leader, also made an appearance in this second video, albeit from a location separate from the girls. Seated in front of a green background with an AK-47 nestling in his arms, Shekau mocked the global outrage his group's actions had sparked. "Just because we kidnapped these young girls, you are making noise? You are making so much noise about Chibok, Chibok, Chibok." He reaffirmed his group's objection to Western education and, as in previous videos, pointedly warned, "Girls, you should go and get married." Then he delivered more distressing news to the Chibok girls' loved ones. "These girls will not leave our hands until you release our brothers in your prisons."

Back in Chibok, the lack of electricity meant the girls' parents couldn't immediately watch the video that was being aired repeatedly by local and international news networks. But they'd heard about it and were desperate to pore over the images. Frantic and clinging to their faith, a handful chose to make the eighty-mile journey to Maiduguri, the capital of Borno State. At long last, they viewed the footage there with the help of local government officials.

But since the majority of the families stayed put in Chibok, the State's Governor, Kashim Shettima, gave instructions for the video to be transferred into "mobile memory devices" (memory sticks) so every parent could see it. Whether in Maiduguri or Chibok, heartbroken parents gathered around screens big and small, desperately scanning the young faces on camera, praying for a sighting of their beloved missing children.

A few days after that second video emerged, François Hollande, then the French president, convened a Paris security summit. Nigeria's president, Goodluck Jonathan, and his regional counterparts, the leaders of Chad, Niger, Cameroon, and Benin, gathered "to discuss fresh strategies for dealing with the security threat posed by Boko Haram." In a rare show of unity among Nigeria and its neighbors, the bloc declared war on Boko Haram and discussed the possibility of a joint rescue operation of the missing girls. President Jonathan forcefully declared, "We are totally committed to finding the girls, wherever they are." He added, "We've been scanning these areas with surveillance aircraft."

Nigeria had long been fighting Boko Haram on the ground and from the air; the campaign at times involved dropping bombs on Sambisa Forest, so the militants had a pretty good idea of what a state response to this mass abduction might look like, long before it even began.

The militants warned the girls early and often about the threat from the sky. "Once you hear planes coming, you must try to hide yourself wherever you are." The girls were told to remain hidden under the tree at all times, for their own safety. "If they see you, they will drop a bomb." Priscilla approached the threats and warnings with a degree of skepticism. Like all the other girls, she refused to believe the Nigerian government would do such a thing.

"You are lying! They will not bomb us. *You*, maybe. But they will never bomb us," the girls said with unmistakable indignation.

Meanwhile, the thought of being held outdoors in the forest for the rest of her life was too much for Priscilla to bear. Within the first month of captivity, she began plotting to escape with a group of girls. All three of them knew what would happen if they were caught, but they'd made up their minds it was worth the risk. When the chosen day came, they waited till Jida was out of sight and the other men were lost in afternoon prayers, at which point the girls slowly and quietly pushed aside the branches that kept them hidden from view and stealthily slipped into the surrounding bushes. Disoriented and afraid within minutes, Priscilla didn't make it far before they were spotted by one of their captors—"Just get back or otherwise I will shoot you!" he threatened. Yelling and gunshots started up almost immediately, and the girls were promptly marched back to camp. With their blooming prison in view, the men dug a series of pits and called the rest of the schoolgirls to gather around, to watch as Priscilla and the other attempted escapees were forced to climb down into what would be their graves. Priscilla's heart thundered as she slid into the hole, while her mind had emptied out all but one thought: *I am going to die.* She looked up at the rest of her schoolmates, the faces of every one of them contorted in pain, smeared with tears. All of them pleading.

"Please, mercy! We beg!"

"Please!"

"Spare them!"

The sound of their pleas for her life were deafening, and the emotional onslaught clearly took the men aback. They now looked down at Priscilla and the others who stood praying and trembling in the pits and faltered. All of a sudden they declared a newfound need to consult with their boss man before taking any further action. Did this mean she might not be killed? Priscilla wondered. In fact, there were no lives taken that day. Instead, Priscilla and her co-conspirators were whipped again and again with lean canes. While they sobbed and screamed, she promised to never leave the camp again. With each merciless blow that fell, they were reminded, "We will kill you if you ever attempt this again."

The fear of death constantly tormented all the girls. But for the Christians among them, it wasn't simply the thought of their lives summarily ending that stalked every waking moment. Embedded in their fears was the deep, irrevocable belief that death would bring with it the moment they would be held accountable for their actions by God. So good deeds and religious faithfulness mattered—above all else. Born into devout Christian homes, they had felt anchored by this faith throughout their existence and had used it to chart a course for life in a turbulent world. Now being unable to joyfully worship, read scripture, or get lost in uninterrupted prayer robbed each girl of her sense of true peace and left in its aftermath a feeling of extreme dislocation. As a result, the lost girls eagerly awaited nightfall each day, when, under the cover of darkness, they would gather together under the tree in the collective joy of worship and prayer. But they had yet to learn that Jida was equal parts caretaker and spy. This inconspicuous man shuffled about the place, peering and prying into everything the girls did. So when he eventually uncovered a nighttime prayer session, he slunk off to inform their captors.

The next day, the captors arrived with a message: "We will kill you if we ever catch you performing Christians prayers again." Priscilla believed every word of the threat. Petrified, they could no longer find it within themselves to gather in the dark in large groups, but they refused to abandon the practice altogether. They continued to look for opportunities to replenish their faith. When the moments presented themselves, Priscilla found they were almost always unannounced and involved no more than two to three girls. They weren't regular occurrences, but these impromptu worship moments provided not only peace and succor to distressed souls, they also brought the spark that kept the spirit of defiance burning within the group.

A month into their captivity, the first rains of May heralded a new source of torment, as well as a battleground, for the girls. Trapped as they were beneath the tree, Priscilla could only watch with growing distress as the ground beneath her feet became water-logged and flooded. Slowly a reservoir of water appeared and in time submerged the girls in waist-high puddles. Jida was dispatched to summon their captors. The men duly appeared to witness the girls' plight, but they brought little to actually ease the girls' suffer-ing. Instead they offered them plastic bags. Flimsy sheets of torn-up polythene were given to the group to protect them during the near-constant downpours, and once the rains eased, the coverings were to be promptly handed back to Jida. Enraged, the girls decided to turn their suffering into a source of aggravation for their captors. Whenever Jida showed up with the flimsy plastic, the girls accepted the sheets without saying a word, then tossed them aside the mo-ment he was out of sight.

Now they waited.

In the middle of the night, when the rains fell and rivers formed around them, the girls let out ear-piercing screams. They shrieked and wailed till men came running from their grass shacks all over the camp.

In a state of panic when they arrived, the men shouted, "What is happening?"

The darkness hid the mischief that filled their eyes, and the girls screamed louder.

"What is wrong with you?"

"It is the rain . . . We are suffering . . . Release us!" they howled, their shrieks fueled by satisfaction.

"Be patient. Just a few more weeks. You will not be here for much longer."

"We are *dying!*" By then their throats were raw and yet their screams grew louder still.

The men struggled to gain control of the situation, alternating between consoling and chiding the girls. This went on till the men ran out of patience and shots rang out in the night. Satisfied, the girls paused and smiled to themselves in the dark. Then they waited long enough for their captors to exhale, wipe the sweat from their brows, and believe they'd quelled the uproar—at which point the girls started screaming all over again.

CHAPTER FIFTEEN

FOR HOURS AT A TIME THE GIRLS SAT IMMERSED IN WATER. THEIR teeth chattered and the cold invaded their soaking hijabs before seeping into their bones. One by one the girls were brought down by chills, coughs, and fever. The rains were still falling two months later in July when the men appeared and roused them from their damp quarters.

"We can see you are tired of this place and that the rainfall has been disturbing you. So let us take you to a new place. Here you'll never have these kinds of challenges."

If the militants had been expecting displays of joy and gratitude, they soon experienced otherwise. The girls exploded in anger.

"What do you mean taking us to a new place? Aren't you taking us back home?" Some of the girls were already crying.

"Don't worry! We are only changing your location because our *oga* is still not back."

By this point, neither Priscilla nor her schoolmates believed a word that came out of the men's mouths. It had been three months since the girls had first been stowed away beneath their arboreal prison, and now the teenagers were rounded up in the sunlight and marched to a new place in the forest. Priscilla walked solemnly, and many of the others cried bitterly along the way. When they stopped fifteen minutes later at their new location, the monstrous tree they'd lived under was still in view.

Two crude single-room structures stood out in the open. This was to be their home. Priscilla had seen "houses" like these countless times before. They were the same ones that littered the landscape of the Boko Haram camp, with no windows, doors, or toilets, only walls made of brown woven grass and wreathed roofs covered in tattered strips of plastic, held in place by several large stones. The men had moved them from the overbearing tree out into the open to spare them the torment of the rain. What they hadn't told the girls till they arrived at this new location was they faced a brand new threat.

"The Nigerian military frequently drops bombs in this place," they announced without emotion.

"What?" the girls shrieked.

"So every day you must wake up early in the morning and leave this place. Go and find a place to sit under these trees that are nearby here."

In their entire three months under the tamarind tree, the girls had heard only the loud whirring of helicopter blades—they'd been unaware of any bomb attacks. Hidden away behind a pile of leaves and branches, they had felt their biggest concern to be the heat and the rain. Now they were being told that they were living under unfriendly skies and could die at any time.

Priscilla, like most of the group, was simply dumbfounded.

Sleep and wake early? She couldn't even see how hundreds of girls would fit into the two small spaces in front of her.

"Half of you will stay in this room!" the men shouted suddenly.

The girls were divided into groups without warning or explanation.

"And the rest of you will be in this other one."

With the living arrangements in place, the men melted away. They retreated to their positions in the distance, from which they monitored the hostages. As with before, it was left to Jida to live with the girls and keep them in check.

Priscilla and Bernice found themselves in the same room, alongside more than one hundred others. Back in Chibok, they'd both been house captains in their respective dorms, so Priscilla had often seen Bernice, a shy, soft-spoken girl, when meetings were called for all the captains—but they'd never spent much time together, and neither girl counted the other as a friend. The inhabitants of the respective spaces busied themselves with plucking the overgrown grass sprawling across their new "home" while there was still daylight. When they eventually willed themselves to lie down on the cold, craggy earth on that first night, their fears were confirmed—it was a very tight squeeze.

Old traditions ushered in this new phase of life for the girls. Just as he'd done every morning for the past three months, Jida's reedy voice accompanied the approaching dawn. He drew the hostages from their cramped spots on the ground to a standing position to pray. Just as before, when it was time for Qur'anic classes, the imam duly appeared and gathered all the girls outside their new dwellings. While Boko Haram's commitment to fostering Islamic fervor remained unwavering, Priscilla and the others quickly realized that several other elements of their existence in Sambisa had suddenly shifted.

Back at the tree, the men had delivered food, water, and firewood. Most days the girls were left wanting more of each, but their basic needs were met. This was no longer the case. Now the school-girls could only count on the men showing up at some point in the day with either rice, beans, pasta, or corn flour, and even then, the delivery times fluctuated wildly. When it came to water and firewood, the girls were completely on their own—those deliveries stopped altogether. It all happened suddenly, and the girls demanded an explanation.

"Why?" they asked the men.

"Because when you first got here you didn't know where you were—that's why we did those things for you. But after all these months, we know you can do these things for yourself."

The girls had an entirely new situation on their hands. When they'd first arrived at the camp in April, the girls had divided themselves into groups of ten at mealtime. Now these mealtime buddy groups were assigned specific duties: Some had the sole mission of heading into the bushes in search of wood. Others set off with plastic containers in hand to collect water they could use to drink and cook. The girls were still refusing in protest to bathe, which under these new conditions was actually a welcome relief because it lessened the girls' water needs. Within the first few days of roaming through the bushes, they discovered a small pond. But the amount of water it provided fell short of their daily requirements. Ultimately, the very rains the girls had feared would be their demise under the tamarind tree had become critical to their survival. They lined up open plastic containers and prayed for the rains to pour down on them.

As the days went by, finding water became a pressing issue. In much the same way, food was also a growing ordeal. The girls didn't have enough to eat. With depressing regularity, the teenagers found themselves sitting out in the open, waiting for hours on end, sometimes all night into the next morning, for deliveries of food that never came. Sometimes the lack of food lasted a few days. Other times, they went a couple of weeks without a proper meal.

The physical impact on the girls was stark. Hunger whittled Priscilla and the others down to skin and bone, leaving them with pallid complexions, gaunt and listless. While the girls' bodies broke down, their captors looked on dispassionately, offering no words of comfort. Instead, they preached forbearance: "You must endure! We cannot go out to loot for supplies with these military boys everywhere. They are all over the place, so you must bear it!"

All they had was their faith and the forest, and now the girls decided to lean on both of them. Before the call to prayers when the luminous predawn light lingered over the forest, small groups of girls crept out of the two rooms and into the bushes in search of kuka leaves. The ancient kuka tree, with its vast, wide trunk and tapered wiry-looking branches, all bent and twisted to form a sort of fantastical headdress, has long been famed for its medicinal and nutritional properties. Dubbed the "Tree of Life" by some, the kuka has provided nourishment and hope to people in Africa, Asia, and Australia throughout the ages, all from the same leaves now sought by the girls. They had to walk for over an hour to reach the nearest kuka trees. When the group finally found them, faint from hunger, everyone knew they had to act fast and get back to camp before it was time for prayers under the watchful eye of Jida. In desperation, the girls scrambled up the handful of kuka trees to gather their precious leaves. Back in the rooms with their treasure, the ravenous girls moved the leaves from the folds of their hijabs onto the ground to dry. Once dried, the ravenous girls ground them into a powder with the help of a smooth rock. They all waited impatiently for the pot, filled with water, to start boiling. This was the welcomed signal that it was time to add the kuka powder. Stirred and left to boil, as soon as the slimy substance cooled down, it was poured into a bowl—the bottom half of a damaged yellow plastic container—and passed around the group. When each girl got her turn, she eagerly slurped down the green slop. Priscilla sucked it down greedily, grateful for the space it filled in her aching stomach.

In her previous life, long before Boko Haram decimated her world, one of Priscilla's favorite pastimes at home had been cooking kuka leaves for her entire family. In fact, few things had filled her with as much pride. Back then, as they all gathered around to eat the popular Nigerian dish she'd so lovingly made with pungent spices, pepper, onions, and meat, none could have foreseen a time when Priscilla's very existence depended on *drinking* those leaves in the presence of a whole new family made up of hundreds of kidnapped sisters. Still, she was thankful for the bonds that knit the group together, borne not of blood but fashioned instead from hardship and suffering. These ties were just as strong as blood relations and held the group close. In fact, as time went by and the girls' discomfort and frustrations mounted, their sense of sisterhood grew even stronger.

At the top of Priscilla's list of frustrations were the living conditions, in particular being forced to sleep on the cold, hard ground. They were without blankets or ground covering, and the exposure to the elements left every joint and muscle in her body stiff and aching. Priscilla dreaded nighttime, when she entered a battle with sleep, fighting against its grasp even though she knew it would ultimately force her to embrace the ground. The girl longed to sleep in a bed under the warmth of a blanket, feel the tenderness of her parents' loving embrace, and savor the taste of a home-cooked meal. Time seemed to move at a pace that made every day feel interminable. The months gradually piled up, as painful yearnings emerged and embedded themselves within the ebb and flow of despair. Priscilla's life in the forest had been stripped of every comfort. All that remained was fear, cold, exhaustion, and hunger.

Her bonds with the other girls, though, became Priscilla's lifeline. When they were first taken, she'd spent almost all of her time with a gang of eleven from her Chibok neighborhood. Being able to share her personal fears with the group became a major source of comfort for her, and this clique in turn leaned on each other for the strength to navigate their despair and survive life in the forest. But alliances were reordered when their captors moved them to the two rooms in the forest and Priscilla and Bernice found themselves together. In the forest the casual friendship between these two girls deepened and blossomed. Soon they were inseparable and spent long hours whispering secrets, giggling, crying, and comforting one another.

When the girls finally decided they wanted to sort through the tangled mass of hair on their heads, Priscilla and Bernice turned to each other. The duo took turns picking through their knotted and twisted hair with sticks carved into prongs. It took hours of pulling and shrieking before they eventually reached the point where they were able to braid each other's manes.

After weeks of deprivation and suffering, the girls suddenly wanted to see what they looked like. With the sun high in the sky and a sense of curiosity burning within, Priscilla and Bernice among handfuls of other girls sidled over to an area not far from their rooms where Boko Haram had abandoned its broken-down motorbikes. The girls knew their captors were watching as they crowded around the bikes' small rearview mirrors. They stared, wide eyed, at their own reflections, almost as if they didn't recognize the faces staring back at them. When Priscilla finally looked in the mirror, she was shocked by how much she had changed. The girl in the mirror looked nothing like the girl who'd been at school in Chibok. From time to time a schoolmate would actually turn up with a broken-off rearview mirror hidden away in her hijab. In those squalid spaces where they lacked everything, the mirror became a prized possession, passed among the girls excitedly. Jida was all too aware of what was happening, but rather than confiscate the mirror, he would gently chide them. "Put it away," he said whenever he spotted them gathered together and engrossed in their reflections. "It will only make you think more about what you have left behind," the old man always added. But for the girls, staring at the round disk was more than a frivolous pastime—it was also a means of reconnecting with the girls they used to be, another lifetime ago.

Still, the day-to-day pace remained much the same. Time ticked by, the days passed, the girls wept and missed home. Hours sometimes leapt past and at other points dragged with a maddening numbness. Nothing much changed.

Then one day the Nigerian government turned up the pressure.

It was after morning prayers. Priscilla, Bernice, and dozens of other girls were in their shack readying themselves for the day ahead. A handful of others were milling about outside, others having already disappeared into the forest to seek refuge from the bombing threat. At first, there was nothing to indicate that a military aircraft might be approaching. By the time Priscilla picked up on the sound of low-level droning, the ground was already shaking and flames had engulfed the girls' second structure. In seconds everyone was fleeing wildly into the forest. Hordes of men appeared the moment they realized a bomb had fallen on one of the shelters. But by the time they got there, the girls were screaming and running uncontrollably everywhere. The men yelled for them to stop and turn back, but nothing was going to make these girls stop. *We have been bombed! What these men have been telling us is true!* Priscilla thought. The girls dispersed, deeper into the forest than they had ever ventured before. The aircraft that dropped the bomb was still hovering above them, and the captives became convinced another bomb would fall shortly.

As the panic subsided, the sound of weeping echoed throughout the forest. News spread to those hiding of three girls being injured by shrapnel during the bombing. Grief and concern for the wounded drew those in hiding back to the camp. Priscilla walked out of the bushes alongside dozens of girls because of the bonds of sisterhood. The trio who'd been seriously hurt required stitches, but in time they recovered. The bombing had severely traumatized the girls. Even though there was one shelter still standing, most of the girls now refused to sleep inside. Sleeping outdoors gave them a better chance of surviving the next bombing. They all knew it was only a matter of time before terror fell from the skies again.

One September morning, a month after the aerial attack, Priscilla listened openmouthed to yet another announcement from their captors.

"We plan to take you home. But first we are going to take you somewhere to relax."

Priscilla and Bernice were thinking the same thing. *More lies. We can't believe them now.*

"Hurry up and pack your things!"

At this point they'd been held for five months, the last two months in this second location. Throughout, they had struggled to find enough to eat or drink. And then the bombing had occurred. The group was eager to move on from this place, though few trusted Boko Haram's promise. Priscilla wanted to believe they would soon be reunited with their loved ones, but she'd been disappointed by these men too many times. So the anxious girl said a little prayer before they set off. "Lord, we do not know where we are going. God, if these men are telling the truth, then show us. If it is a lie, God, show us."

It was midmorning when Priscilla and the others were ushered into the fleet of waiting vehicles. The girls were in a state of turmoil but offered no resistance. Over the course of the many hours they traveled, the militants shared no more information about where they were going or when they would be reunited with their loved ones. Yet most of the girls in Priscilla's truck couldn't stop feelings of excitement from taking over. The mood in the vehicle was light, with a great deal of chatter and laughter.

Priscilla sat quietly throughout, preparing herself for whatever happened next. She watched as the landscape around them changed. The claustrophobia of Sambisa slowly fell away, and the dirt track eventually came to resemble a road. When the Boko Haram convoy pulled into the town of Gwoza, it was past eleven at night. Most people were already asleep, and even those who were awake had no idea Boko Haram had brought the world's most famous hostages to this militant enclave in Borno State, south of its capital, Maiduguri. The girls themselves had no idea they were now closer than they had ever been to their homes in Chibok. After the militants had captured Gwoza in August 2014, they'd slaughtered or driven out most of the civilians from this town in Nigeria's northeast. By the time the men turned up there with the girls, it was mostly empty. Those who remained were loyalists or militants themselves.

The convoy stopped outside a large compound surrounded by high walls. The gate barring entry was painted black.

The men yelled, "Come down!"

The girls did as they were told. As they stood outside, Priscilla looked around the place, and the first alarm bells went off in her head. *Why are we to get out of the vehicles here?*

The whole place was eerily silent.

"You must now enter this house," the men said.

"To do what?" challenged the girls.

"*Enter!*"

The gate was suddenly open. Panic immediately surged throughout Priscilla's body. The men were herding the girls through, and momentum made it difficult for Priscilla or any other girl to refuse to cross the threshold.

Now the captives found themselves standing in a large compound occupied by a massive eight-bedroom house.

"Go inside the house."

"No."

"Why are you just standing here in the compound?"

"We won't enter the house of someone we don't know!"

"Stop playing games. Enter right now!"

"No!"

The girls would not be moved. Even though the men screamed and shouted, Priscilla and the others eventually dropped to the ground and remained there for the rest of the night. Their captors eyed them in silence.

When rain blanketed Gwoza the next day, the girls decided to take shelter on the veranda, and there they remained for their second night in the town. On the third evening, the men came with angry faces and demanded the group enter the house.

"You will not sleep here! You must enter immediately!"

The response was the same. "No, we will not."

At this stage, only a fraction of the Chibok girls were in Gwoza. For reasons never explained, the men had divided the hostages into three batches for the journey. Priscilla had arrived with the first batch, who refused to go past the veranda. More girls arrived on the fourth night, and this marked the end of their captors' patience. On that night the men appeared on the veranda with long, slender canes in their hands. Having decided the time for coaxing and cajoling was over, the men decided to beat the girls mercilessly until the holdouts gave in. They moved among the group with arms flailing as they loudly and sternly ordered everyone into the house. Priscilla wept uncontrollably, not just from the searing pain bolting through her body, but also from knowing they had lost. They had no choice. Priscilla ran indoors surrounded by other weeping girls.

As distressed as the girls were, they couldn't help but notice how different this place was from their previous shelter. The house was illuminated by electricity, allowing Priscilla to take in the sofas, tables, and chairs. In the kitchen, a toaster, kettle, stove, and fridge stood ready to be used, and when the taps were turned on, water came rushing out. In the bathrooms, there were showers, working toilets, and more water than the girls knew what to do with. When Priscilla and Bernice caught sight of a woman's bra and panties hanging in one of the bathrooms, they gave each other puzzled looks. They did the same thing when they spotted a meal half-eaten and clearly abandoned in a hurry. But with her legs and back still smarting from the beating, Priscilla asked no questions.

The house itself seemed like it was world away from the cramped conditions Priscilla had endured in the forest. The men left it to the girls to decide in which one of the eight bedrooms they wanted to lay their heads at the end of each day. The one room with a bed was automatically handed over to Deborah, who was expecting a baby. She'd been married just a few weeks when Boko Haram had attacked the school, and when they carried her off that night she already knew she was pregnant. Meanwhile, the various cliques moved into the other seven empty bedrooms. A bare floor without blankets or pillows was once again their resting place. But for the first time in five months they would not fall asleep exposed to the elements, and the sun going down would no longer trigger fears of what would emerge from the bushes once the day's light was gone.

Life in a comfortable house in town had its own surreal quality. Now Priscilla could bathe whenever she wanted to, an action all the girls finally embraced after months of personal objections. She chose to ignore the gleaming showerhead, and for the first time in months Priscilla was able to fill a bucket with water, enjoy working up a lather with her small bar of soap, and slowly wash herself clean in the privacy of a bathroom. After being grimy for so long, the relief she felt made the nightmare of her captivity a little more bearable on that particular day. The girls could also speak freely among themselves because no male stepped foot in the house while they were there—the farthest they got was the outdoor veranda, where you'd find the imam each day teaching Qur'anic studies.

The girls could cook food whenever they wanted, and rest or sleep without anyone's permission. But for all these acts that underscored autonomy and personal choice, the one thing the girls did not have was freedom. From the moment they moved into the large home, they were fully trapped. Now in town, there was no need to go in search of water or firewood, chores the girls loathed. But the unintended consequence was that the girls never moved beyond the front gate. The fact that Gwoza was close to large urban centers like Bama and Maiduguri seemed to have made the men more fearful of an attack or a rescue attempt for the girls. They positioned fighters to stand guard at every window, every door, and around the entire wall surrounding the house.

Unexpectedly, the imam gave each one of them a journal to aid with their Qur'anic studies. But Priscilla and dozens of others found a different use for the tattered books. She now transferred the writings she'd amassed on those scraps of paper collected in the forest to her treasured notebook. Once the transfer was complete, Priscilla filled a bowl with water and the paper and watched her captured feelings disappear before her eyes. She wrote whenever possible and found comfort in pouring her pain onto the flimsy pages. Like all the other secret scribes, Priscilla stashed her book in various hiding places throughout the bedroom they shared. She knew if the secret writings were ever discovered she'd be in serious trouble, but Priscilla kept writing, convinced this was a risk worth taking.

Life in town lacked almost all the physical hardships that had shaped and tormented the girls' existence beneath the gargantuan tree and sleeping near the two-room shelters out in the open. But nothing about their existence was normal. The girls had been in captivity for eight and a half months by the time Christmas came around. Though they'd largely stopped caring about the days of the week, or even the time of day, the high points in the Christian calendar still meant a great deal. So much so, the group tried to keep track of those dates and where they fell. Christmas was the most special of all, a time when bonds between family, friends, and neighbors were strengthened through shared meals and exuberant celebrations. All over Chibok, people got together and split the cost of buying a cow to slaughter for the occasion. The sharing of the uncooked beef among houses is only part of the tradition, perhaps the least important part—the essence of this communion lies in the sharing of the cooked meat among all those who paid for the cow and even those who didn't. Muslims in the community are also given plates of food and invited to share in the town-wide celebration. Those Christmas memories of past festivities flooded Priscilla's mind—she pictured the new dresses every child always excitedly received, the elaborate braids the girls wore in their hair, and the sound of vibrant singing that rose to the roof of every Chibok church that special day.

But now that she found herself in the hands of a bunch of Islamic fanatics, determined to destroy her faith, Priscilla mourned the fact that there could be no public acknowledgment of Christmas and wept bitterly. She longed for the sound of hymns and joyful activity. And her heart grew heavier still as the girls whispered Christmas greetings to each other before retreating to pray individually in secret. All her life, Christmas had been a collective experience, a holiday that more than any other captured the communal spirit of life in Chibok—a place where faith, joy, and loss are equally shared.

In Gwoza, the girls experienced emotional upset on an unparalleled level. The reason? This is where the talk of marriage really began.

For the entire time the girls were held in the forest, the men stayed away from the subject, most likely because the few times they'd dared broach it, a couple of the girls had run off in floods of tears. But now their captors felt differently.

The sight of a large group of militants waiting for the girls on the veranda didn't set off any alarm bells. As far as Priscilla was concerned, they'd been called outside to hear an announcement. Nothing prepared her for the subject matter.

"We have come here because we just want to announce to you,

for those of you who will agree. You have been with us for a long time and haven't made it home. So now there is no way for you to go back. So it is a better option for you to think about it and then get married. If you go through with it, then your husband can take you home to your people."

The shock among the girls triggered crying and loud shouting: "No, No, No!"

Shocked by the strength of their refusal, the men quickly left without saying anything more.

But they returned the next day. This time their statement was brief. "If you agree to marriage, then come and stand to the side." Much to Priscilla's surprise, twelve of the original twenty Muslim girls from Chibok decided to make marriage their next life chapter.

Now that their feelings were known, they were whisked out of the house and placed into a smaller unit just next door. For the men seeking to recruit wives, their actions followed a formula. Every couple of days the men reappeared and made the same pitch to the girls. And with each visit they netted more. Soon there were at least fifty of them living next door, waiting for their suitors to appear, all the while nursing the belief that married life would be better and eventually set them on a path back to their families. Priscilla could hear their laughter through the brittle walls, and whenever the wives-to-be found themselves at the windows, they waved merrily.

For Priscilla, who'd never even had a boyfriend, because her father hadn't allowed it, marrying one of these insurgents was out of the question. But to dozens of girls who'd converted to Islam during their first year in captivity, the thought of being wed to one of their captors wasn't abhorrent. In the days that followed, these girls put their names down for a spouse. For as long as they remained willing but unmarried, the militants kept the girls apart, fearful that holdouts like Priscilla would manage to change their minds. But in time, all of them were married off and promptly disappeared without saying goodbye or leaving any clues to where they'd gone.

As for the remaining unwed Chibok girls, Boko Haram's strategy for marriage was quite simple. First, cajole. If that didn't produce results, then beat the girls or put them to work. The pressure was constant. But when it came to those like Priscilla, the men eventually changed their tactics and began to peel the girls away from the wider group in the belief they'd have a better chance of selling the idea if the conversation didn't take place in front of an audience. Jida was the one who approached Priscilla.

"You should marry. . . ."

"It is better to get married because it will make life more comfortable for you."

"When you have your own house nobody will rule over you. . . ."

"You will have your own authority to do what you want—it will be better than this."

It didn't matter to Priscilla whether she was alone or in a group. Her answer was always the same, a short, sharp no.

There were painful consequences for refusing. Boko Haram began to dole out beatings to the defiant, which eventually became regular occurrences. Priscilla took the cane lashes without complaining, praying the whole time, "Lord, protect me. I don't want to get married!"

The beatings were just one new twist. The other involved using the recalcitrant ones to serve the new Chibok wives. Every day the men turned up at the girls' house to assign chores to the unmarried "slaves," who busied themselves doing their mistresses' laundry or delivering messages on their behalf. All the while, the newlyweds were supposedly busy with their Islamic studies. Priscilla refused to be drawn into this new state of affairs, and each time they chose her for work duty, she quietly but firmly refused, muttering something about having a headache and feeling too weak to work. In time it was clear she was faking, but there were plenty of other girls to choose from, so ultimately the men left her alone.

The birth of baby Amos brought some measure of relief to the strained relations between the two groups of girls. After briefly complaining of stomach pains, Deborah had retreated to her room and within a short time had given birth, with the help of a handful of girls who'd never delivered a baby before. Nervousness kept Priscilla away from what was happening, but she rejoiced with all the others when she learned Amos had been born without any complications. The chubby little one soon became everyone's baby and they all took turns caring for him. He survived on Deborah's breast milk, was never ill, and received all the clothing he needed from their captors, as well as gifts from the girls who had moved next door.

Still, the fact that some of the girls had married their abductors and were now treating their former classmates as slaves sorely tested the bonds of kinship. Priscilla viewed the situation with sadness rather than rage. When she looked at the choices her classmates had made, she didn't see acts of free will. In her mind, the decision to marry hadn't been made easily by any of her friends. These were girls who simply couldn't bear the pressure. So whenever Chibok wives turned up at the girls' house to hang out and have their hair braided, they received a warm welcome and the conversation between the girls remained friendly.

The only time tensions mounted was when talk turned to marriage.

"You should agree to marriage. Your life will become easier," the wives coaxed gently.

"Stop talking!" yelled the holdouts. "Stop talking about this one. We don't want this kind of talking."

"Okay, okay, it is not by force, it is by choice," the brides responded, hoping to ease the tension in the room before quickly changing the subject.

While Priscilla believed the girls had married due to pressure and torment, she searched their faces for the telltale signs of regret and misery. At first she couldn't find any. But as the days went by, their once bright smiles dimmed and their eyes grew cloudy whenever the subject of marriage came up. The wives never explained what had stolen the light from their eyes. But they did say this: "If I had known the truth, I never would have agreed to marriage."

CHAPTER SIXTEEN

TWO YEARS AFTER THE ABDUCTION OF THE CHIBOK GIRLS, AISHA Yesufu never thought she'd still be wearing her red hijab or taking part in marches and sit-ins. In fact, when the girls were first taken, she'd confidently told people they'd all be home within two weeks. Back then, a friend had given her a red wristband inscribed with CHIBOK GIRLS APRIL 14 2014, to commemorate the tragedy, and as she slipped on the band, she pledged, "I will never remove it until all the girls have been found." Then she waited and the months went by, but no girls came back. One day toward the end of 2014, as Aisha sat at home in Abuja bitterly contemplating the growing pile of days and the lack of information from the government, her then twelve-year-old daughter, Aliyyah, delivered a devastating blow. "Mummy, you know if any of the Chibok girls was an American, she would have been brought back by now." Barely a teenager, the young girl spoke calmly, without any emotion. On hearing those words, Aisha was wracked with torment. *My twelve-year-old daughter has come to the conclusion her life is worth less than an American . . . That is the reality.* When 2016 came around, Aisha's plastic bracelet was still in place, by now a mocking reminder of the faith she'd once held in her government's claims it would do everything possible to reunite the girls with their families.

As she took her daily position at the Unity Fountain for the Bring Back Our Girls sit-in, she saw the number of attendees ebb and flow. There were days when barely a dozen people turned up, but Aisha was always there, and at some point her thoughts always drifted to her own children, in particular to her daughter, Aliyyah. Aisha marveled at how her daughter's young life had changed in the years since the Bring Back Our Girls protests had taken over her existence. Aliyyah was moving forward in school, having new experiences, and nurturing new dreams. But there were no stories of progress for the stolen girls—their lives had been truncated, and their parents' existence hollowed out. Invariably, Aisha's mind also wandered back to the very beginning, that rain-soaked night at the Unity Fountain when parents of the missing Chibok community members and people like herself who had refused to accept this injustice had all said a defiant yes, to launching daily Bring Back Our Girls demonstrations. But never in a million years had Aisha expected them to still be sitting in the same place all these years later, or for the parents of the missing girls to have been abandoned first by the government of Goodluck Jonathan and then that of his successor, Muhammadu Buhari. Aisha absorbed all the parents' pain, and their lamentations never left her.

"Every time I hear someone say it is a scam," cried one Chibok mother, "I ask myself, Does that mean my eighteen-year-old daughter never existed? Because I had a daughter who was eighteen, whom I sent to school, and she never came back to me."

"The government used to fine us for not sending our children to school. But now we have sent our children to school and they have been taken away—who is going to fine the government?" said another father mournfully.

"My daughter always said she was going to university so she could come back and look after me. Is it with the terrorists she is now looking after me?" a different mother mourned.

Under President Jonathan, the government's response to the Chibok abductions was one of indifference and denial. The president decided early on that events in Chibok were a hoax, one devised to embarrass and ultimately drive him from office, so his administration was never a source of comfort for the devastated parents and community. In fact, on April 15, 2014, the day after news of the girls' abduction broke, President Jonathan had been seen out in public, happily singing and dancing at a political rally in the northern state of Kano. He said nothing publicly about the girls for nineteen days, till a question about the events in Chibok was posed to him on May 4 during a routine television appearance.

At the same time, First Lady Patience Jonathan had done her part to sow discord into the public debate surrounding the missing girls. On May 5, during an all-night meeting with some mothers of the missing girls and their supporters, Patience had lashed out at the heartbroken women. "We, the Nigerian women, are saying that no child is missing in Borno State. If any child is missing, let the governor go and look for them. There is nothing we can do again." Hours after the meeting had ended two attendees, Naomi Mutuah and Saratu Angus Ndirpaya, representatives of the Chibok community who'd organized a series of protests against the Nigerian's government's response to the abduction, were detained by Nigerian state security officials and driven to a police station, reportedly on the orders of Patience Jonathan. Saratu later described to journalists and a number of Chibok community elders the full-blown anger directed toward her and Naomi by the first lady, who told them in the middle of the crowded room that "they had no right to protest," because they didn't have children among the missing girls. The first lady's media assistant later disputed the multiple public accounts of Patience's involvement in the arrest of these two Bring Back Our Girls activists.

The whole time Aisha looked on, and her shock slowly turned to angry disbelief as the first couple opened up a divide in Nigerian society. She made no secret of her objections. "That is one of the most horrendous things the government of Goodluck Ebele Jonathan did, to make people doubt there was an abduction. Instead of trying to get everyone to come together, he ended up separating people." On May 26, 2014, forty-three days after the girls disappeared, the chief of defense staff, Air Marshal Alex Badeh, proudly announced in front of a bank of TV cameras, "The good news for the parents of the girls is that we know where they are but we cannot tell you. We cannot come and tell you the military's secret. Just leave us alone to do our work. We are going to get the girls back." The world waited. No girls returned. Bring Back Our Girls refused to back down and continued to ask questions and demand details of the government's efforts to free the captives. The answers never came, and the state's position on negotiating with Boko Haram and accepting offers of international assistance to rescue the girls remained unclear. But one thing wasn't in doubt: the Jonathan administration's position that the Bring Back Our Girls movement, including Oby, Aisha, and the rest of the protestors, was without exception the enemy.

Seemingly overnight Aisha found herself the target of online intimidation from Internet trolls who claimed the Bring Back Our Girls movement was in cahoots with the opposition and working to derail President Jonathan's reelection chances. The online abuse Aisha and the other activists experienced was near constant, and on more than one occasion that online intimidation crossed over into the real world. Ugly scenes of pushing and shoving between

Bring Back Our Girls activists and thugs for hire played out at the Unity Fountain.

For Muhammadu Buhari, President Jonathan's main political challenger in the 2015 elections, the abducted girls were the perfect campaign issue to drive a wedge between Jonathan and voters. It was a foolproof narrative gifted to the opposition. *Goodluck Jonathan lost 219 girls on his watch, from a part of the country under a state of emergency. He is weak and can't be trusted to keep the nation safe, and he certainly doesn't care about the poor and those living in the Muslim north.* Everywhere Buhari went, every time he opened his mouth, Aisha heard "Chibok girls this, Chibok girls that, Chibok girls, I'm going to bring them back." Sure enough, the seventy-two-year-old former military ruler rode to victory months later with a pledge to defeat Boko Haram, making him the first opposition figure to win a presidential election in Nigeria since its independence in 1960. On May 29, 2015, Muhammadu Buhari was sworn in as the fifteenth president of Nigeria in Abuja's Eagle Square. This latest chapter in the nation's long, turbulent history was marked by celebratory dancing, doves released to symbolize peace, and a declaration from the new president: "We cannot claim to have defeated Boko Haram without rescuing the Chibok girls and all other innocent persons held hostage by insurgents." He added, "This government will do all it can to rescue them alive."

Aisha watched these scenes on her TV screen like millions of other Nigerians, and her heart leapt in her chest. Finally the Bring Back Our Girls movement had a president who acknowledged freely and openly that the Chibok mass abduction had happened and, unlike Goodluck Jonathan, was committed to ending this long-running nightmare for the girls' parents. When the new president met with Aisha, some of the other BBOG activists, and two Chibok parents a couple of weeks later, on July 18, 2015, her heart swelled with joy as she watched Buhari take notes, provide words of comfort to the grieving parents, and once again reiterate his commitment to rescuing the girls. As far as Aisha was concerned it was an amazing meeting and she left on an incredible high.

But then President Buhari declared on December 24, 2015, that despite continued suicide bombings by Boko Haram, the Nigerian military had "technically . . . won the war" against the insurgent group, BBOG activists were taken aback. During his inaugural address, Buhari's definition of victory over Boko Haram had included the return of the Chibok girls. What had changed?

When news emerged of President Buhari's first presidential media chat on December 30, 2015, Aisha saw it as an opportunity to finally get an update on efforts to find the girls. The activists all gathered around their television sets and waited as the president fielded questions from a panel of journalists during the live televised event in Abuja. Finally the questions moved on to the Chibok girls and Boko Haram:

Question: "Do we know for a fact that the Chibok girls are alive, they are okay, and they are in this location, that location, or wherever it is they are—do we have any credible information?"

Buhari: "Not credible information. I am working with Niger, with Chad, and with Cameroon, and I assure you the question of the Chibok girls is in all our minds for even humanitarian reasons.

"But there is no firm intelligence where those girls physically are and what condition they are in. But what we believe from our intelligence they keep shifting them around so they are not taken by surprise and they get freed and they are not kept with a whole lot of . . . they are not kept in one place, we don't know how many divisions they made of them and where they are."

Question: "So in essence you don't have any cogent intelligence, any credible intelligence to say the Chibok girls are still alive?"

Buhari: "Or whether they are in one place . . . that's right and that's the honest truth."

Aisha felt sick to her stomach. Surely the president couldn't have meant what he just said. Buhari was the one they'd been pinning their hopes on. He'd pledged to "fight" for the girls. There was no success against Boko Haram without the girls, those were his words. The president's statement about a lack of "credible" intelligence brought to mind vague statements made in the past by officials in the previous administration. Bring Back Our Girls was infuriated by his casual-sounding statements and what came across as a distinct lack of urgency for any efforts to find the girls. It sent shockwaves throughout the entire movement. BBOG's cofounder Oby Ezekwesili made clear Buhari's position was unacceptable. "President Buhari is a very serious-minded person. For him to now say [there is a] lack of credible intelligence, that was totally not going to work. If there is a lack of credible intelligence, then get it—get the credible intelligence, find it, discover it, do everything to get it."

BBOG demanded a meeting with President Buhari, and within days the date was set, for January 14, 2016. Word of the meeting got back to Chibok, and over 130 parents expressed their desire to attend. Many were forced to sell their cattle to afford the cost of traveling down to Abuja. They departed Chibok on January 13 and were promptly arrested by the local military for the baffling reason of failing to secure clearance to leave the area. Aisha could make no sense of the military's actions. After a great deal of wrangling they were finally released, and by the time the parents caught up with the rest of the BBOG activists, Aisha and the others were standing at the gates of the presidential villa waiting to be shown in for their scheduled meeting with President Buhari. Attempts made by government officials to cancel the meeting and to send the parents and activists back were loudly rejected.

Eventually the presidential spokesman Garba Shehu relented and led the large group into a banquet hall. Already present was a high-level delegation of ministers, including the heads of women's affairs, defense, the national security adviser, and the chief of defense staff. Aisha and the others quickly took a seat in the chairs provided and waited. The mood in the room was tense as both delegations eyed each other suspiciously. Before long one of the ministers spoke up.

"We've been sent by the president to meet with you," he said.

"We've come to meet with the president. We have with us more than 130 Chibok parents who made the long journey to meet with the president," replied the BBOG activists.

"The president is in a meeting."

"That's okay, we'll wait. No matter how long it takes."

And with that note of defiance the BBOG activists and Chibok parents settled in—all of which angered the minister of women's affairs, Aisha al-Hassan, who openly berated the parents, calling them "ungrateful" for all that the Buhari government had done for them.

Aisha Yesufu took deep breaths and tried to stay calm.

Al-Hassan continued: "You should now stop with this protesting and leave this issue of your missing children in God's hands."

The parents looked startled and barely knew where to look once the words had left the minister's mouth. Aisha Yesufu felt her head snap as she turned to glare at the minister. "You lost an election but took your case to court. Why didn't you leave it to God?" She was seething as she spoke. The two women glared at one another before an aide coaxed the minister to step away from Aisha, who was ready for whatever came next.

They had been waiting over an hour when an official suddenly announced that the president would see them. A sense of relief spread out among the parents and the BBOG activists. Aisha sat up, eager for the opportunity to face President Buhari. After all, in the last meeting they'd had with him the previous year after his inauguration, he'd spoken with such warmth and kindness to the parents and activists. Aisha waited, and when the president entered the room, she did not recognize him. Buhari arrived in a clear state of anger and immediately the assembled media was ordered out of the room. The president glared at the parents and activists with open hostility. As Aisha's shock subsided, she felt pain rise up to take its place. She couldn't believe what was happening. After much cajoling the president grudgingly agreed to hear from a Chibok parent, a representative from BBOG, and a member of the Chibok community association. He listened impassively to stories of family heartache, a community struggling to move forward in the absence of its children, and BBOG's request for the government to make the search for the girls a priority once more.

By the time he spoke, the president was so angry Aisha had to pinch herself to make sure she wasn't in a bad dream. Looking over at the Chibok parents, Buhari practically spat out his words. "This administration has done a great deal for you and yet you are not appreciative. There is so much I have done for this country. There is so much corruption here and I have recovered those monies. . . ."

Aisha couldn't understand why he was talking about corruption to Chibok parents, and then he shifted to the Niger delta. *What has any of this got to do with these poor people?* Aisha tried her best to hide her shock and pain, while the parents looked like their souls had been taken from them. They sat wide eyed and too afraid to move as the president dismissed their plight and the anguish they had battled for almost eighteen months.

Buhari continued to speak. "I have reached the peak of my career as a military man and as a politician." With that he stood up, opened up his hand, and let the microphone drop to the table with a thud. And then he was gone.

The parents and the BBOG representatives were bewildered by what had just happened. Aisha rejected presidential protocols and remained seated, while the rest of the room scrambled to its feet when it dawned on everyone the president was abruptly leaving.

The Chibok parents had arrived with so much hope for this meeting, buoyed by everything Buhari had said on the campaign trail. Now they looked spent and utterly devastated. They hadn't received a single kind word or expression of commitment to finding their daughters. Nothing.

On April 14, 2016, a line was drawn in the sand between the Bring Back Our Girls movement and the Buhari presidency. This was the moment Buhari cast BBOG as the enemy of the government. And for Aisha, it was the day she told herself *Muhammadu Buhari ceased to be my president.*

CHAPTER SEVENTEEN

THE ABDUCTION OF THE 276 GIRLS FROM CHIBOK WAS A TRAGEDY, one that engulfed the lives of the girls, their families, and their community. But beyond the event's tragic consequences, this is also a story about voices being ignored and silenced.

Boko Haram's unbending opposition to girls' education is, in essence, an expression of its desire to silence them. To deny females a voice is to take away their ability to challenge the very practices and norms that subjugate and harm them. Successive Nigerian governments shaped a response to this tragedy that included minimizing and ignoring the voices of those fighting for the girls' return. And with the international media attaching so little importance to the voices of Africans, news bosses easily moved on and global audiences tuned out.

All of this has driven me to use my own voice to keep this story on people's minds. I also understand that the only reason I'm able to take this stance and speak up is because I've been empowered by education, and that I was born to an educated mother.

I don't need data to make the case that education is one of life's greatest differentiators. I have to look no further than my own mother's life to see how it alters life's outcomes. One educated girl can change everything.

My mother grew up in the small, underdeveloped Sierra Leonean town of Rotifunk with two brothers, a sister, her father with his two wives, and half siblings of all ages. They were a family of meager means, strong Islamic faith, and myriad rivalries and petty jealousies between the wives—my grandmother, Mammy Iye, and the older, first wife, Mammy Yenkin. The battles between these two women spanned my mother's childhood. Mammy Yenkin constantly tried to push Mammy Iye and her children to the margins of my grandfather's affections in order to gain favor for her own children. And while my grandfather Pa Amadou Conteh may have been open to manipulation in certain areas, he stood firm on the issue of his children going to school. Even though neither he nor his wives were educated, he made sure that when every single one of his nine children came of age, they were enrolled in the local primary school. They were all given the same opportunities. But one by one, my mother watched as her siblings fell behind or lost interest in their studies, and then dropped out of school altogether. In contrast, my mother, Kadi, was a devoted and gifted scholar who soared academically.

When the time came for high school, she packed her bags for the Magburaka Government Secondary School for Girls, more commonly referred to as "Mathora," the first public girls' school in the north of the country, hundreds of miles from her home. Without hesitation, Kadi waved goodbye to all she'd known and loved and headed off to boarding school. There she developed into a fiercely independent young woman, one who amassed prizes and scholarships. When her time at Mathora was over, she made her way to the capital of Sierra Leone, Freetown. Here, she enrolled at another high school for her A-level qualifications, which paved the way for her to study English language and literature at Fourah Bay College (FBC), part of the University of Sierra Leone.

My mother entered college in 1970, when hemlines were high and the nation's politics were in turmoil. Sierra Leone's independence from the British had been achieved just nine years earlier, in 1961. My mother embraced the fashion of the times, as well as the vibrant college scene. Three years later, in 1973, she secured a bachelor's degree with honors.

Her degree completed, she had no intention of slowing down.

Thanks to a scholarship, she was off to England next, where the heels were stacked and the pants flared. Kadi soon had a large Afro and her master's degree in African literature from the University of Sheffield in 1974. Marriage to my father, who'd been studying law in England, soon followed, as did the births of my sister, Jane, and me in London, in 1974 and 1976 respectively. By the early 1980s, when everyone else was embracing large shoulder pads, my mother wore a Jheri curl, was pregnant with my brother Mamud, and was finishing up her PhD at the University of London.

During this time I saw my father only periodically, because he was working in Sierra Leone as the legal adviser for the Sierra Leone Produce Marketing Board, a national import-export company. In 1983, with Kadi's doctorate in hand, my parents decided it was time for the family to be reunited in Sierra Leone and for their professional lives to begin in earnest. So we swapped London for Freetown, a decision that as a seven-year-old I found shockingly unpleasant and totally unnecessary.

My mother's homecoming was a return to her roots, but years of academic achievement meant she'd blossomed into something different from the rest of her family. She returned to lecture English at her alma mater, Fourah Bay College, and her professional success now meant she bore the financial responsibility and decision-making burden of caring for her parents, siblings, and countless other relatives, all of them living lives hamstrung by little to no education.

Before the move back to Sierra Leone, I had no memories of these relatives. My very first memory of my grandmother Mammy Iye is from the night of our arrival. My young brain couldn't process why this old, wrinkled individual, dressed in peculiar colorful clothing, speaking a language I didn't know, was crying and incessantly touching my face and head.

In time I grew to adore this beautiful, fragile-looking woman, who brought me sugarcane, mangoes, and other sweet, sticky treats whenever she visited. Our conversations always required the help of a relative to translate, as my proficiency in Temne, our tribal language, remained poor and her grasp of English elementary.

My mother and grandmother couldn't have been more different. Mammy Iye was afraid to speak much louder than a whisper and was seldom disagreeable, even to advocate for her own best interests. This meant many of life's most important decisions—when to marry, whom to marry, how many children to bear—were not hers to make. Kadi, though, was a force of nature. She had a clear sense of self and no shortage of personal conviction. Growing up, I rarely welcomed my father's words "it's up to your mother," as attempts to coerce her were futile.

For all their differences, my mother and grandmother remained alike in one critical way: they both possessed an unshakable faith in God. Both believed deeply in the fundamental precepts of Islam: prayer, fasting, giving to charity, and never doubting that whatever happened was ultimately the will of God. Education had led my mother to places that might as well have been another planet as far as my grandmother was concerned, but it never affected their relationship, and they remained adoring of each other.

Everything in Sierra Leone's patriarchal society directs women and girls to be quiet, docile, and subservient to men. But with Kadi as my bulwark, those norms never infiltrated my childhood. Much to my father's chagrin, she insisted they have separate bank accounts for their respective salaries and a joint account for household expenses. The kitchen was another battleground, but my mother held her line. She would cook only on the weekends. My father grumbled whenever he got the chance, but he accepted it. During the week, all meals and school lunches for my brother and I were prepared by a cook, one of the many relatives who lived with us. Most weekends, though, Kadi would serve up huge breakfast spreads of crepes, eggs, bacon, and sausages. The people I loved most in the world sat around that dining table. As I watched my parents playfully tease and bicker, I was the happiest girl in the world.

That is, until my father died at age forty.

In time, our life assumed a new normal. We went back to school and Kadi returned to work, but she now occupied an even bigger space in my life. She was both mum and dad.

Regularly, friends raised the subject of her remarrying. "I don't want to deal with some man telling me how to raise my kids or having expectations of me going into the kitchen to cook for him. That's just not going to happen," she defiantly said.

Kadi wouldn't be controlled or contained, nor would she allow me to be. While other girls my age found themselves being restricted as puberty set in, my physical freedom was guaranteed. One summer while visiting in England, I complained I was bored. Kadi headed to the local library and researched residential summer camps. Soon I was on my way to camp in the English countryside, and for the next few summers without fail, my mother packed my cases and sent me off to be with kids from all over the world—a concept entirely foreign to our Sierra Leonean culture. When my love affair with acting first took hold, she whole-heartedly supported my passion, allowing me to stay late after school and rehearse on weekends with unknown groups of kids—always pushing me forward, encouraging new and varied interests.

Meanwhile when Kadi's friends talked of circumcising their daughters, she rejected the discussion without hesitation or apology. The practice of partially or totally removing the female genitalia, known as female genital mutilation or cutting (FGM/C) is a coming-of-age rite in Sierra Leone, with deep roots entwining culture and politics. Though its origins remain a mystery, UNICEF estimates up to 90 percent of Sierra Leonean women are subjected to genital cutting. It has long been performed as a part of rituals to mark the transition to adulthood and initiation into Bondo— the women's "secret societies"—and despite concerted local and international efforts to stamp it out, Sierra Leone remains one of twenty-eight African countries where this practice continues. But despite the social pressure on mothers and the public ridicule of girls who aren't "cut," Kadi steadfastly refused to subject me to the painful rite of passage she'd endured as a teenager. My mother placed no limitations on my imagination or sense of what I could attain. As far as she was concerned, with an indomitable will, a plan, a willingness to work hard, and God's blessings, everything remained within reach.

At sixteen years old, I was one of a handful of black students attending the Lebanese International School (LIS), a private high school in Freetown. Kadi had yanked me out of my public school because of the near-constant teachers' strikes and the falling academic standards. On April 29, 1992, I was in class at LIS trying to pay attention to the teacher droning on. It was a bright morning and shaping up to be another hot April day. Out of the corner of my eye a couple of young Lebanese men ran through the school gate. At first I ignored the distraction, but then more arrived, shouting in Arabic. Something was very wrong.

One of my Lebanese classmates yelled out in Arabic to the

multiplying stream of running men, and a frantic conversation ensued. When they were done, the non-Arabic speakers in our class pounced.

"What's going on? What's happening?" we asked.

"There's been a coup. Soldiers have taken over State House," a classmate said.

State House, the seat of the executive branch of the Sierra Leonean government, was located only a couple of miles away. As the Lebanese have long been custodians of much of the country's commercial wealth, we all knew the school was a magnet for looters if widespread trouble broke out. No one waited for the teacher to wrap up. We took matters into our own hands and dismissed ourselves.

Unable to make it home due to the distance from school, my only other option was to go home with my cousin Maggie, who also attended LIS and was in the year below. With the sound of gunshots and yelling in the air, close to a dozen of us climbed into a classmate's SUV, which was handily parked out front. We sat on each other's laps, crouched on the floor, and even sat in the trunk. As we pulled out of the school drive and headed in the opposite direction to the sounds of chaos, we were terrified and too afraid to say much besides our prayers.

The days that followed were full of mayhem and widespread fear. We learned the sitting president, Joseph Momoh, had fled to neighboring Guinea, family friends had been arrested, the National Provisional Ruling Party (NPRC) was in charge, and that a twenty-five-year-old army junior, Captain Valentine Strasser, was now president, the youngest head of state in the world. Countless questions were triggered. What did NPRC and Strasser plan to do next? How would the international community respond? How would this new military government tackle the country's long-running civil war against rebels who'd taken control of the country's east and its diamond mines?

I finally made it home about a week later, when it felt safer to move about the streets. Late one night during this period of heightened fear, a number of cars pulled into our driveway unannounced. A power outage had swept the neighborhood. It was so dark you couldn't see your own hand stretched out in front of your face. Everyone in the house trembled in the darkness, too afraid to make a sound as the heavy footsteps approached our single-story home.

"We want to speak to Dr. Kadi Sesay," a loud male voice announced.

All the windows were closed, the curtains drawn, and the house completely dark. We sat terrified and silent in the living room.

"It is nothing bad," the voice insisted. "Don't be afraid. We just want to talk to you."

None of us made a sound. The unidentified man waited for a few more minutes before he gave up and returned to the vehicles. Seconds later we heard them roar off into the darkness.

Later, we discovered that Kadi's reputation for being independently minded and willing to speak up for the truth had brought her to the attention of the NPRC military junta. They were seeking her help with their stated goal of transitioning the country from military rule back to a civilian government, in due course. A series of conversations between them and my mother ensued, and eventually she agreed to quit her position at the university, where she was a senior lecturer and the first woman to serve as the head of the English faculty, to head up the National Commission for Democracy.

This was 1994. In 1996, fellow NPRC soldiers ousted Strasser in a coup and Julius Maada Bio assumed the presidency. The elections he called for brought a new president, Ahmed Tejan Kabbah, to power. Kabbah appointed my mother to the position of minister of development and economic planning during his first term. After his reelection to a second term in 2002, my mother was given a new portfolio, minister of trade and industry. Neither position had ever been held by a woman before.

By the time my mother became a politician, I was going to school in England. I watched from afar in amazement as she took to the male-dominated arena of African politics. She was a member of the president's cabinet and sat at the heart of government as a fierce feminist and advocate for the advancement and protection of women, girls, and the poor. She was part of the government's negotiating team in Lomé, Togo, that wrangled with rebels to secure the contentious peace deal that marked the end of Sierra Leone's eleven-year civil war in 2002. Her audacity and unwavering belief in doing the right thing, even if controversial and hard, continued to motivate me.

As I navigated my way through Cambridge University, where I was studying English, she inspired me to disrupt my college life and advocate for a fairer, more respectful treatment of female students, and to start an incendiary college magazine loathed by the male students far and wide.

When her political party, the Sierra Leone People's Party, or SLPP, was swept from power in 2007, my mother settled into the role of an opposition politician and party elder. I hoped the turn of events would make her slow down a little, maybe even leave the country and take a job with an international body like the United Nations. The idea of leaving the country she loved deeply was unappealing, and she quickly dismissed it whenever I or anybody else suggested it.

Instead she once again embraced Sierra Leone's byzantine politics and set her sights on becoming the SLPP's presidential nominee in the 2012 elections. She lost the race to Julius Maada Bio, but instead of turning away in anger, she became his running mate, making her the first female vice-presidential nominee in Sierra Leone's history. Amid widespread allegations of vote rigging and electoral fraud, the SLPP lost once more at the polls in 2012. But my mother and Bio remained undeterred, buoyed by the conviction they were the pair to set the country on a new path, and they set their sights on the next vote, in March 2018.

When my poor, uneducated grandmother Mammy Iye gave birth to my mum in 1949 in sleepy Rotifunk, a place not much different from Chibok, no one could have known she'd brought into the world a girl who would go on to reach the heights of academia and settle in the nation's history books. It was a path unforeseen at her birth, but one carved out by education and an enduring faith that kept Kadi strong the entire way.

I am a beneficiary of her journey, educated and emboldened to fight for girls from places like Chibok, so they too may one day move through the world with voices unchecked.

CHAPTER EIGHTEEN

FOR PRISCILLA, REGARDLESS OF WHETHER IT WAS IN THE FOREST OR town, there was no getting used to life in captivity. Living in Gwoza meant she'd swapped lying on the cold, hard ground in the forest for the cold, hard concrete floor in the house, but she hated her situation just as much. Not a day went by when Priscilla and the other girls didn't shed tears for the life and loved ones they'd been taken from. But there were days in captivity when laughter also broke through and for the briefest of moments, the clouds of grief lifted. On those occasions the girls would often be sitting out on the veranda and memories of life in Chibok would set off ripples of laughter. During those few minutes they chuckled freely and temporarily forgot where they were, and the fact that they weren't actually free.

The Nigerian military's effort to crush the terror group was a constant source of danger and tension. At the heart of their strategy lay aerial bombardments—a tactic wholly incongruent with the government's stated goal of doing everything possible to find the Chibok captives and bringing them home safely. Bombs routinely fell all around the girls. Priscilla and her schoolmates learned to differentiate the low rumblings of surveillance aircraft from the loud, oppressive vibrations of fighter jets and could make a determination within seconds about the likelihood of a bomb falling near them. But there were occasions when they didn't get it right and what was thought to be a surveillance aircraft turned out to be a bomber; these were the instances when the girls failed to get out of the house in time. Within minutes, hundreds of them would be sent running through the Gwoza compound as the roof of the veranda collapsed, windows were blown to bits, and some of their friends lay in pools of blood, injured by shrapnel fragments flying through the air.

Priscilla was permanently on edge. Just as she feared the bombs falling from the skies without warning, she feared in equal measure the danger lurking much closer: the possibility her captors would force her to convert to Islam and marry her off to one of their own. So she stayed in the room where they all slept, refusing to wander into other parts of the house unless it was absolutely necessary.

Priscilla came up with a simple, two-pronged plan for survival. First: remain quiet and prayerful.

When the girls voted for leaders among them to negotiate with their captors for additional soap or to ask for conditions to be improved, Priscilla made sure she was never included. She'd noticed a trend. All the girls who'd taken on the role of the group's spokesperson in dealings with Boko Haram were suddenly married off to them.

Shortly after the eighty-two girls were released in May 2017, they were taken to the presidential villa in Abuja to meet President Muhammadu Buhari, amid a sea of media.

In the immediate aftermath of their release, the twenty-one girls and their families are presented to the Nigerian president in an elaborate media event.

Dorcas Yacubu, the youngest girl abducted, still in captivity.

On July 5, 2017, I made a secret visit to the rehabilitation center housing the twenty-one girls and the newly freed group of eighty-two. This was the first time I'd met the recently released schoolgirls.

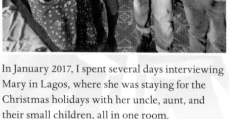

In January 2017, I spent several days interviewing Mary in Lagos, where she was staying for the Christmas holidays with her uncle, aunt, and their small children, all in one room.

A heavy ring of Nigerian security stands guard as the twenty-one girls and I prepare to leave Yola for Chibok, December 23, 2016.

Due to security concerns, the Nigerian authorities made the decision to spend the night in Yola with the twenty-one newly freed girls before setting off for Chibok the next morning.

Giggling and bursting with excitement, the twenty-one girls board a bus for the short journey from an Abuja airport terminal to the plane waiting on the tarmac.

In our second meeting since their release in October 2016, many of the twenty-one freed girls quickly gathered around me to take a selfie, before we left Abuja for Chibok on December 22, 2016.

On October 19, 2016, six days after the twenty-one girls were released, I meet them for the first time at the presidential villa in Abuja.

Anxious family members wait in the heat to be reunited with their girls on their first visit home to Chibok since their release, December 23, 2016.

The girls rejoice as they are reunited with loved ones in Chibok.

Moments before leaving Yola for Chibok, the girls are told to pose for a picture with the governor of the state, Jibrilla Bindow, December 23, 2016.

The twenty-one freed girls excitedly leave the rehabilitation center they'd been housed in, ahead of the trip home to Chibok, December 22, 2016.

(above) Emotions run high as the twenty-one freed girls are reunited with loved ones in Chibok for the first time since their abduction in 2014.

(left) Born to Deborah while in captivity, baby Amos emerged happy and without any significant health complaints.

The twenty-one girls disembark at the Abuja airport and make their way to the terminal to check in for their flight to Yola, December 22, 2016.

During a quick stop in Mararaba Mubi to refuel, I quickly record my thoughts on the journey to Chibok for my CNN report.

Parents of the newly returned twenty-one Chibok girls wait in the harsh sun to enter the compound and be reunited with their daughters.

Adamawa State Governor Bindow and the twenty-one freed girls, moments before the girls departed Yola for Chibok.

The girls enjoy cookies and soda, their first sugary treats since their kidnapping nearly two and a half years earlier.

The newly freed twenty-one, still in the drab hijabs they had been forced to wear in captivity, are transported from Banki, the location of their release.

I try to console a distraught Madame Yanna as she mourns the ongoing captivity of her daughter, Rifkatu Galang.

The girls' parents listen patiently as a Nigerian military official tells them that most of their daughters will not be allowed home for Christmas after all, due to the ongoing Boko Haram security concerns.

Twenty-one-year-old Saa, currently living and studying in the United States.

Secondly: remain as inconspicuous as possible and minimize all contact with the men.

In March 2015, six months after the girls first arrived in Gwoza, the militants decided to move them back into the forest. At this point, they'd been separated from their families for almost a year. The men gave the girls no explanation for the decision, but it was more than likely triggered by the growing pressure caused by the intensifying military campaign to reclaim Gwoza, which was widely referred to as the group's headquarters. In the months leading up to the relocation, there'd also been media reports of the girls being spotted in Gwoza by former Boko Haram abductees who were also once held in the town.

In fact, back on April 14, 2015, exactly one year after the girls had disappeared, the BBC reported the accounts of four unnamed eyewitnesses who claimed to have seen some of the Chibok girls in Gwoza. One of them described seeing the girls in their hijabs being escorted by the militants. "They said they were the Chibok girls kept in a big house," the eyewitness reportedly claimed. "We just happened to be on the same road as them." Boko Haram knew it needed to move the girls.

When they were all loaded in the vehicles, Priscilla noticed that the group was smaller—they were leaving close to fifty of their schoolmates who were all wives now and part of Boko Haram's dangerous world.

The girls departed Gwoza first thing that morning and were on the move without stopping throughout the day, plunging deep into the forest. When the vehicles finally arrived at their new location, the landscape was by now all too familiar to Priscilla. Shacks of woven grass dotted the camp, along with the terror group's standard paraphernalia: broken-down vehicles, discarded motorbikes, and women who flitted about like dark-robed ghosts. In this camp, the girls would be spread out across five small shacks and within days consumed by efforts to find water, firewood, and enough to eat. Now that they were back in the forest, the men were content once more to leave Jida in charge, while they pulled back to their cluster of homes. Their overseer found himself a spot nearby and quietly monitored his charges, unconcerned that they'd be able to slip away. As a result, Priscilla discovered she was allowed to move about the place.

The captors' one remaining concern involved the Chibok school uniforms. The girls had held on to their brightly hued blouses and wrappers, keeping them hidden during their long eleven months in captivity. In this new open-air setting, the men noticed that groups of the teenagers were slipping off their hijabs and sitting together in their school uniforms in the middle of the day as planes patrolled overhead.

Priscilla and the other girls were, of course, doing this intentionally. They'd spotted the stepped-up aerial traffic and decided that exposing their school uniforms to the eyes in the sky could well be their best chance of being rescued. The men, catching on, rounded them up days later and handed them reams of fabric.

"Hand us your school uniforms!" the men snapped.

Priscilla's heart sank.

The men waited impatiently for the girls to return with their variously colored wrappers and blouses. With great satisfaction the men laid all the garments on the ground in a pile and set fire to them while the girls did their best to stifle their cries. Now that the uniforms were gone, the men felt confident they'd eliminated the risk of the girls' being spotted by aerial surveillance or by soldiers on the ground; they'd lost their only distinguishable feature.

While the bonfire raged, the girls' captors gave them new instructions. "Take these wrappers now and make your own clothing."

Priscilla stared incredulously at the bundles of fabric being handed out. For someone like her, who'd never sewn anything in her life, being told to make something to wear was one of the most ridiculous statements she'd ever heard, and ordinarily she would have chuckled at the very suggestion. But all that was ordinary or normal had long ago disappeared from Priscilla's life, now lost in the forest, where she and Bernice sat side by side and slowly figured out to how to make their own smocks.

After eleven months in this fourth location, the men appeared one night with determined looks on their faces and a new announcement.

"There are always planes in the skies here. So let's move to a place where this will no longer be a problem. Pack your things, so we can go." The girls had very little to gather: most of them had only one hijab each and a pair of slippers that were already on their feet. Only a handful of them even had underwear at this stage. In fact, each girl's most prized possession was the yellow plastic container she used for drinking. So the girls were packed and ready to go within minutes.

The journey to their new home took two whole days, and along the way Priscilla and Bernice grew increasingly fearful of what would be waiting for them when the vehicles finally stopped.

This latest camp looked much like all the other places they'd been held captive, only now the girls were spread among three one-room shacks. And there was no Jida! At the time Priscilla and the others were awoken in the middle of the night and told to quickly gather their belongings, they had been focused on moving as quickly as possible. It wasn't until they arrived at the new camp that Priscilla had realized Jida wasn't with them. None of the men acknowledged his absence or ever mentioned him again. Once their captors retreated the girls were truly on their own. The men very rarely came by to check on them after that first night, and food deliveries became increasingly rare too. The only constant in this new, isolated existence was the appearance of an imam, which still happened in the early afternoon each day. But once he was gone, there were no more visitors.

Life here was the most difficult it had been for the girls up till that point. They had little clean water to drink and so little to eat that in moments of desperation they wandered into the forest in search of food. Unable to find any kuka, the girls plucked the leaves from wild-looking tamarind trees that were bereft of their fruit, because they weren't in season. They excitedly boiled them down and then relished the sour-tasting water. Priscilla felt like she was starving to death, there among the three shacks. At one stage the girls were without food for six whole weeks. Then the green fruits of the tamarind tree were their sole source of comfort.

The men may have thought they were bringing their captives to a place with less overhead traffic, but in that sense, the new camp actually ended up being far worse than anywhere else they'd been kept. Sleep became a rare occurrence for Priscilla as bombs fell nearby throughout the night. Every day, for hours at a time, planes and helicopters dropped missiles and the earth beneath their feet shook as the girls trembled and prayed for God's protection.

Priscilla was stunned to hear they were being moved once more. It was October 2016, and they were approaching nearly two and a half years in captivity. She listened impassively as the men told them to leave everything behind and promised they'd be safer in the next place.

"The planes know where we are. So we're now going to a place the planes don't know about." The men sounded optimistic as they spoke.

Unmoved by anything she'd heard, Priscilla just sat on the ground and stared into space.

Around seven o'clock that evening, the men and girls were gathered and poised to set off. *Where are all the cars?* Priscilla wondered. She quickly learned the vehicles would not be part of this journey. They would be walking. There was a little light when they began, but soon they moved silently in the dark through Sambisa.

They walked all night without food or water, and when the sun rose the next day the girls were so parched they drank from puddles they found along the way. They walked for two more days in the heat and through clouds of dust, yet when they finally arrived at their destination around seven a.m., there was nothing. No woven shacks, no camp off in the distance, no sounds of radio or the low rumble of generators. There was no one there. Nothing, apart from a tall and lean tamarind tree.

Priscilla and Bernice whispered to each other, trying to figure out why they had been taken to such a place. *What is about to happen to us?*

"Go and sit under the tree!" the men shouted.

Unlike the colossal tamarind tree that had marked the beginning of their life in Boko Haram captivity, the tree they now scrambled to sit beneath was unremarkable in every way. With great relief and gratitude Priscilla and Bernice received the food and water the men suddenly appeared with. The militants quickly backed away and the girls stayed under the tree.

When the sun had gone and the day edged to a close, a new group of men appeared to address the girls. There were about fifty of them, and most wore military-style clothing and were armed, except for the one man who appeared to be in charge. He wore white from head to toe and had no weapon. Their demeanor made the girls uneasy. To Priscilla, they looked like they were there to make arrests.

The man in white started to speak.

"Everybody gather together. We have an announcement. We have made a plan with the Nigerian government, and we are going to free twenty girls—that is the number that we agreed to. But we have decided to add one extra, as a gift to Nigeria."

At the time the announcement was taking place, Priscilla and Bernice were fast asleep on the forest floor and they missed the man's speech. The girls seated all around them were giddy with joy, but also a little apprehensive. *Who would be chosen?* The girls struggled to remain calm while they waited for the selections to be made. With hopes of being picked, one of the girls tried to quickly move from the back to the front of the group. As she rushed passed, she brushed Priscilla and woke her. Rubbing the sleep from her eyes and stretching her long limbs, Priscilla noticed the group of men standing together addressing the girls and the anxious look on her schoolmates' faces.

"What is happening?" she asked the girl sitting next to her. The girl explained to Priscilla that they were on the brink of choosing twenty-one girls to return to their families. Priscilla wanted to leap up and jump for joy. "Thank you, God! Thank you, God! Please make this happen!" she exclaimed. She was still giving thanks when the man in white spoke again.

"Who has paper and pen?" he asked, his eyes scanning the group.

Priscilla was torn. She had ignored the men's instructions to leave everything behind when they'd left the last camp. Priscilla had not only packed her notebook, she'd brought along a pen for good measure. The last thing she wanted was to get into trouble. *Should I say have a pen and paper or just keep my mouth shut?*

"I have some," Priscilla's voice rang out.

"Who?"

"Me, I have pen and paper." Priscilla's mouth was suddenly dry. She could hear her heartbeat in her ears.

"Come up here!"

All she could think was *What have I gotten myself into now?*

There were fifty pairs of male eyes staring at Priscilla as she walked toward the front of the group. She nervously clutched her frayed notebook and pen and kept praying to be spared punishment for not doing as she was told.

When she was standing directly in front of the man in white, Priscilla tore a few limp pages from her book. She handed the paper and her pen over to man, who continued to stare at her as he slowly took the items from her outstretched hand.

"What is your name?" he asked gently.

"Priscilla."

Seconds later, her name was written on one of her sheets of paper.

"Go and sit over there," one of the men told her.

But now that she'd been chosen, Priscilla was too nervous to sit. Fearful of losing her spot, she moved to the side but remained standing.

Priscilla looked at the rest of her sisters seated under the tamarind tree. Every one of them had a pleading look in her eyes. Many of them were muttering under the breath, praying for this to be their moment.

The men used their flashlight to make their selections, swinging the beam from one face to another. The chosen ones tended to be the girls who sat quietly. Priscilla noticed that those who tried to push to the front or to go out of their way to be noticed were ignored. Bernice had also been asleep. By the time she woke up, Priscilla was already standing at the front of the group with her name top of the list. Bernice too asked a girl seated close by to explain what she was looking at. She watched calmly and told herself if that if it was God's will, she would be picked. Moments later Bernice felt the glare of the flashlight on her face.

"What is your name?"

"Bernice."

"Get up and stand over here, with these other girls."

When the list of girls was complete, each name was read aloud. Priscilla's name had been deliberately left off because the men intended to reveal her as number twenty-one, a surprise at their meeting with the Nigerian authorities. With the roll call over, the man in white looked at the dozens of heartbroken girls who hadn't been chosen.

"Be patient," he coaxed. "If we go with these girls and the agreement we have made with the government goes through, then you will be joining your friends very soon."

The girls wanted to believe him, but it was difficult given all they'd been through. Some were sobbing wildly when the man in white shouted, "Let's go!"

Priscilla and Bernice needed to say goodbye. They longed to hug the girls they'd sat and wept in the darkness with and cared for in times of sickness, but they weren't allowed.

"No! Let's go now!"

All of the girls were crying hysterically.

"Don't worry," those left behind said. "We will follow you if it is our time."

Priscilla cried for the sisters she was leaving behind and also because of the deep fear she felt within. *Are we really being taken home?* She'd been praying for this day for such a long time, and now she was soaked in grief and thoroughly confused about how things would actually play out.

The men and the twenty-one chosen girls walked for a few minutes, until they could no longer hear the rest of the girls weeping.

"Wait here," the men instructed.

Within the hour, they heard the sound of vehicles approaching. A line of ten Hilux pickup trucks moved toward them, and the chosen ones were divided into small groups and spread out among the cars. They drove through Sambisa for the next four days before stopping.

"We are stopping here to wait for somebody. This person will be our escort. So come down." After days of being cooped up in cramped vehicles, the girls welcomed a break in the journey.

This Boko Haram camp was not like the scores of others populating Sambisa. Over the next three days, the twenty-one huddled together, watching camp life unfold in the distance and waiting for their next set of instructions.

Finally, the "escort" arrived in the middle of the night while most of the girls slept. Priscilla and Bernice had stayed up, lost in conversation, and suddenly they heard angry voices.

"Let's go!" a man was shouting. His rough tone made the two girls uneasy. They quickly shook the others in the group awake.

The girls were hastily loaded into the waiting vehicles and within seconds were bolting through the dark forest. From the safety of the truck, Priscilla watched the branches sway wildly as the vehicles pushed past them. But the forest's dense, suffocating vegetation began to thin out as they moved beyond Sambisa's boundaries. They'd been driving for a few hours when the militants decided to tell Priscilla what they planned to do with her.

"We are going drop the twenty girls along the way. But you will continue on with us. You will be the one to do the talking when we meet the government people."

Priscilla was startled by the plan and the weight of expectation on her young shoulders. She didn't understand why she'd been chosen. *What will happen to me once I arrive?* she asked herself. By now the teenager was trembling, but none of the men shared what they did or didn't know about what lay in store for her when she reached their destination. There was only one certainty in this situation of unknowns: she was being used as a human shield. Priscilla was their fail-safe in the event the Nigerian military was luring the militants into a trap rather than the preagreed handover. But she knew that in this matter, as with so many others she'd encountered during her years in captivity, she had very little choice.

Several hours later the convey came to a stop on the side of the road. This was where the twenty girls and all the vehicles were to remain. The rest of Priscilla's journey would be completed with the militants on foot. When they set off, it was before dawn.

She walked through the darkness at the heart of a crowd made up of fifty armed men. Hours later, when the heat of the day had drenched her in sweat, Priscilla turned to look back at the scene, and her breath caught in her throat. She'd known that, as they walked, they were going past myriad Boko Haram camps deep in the forest. What she failed to realize was that each time they'd gone past a settlement, dozens of men had dropped everything they were doing and joined the procession, amassing what was clearly meant to be a show of force. In due course, Priscilla's tall, bony frame was surrounded by hundreds of militants, some following along on foot, while the tinny whine of motorbikes carrying others also filled the air.

Their destination was a wide-open clearing on the outskirts of Banki, a town bordering Cameroon in southeastern Borno State. Back in 2014, Banki had made national headlines after Boko Haram burst into the town, kicked out the Nigerian armed forces, and seized control of the strategically important location. However, by 2015, control had reverted once more to the Nigerian military. In that way, Banki had become a symbol of the ebb and flow of the battle between the Nigerian armed forces and Boko Haram, as well as further evidence of the long-lasting damage caused by the terror group. What had once been a town abuzz with life and possibility had been transformed into endless miles of squalid camp, housing tens of thousands of Nigerians, all of them displaced by Boko Haram's never-ending campaign of violent disruption.

The clearing for the meet-up was empty when Priscilla and her entourage stepped out of the forest. As Priscilla looked up, she saw a ball of smoking fire coming toward her, sending the men around her scattering in all directions.

A terrified-looking man curled into a ball at her feet and urged, "Lie down! Lie down! Make sure you pray because this might be your final prayer."

But rather than press her body flat to the ground, Priscilla chose to kneel. With her hands held aloft, she bowed her head and prayed. She begged God to save her life as the smoking projectile spun toward her, but it passed overhead, exploding in the bushes behind her.

A strange quiet descended on the clearing. Soon the men who'd scattered were back, casting furtive glances about the place in search of the officials they'd been negotiating with. They waited. When no one showed up after an hour, the men decided to make a phone call on a cell phone someone had stashed away in his pocket.

"We are waiting—where are you?" the militant asked gruffly. The conversation was brief and then everyone went back to waiting.

Eventually five vehicles drove toward the clearing, all bearing the iconic logo of the International Committee of the Red Cross. Half a dozen men, some Nigerian, others European, climbed out of the cars. Among them was Zannah Mustapha, a tall, thin northern Nigerian man with thick-rimmed glasses. This influential former lawyer in his late fifties had played a critical role, alongside three secret Swiss negotiators, in negotiations with Boko Haram for the release of these twenty-one girls. The talks had been painstaking, but Mustapha had remained hopeful the entire time. Much of that confidence was due to the relationship he had established with Boko Haram back in 2007, after he first came across a preradicalized Mohammed Yusuf, in a mosque in Maiduguri where they were both living at the time. Boko Haram's trust of Mustapha deepened when he launched the Future Prowess Islamic Foundation School that same year, to educate the children and support victims of all sides of the insurgency. To date he provides free education, uniforms, meals, and health care for all who are enrolled. Over the years Mustapha has become a lifeline for growing numbers of Boko Haram widows and orphans displaced by the conflict. His efforts to negotiate the release of the twenty-one girls was triggered by President Buhari's 2016 statement at the United Nations, in which he expressed a willingness to negotiate with Boko Haram and welcomed "intermediaries such as UN outfits to step in." This created the opening for Mustapha's outreach to the group. "Nobody contacted me to do this in the first place," he said. "I felt it was necessary to do what I did as a humanitarian. I was not influenced by anybody from either side." The process led by Mustapha and a number of Swiss negotiators took only a few weeks, though it required a series of confidence-building measures to arrive at an agreement. But this lawyer turned humanitarian, who has won a host of awards for his work, has always been quick to stress that the real mediation that resulted in the release of Priscilla and the others was initiated and coordinated by the Nigerian government. And whenever he's been asked to shed some light on what Boko Haram received in exchange for giving up the twenty-one girls, Zannah Mustapha has always politely demurred.

On October 13, 2016, Mustapha and one of his Swiss colleagues walked to the middle of the clearing, where ten armed militants joined them. The men from the forest were strikingly upbeat as they exchanged pleasantries with the newcomers. Next they moved right on to the matter at hand. "We have already brought your girls. And we brought one to show you that they are around," the man said and pointed at Priscilla. He went on, "So here is the girl. Let's greet her."

Priscilla swallowed hard, and her eyes widened as the men came toward her. She nodded her head respectfully and bent her knees when they were finally in front of her.

"Who are you?" one of the men asked her.

Priscilla was so nervous she could barely raise her voice above a whisper. "I am one of the Chibok girls."

"Don't be afraid. We are here to rescue you. But where are the others?"

"The rest are with the boys, far off from here."

"Be patient," urged Zannah as he gave a tender smile to the frightened girl.

Priscilla's captors piped up once more. "This girl we have brought here today, but her name is not on the list. We only promised to release twenty people, but we brought her as a gift to Nigeria. So even if this ends up in a battle, she will be freed. We made that promise and we will keep it. We are gifting her to you, Zannah Mustapha—she is yours and a gift to Nigeria."

Priscilla wasn't bothered by the militant's talk of her being a "gift." Priscilla cared about only one thing—getting home to her loved ones. At this stage, whatever came out of the mouths of these armed men were just words. Now Zannah Mustapha took her hand and Priscilla began to cry, moved to tears by the prospect of being so close to freedom and the kindness of this stranger. Priscilla was still crying gently when one of the militants said to a fellow fighter, "Go and bring those girls."

About an hour later, dozens of Boko Haram fighters materialized from the bushes. By their sides were twenty frightened-looking girls from Chibok. They approached slowly. A handful of words were exchanged between the militants and negotiators to confirm the agreement. All twenty-one girls were too afraid to even breathe at this point. They all just stood silently, waiting, wanting all of it to be over.

"OK ladies, the moment you hear your name—it is the end," said their kidnappers.

Zannah Mustapha now turned to Priscilla and instructed her to read the names on the list he handed to her. As she read their names, each girl acknowledged herself before stepping out of the clutches of Boko Haram and into a new future. Every one of them was immediately whisked toward a waiting vehicle.

After Priscilla had finished reading the list, she stood alone in the clearing, seemingly forgotten. Zannah Mustapha and his Swiss colleague were deep in conversation, and the militants were poised to head back into the forest. The Boko boys noticed she'd been overlooked and quickly yelled out to the departing negotiators, "Ah, you have forgotten Priscilla for us!"

Embarrassed, Zannah Mustapha spun on his heels and rushed toward her. "Ah, how will we forget her? She is our bonus!"

Priscilla couldn't believe she was actually free as she walked toward the parked vehicles. All the girls were in the cars except Bernice. She had been standing anxiously, refusing to get in the car without her friend. Priscilla smiled warmly and giggled when she caught sight of Bernice. They were finally by each other's side, and nothing more needed to be said.

When the convoy of Red Cross vehicles pulled away from the clearing, none of the twenty-one girls could quite grasp the fact that their ordeal was over—one day short of two and a half years in captivity. In Priscilla's car the girls chatted excitedly. But dark thoughts also lingered. *Is this really happening? Will I find my parents alive?* When they had been held in the house in Gwoza, the men had told them repeatedly that their parents were all dead, as a tactic to pressure the girls into marriage. Now Priscilla and Bernice couldn't shake the fear of not having a family to come back to.

They drove the short distance from the handover location into Banki town itself and then onto a military airstrip, where a helicopter sat waiting. None of the girls had ever been in a helicopter, or any kind of aircraft, before that day. Yet they were so full of adrenaline and relief, they weren't even capable of being afraid when they clambered aboard. They couldn't help but chuckle darkly to each other as they strapped themselves in. They had spent years watching aircraft drop bombs on their heads while they were in captivity. And now they were inside a helicopter going home! As the helicopter packed with the twenty-one girls and baby Amos rose into the skies, Priscilla started to truly believe that she might really be free. In the blink of an eye, she'd gone from living as a captured Chibok schoolgirl to reclaiming her freedom in a bush clearing on the outskirts of Banki. For the first time in more than nine hundred days, Rebecca could begin to think about her future with something other than dread in her heart.

The helicopter made the short trip to Maiduguri, the capital of Borno State, pausing briefly on the tarmac before heading to Kaduna, the capital city of Kaduna State in northwestern Nigeria. The government's original plan of leaving the girls there for medical checkups was firmly rejected by President Buhari—who demanded the girls be taken to the capital, Abuja, immediately.

The moment the doors of the aircraft opened in Abuja, the girls were transported to the Department of State Security (DSS), Nigeria's equivalent of the FBI. The teenagers confronted a mash-up of smiling faces belonging to strangers, stern security officials, medical personnel, and endless questions. At the DSS they were out of harm's way. Access in and out of the organization's complex was closely monitored twenty-four hours a day. There was a hospital on the grounds, usually reserved for members of the Nigerian military, but on that day the doctors and nurses were standing by to welcome the Chibok girls.

Upon settling, the very first thing the girls asked for was a Bible. For two and a half years they'd been unable to worship freely. Now that they'd regained their freedom, giving thanks to God for answered prayers was their most pressing priority. They also had brand-new, beautifully bright outfits waiting for them.

The girls were in no way prepared for the crush of people waiting to welcome them at DSS headquarters. The twenty-one were led into a white-walled, brightly lit room where they sat quietly as people poured in. A host of VIPs—the vice-president of Nigeria, Professor Yemi Osinbajo, and his wife, Oludolapo; alongside Aisha al-Hassan, the minister of women's affairs; and Lai Mohammed, the minister of information and culture—were all on hand. Each girl was tenderly embraced and met with kind, reassuring words.

Warmth and gentleness had been absent from their lives for such a long time. Now faced with this kindness from strangers, all the painful emotions they'd kept under control spilled out into the open. Officials did their best to comfort the girls, seeing their hurt and distress. Meanwhile, a horde of journalists invited to capture the long-awaited return of these Chibok girls were crammed into the back of the room. This was a victory for the government of Muhammadu Buhari. The administration understood all too well the value of these images to Nigerians as well as to foreign governments and the broader international community.

But the girls' parents were conspicuously absent from the crowd. The girls had been freed on Thursday, October 13, 2016, and even though news had reached the Chibok community that same day, most of their parents didn't have the money readily available to cover the cost for a five-hundred-mile journey to the nation's capital—not to mention they'd have to travel along a road that remained a target for their daughters' abductors. The government ultimately stepped in and paid the families' travel costs, but it would take days for them to arrive. Meanwhile, all the girls and baby Amos were subjected to a battery of physical tests and reams of questions to assess their state of mind. The sight of their emaciated bodies and ashen complexions left no room for doubt. These girls had suffered extreme starvation and deprivation, but many more tests were conducted to gain a full picture of their health and well-being. Throughout the poking, pulling, and inspecting, Priscilla's mind remained preoccupied with just one thought: seeing her parents.

Like the other girls, Priscilla would have to wait until Sunday—two full days—before she could embrace her mother and father. When the moment finally came, it was at a specially arranged Thanksgiving service. At last, all the parents and daughters gazed on faces they'd long feared were lost to them forever. Under the cream-colored canopies erected to protect the families and specially invited VIPs from the unfriendly skies, mothers and fathers clung to their painfully thin daughters for the first time in years. They cradled their children like they were fragile newborns, as if the opening up of any space between them might allow something terrible to happen once more.

One father rocked his child protectively while she sat in his lap. Another held his fragile-boned daughter high above his head in joyful thanks. Priscilla's mother could hardly stand the force of her own sobbing, leaving her doubled over yet refusing to let go of her beloved daughter. Her father stared at his Priscilla through bloodshot eyes; his chest rose and fell heavily while he cried. When they moved beyond the tents, into the open courtyard, no one seemed to care about the intermittent rain, maybe because their faces were already soaked with tears. The merging of unbridled joy and the agony of lost years produced a heartrending wailing that reverberated throughout the courtyard.

At the heart of this reunion ceremony, these wounded, damaged people raised prayers of thanks and songs of praise. For Chibok's devoutly Christian community, there could be no better way to formally mark their children's return from the clutches of evil than through prayer. The girls themselves led some of those prayers and spoke of how faith had kept them alive in the dead of night in that forest. It was this same faith that provided comfort to the girls' parents when much of the world had turned away from their suffering.

And then, once the prayers were completed, the euphoria in the room and the celebratory drumming pulled everyone to their feet. As palms beat the drums harder, the music grew louder and everyone moved rhythmically, singing songs of old from Chibok, a home the twenty-one had visited only in their minds over the past two and a half years. They were still a distance from that long-awaited homecoming.

At first, the girls in their beautiful new outfits stood in rows, dancing in unison to the accelerating drumbeat. Faster and faster they moved, with arms swaying side to side, their feet leaping deftly across the brick-lined courtyard and their throats outstretched to the heavens, letting their voices rise high in the Abuja skies. As the emotion and percussion took over, the lines separating the dancers and giving the group order quickly melted away, leaving parents, daughters, and VIPs dancing freely and joyfully intermingled. Soon the scene was a swirl of undulating bodies, ecstatic faces, and a collage of bright and vibrant color. They moved together instinctively, celebrating the return of their stolen daughters, as one reunited Chibok family.

CHAPTER NINETEEN

I WOKE UP ON OCTOBER 13, 2016, IN NEW YORK, FAR AWAY FROM MY home in Los Angeles. I'd been on the East Coast for a multiday publicity blitz to promote *We Will Rise: Michelle Obama's Mission to Educate Girls Around the World*, a CNN-produced documentary I was featured in alongside the former first lady and the actresses Meryl Streep and Freida Pinto. When I opened my eyes just before nine, I was bone tired and looking forward to enjoying the dregs of summer on a rare day off in the big city.

What I wasn't expecting that day was the news of twenty-one Chibok schoolgirls being released. I actually stumbled on it while absentmindedly scrolling through social media. Still bleary eyed and barely awake, I wasn't wearing my glasses or contacts lenses, so a part of me thought it had to be a mistake. In my confusion, it seemed impossible that the Nigerian government could have secured the mass release without the news leaking out beforehand. Once I confirmed that the girls had actually been freed, I felt a rush of emotions: heart-thumping joy, shock, relief, and an undeniable sadness that came from knowing they were but a small fraction of the 219 schoolgirls Boko Haram had taken that April night nearly two and a half years earlier.

Long after most people had stopped paying attention, I'd remained consumed by what had happened to the girls. Six months earlier, as the second anniversary of the mass abduction had approached, I had been forced to confront the fact that the world hadn't seen or heard anything substantive about them in months. Their loved ones, like everyone else, were completely in the dark. At that point, no one knew whether the girls were even alive, and if they were still being held in Nigeria or if they'd been smuggled across that country's borders, as was long rumored. It was said that the Buhari government was negotiating with Boko Haram to bring the teenagers home. Was that actually true? Just as with the previous administration of Goodluck Jonathan, no one could get meaningful information from the current government.

A flurry of developments had recently revived global public interest in the tragedy, albeit only briefly. CNN's public release of a proof-of-life video on April 14, 2016, the second anniversary of the Chibok abductions, was followed by the discovery on May 18 of the first of the missing Chibok schoolgirls—Amina Ali Nkeki, who was found that night on the edges of Sambisa Forest by members of the Civilian Joint Task Force, the vigilante group set up to help fight Boko Haram. She carried in her arms a baby girl, and by her side was a young man who claimed to be her husband. It all generated a stream of headlines, as did the emergence of another hostage video later in August. But my list of questions about the girls' fate remained endless and basically unanswered.

Now I found myself in a New York hotel room processing the

extraordinary news that a group of twenty-one had been released. Within minutes I knew I had to get to Nigeria; nothing else mattered to me. Several frantic emails and begging phone calls later, I had the green light from my bosses in Atlanta and I was booked on a flight from JFK to Abuja for that evening. As I looked around my messy room, I focused on the two large suitcases, lying open on the floor, both piled high with spiky heels and colorful dresses, clothes suitable for a media blitz but useless for a journalist on assignment in Nigeria.

I was in a race against the clock and off to a poor start, but before I could do anything else, I needed to speak to my mother. I dialed her number hurriedly. She picked up after a few rings and I breathed a sigh of relief as her warm, deep voice flooded my senses. We could barely contain our excitement during the brief conversation. We'd talked about what this moment might be like, when the girls might be freed, but now we had to acknowledge that it was tinged with significant sadness because only a small fraction of them had been released. My mother wholeheartedly approved of my snap decision to drop everything and head to Nigeria to meet my "sisters," as she often called the Chibok girls. She also believed my presence would help put the story back on people's radar, though when I cast an eye on CNN USA's coverage that morning there was no mention of the story to support that optimism. That October, the network was in the throes of election fever and Trump mania. With the US presidential vote a few short weeks away, the shows that morning were covering the same news as they had been all year long, dominated by an endless procession of political pundits. I tried to keep my growing disappointment in check. I told myself that the story would become a priority for my bosses once CNN's reporting teams were back on the ground again in Nigeria. I was convinced the network would be just as invested as it had been back in 2014.

By the time I boarded my flight that night, I was drenched in sweat and wondering whether my heart would ever slow down. I'd been rushing around at breakneck speed the entire day and getting to the airport had been an ordeal. Nonetheless, I'd made it. Once I was settled into my seat, I allowed feelings of triumph to take over. I thought about the twenty-one girls savoring their freedom for the first time in two and a half years, and I felt a rush of excitement. I couldn't wait to meet them.

I still wasn't sure how I was going to make that happen. Based on the level of difficulty other journalists had experienced in trying to get to Amina, the Chibok girl who'd escaped to freedom in May, I knew that this wasn't going to be easy. The Nkeki family had been complaining for months about their severely limited access to their daughter. Despite the rising family tensions and intensifying questions from journalists, the Nigerian government's public position never wavered. The Defense Ministry's spokesman, Brigadier General Rabe Abubakar, announced, "We have to safeguard her and give her all the necessary security for her to recuperate well." And with that brief, uncompromising statement, Amina remained out of public view and essentially out of reach in an undisclosed location in the Nigerian capital.

Now there were twenty-one freed girls. It seemed a foregone conclusion that the government would have rings of security surrounding them. All of this set the stage for a monumental battle as journalists from around the world sought access to them. As the plane carried me across the world, I was also wondering about my volatile relationship with former president Goodluck Jonathan and his administration. Had the deeply embedded ill will toward me by previous officials found a home within the new administration? I had no way of knowing. But by the time I finally fell asleep on the plane, I'd made up my mind. It didn't matter how Buhari officials felt about me. One way or another, I was going to pull off a meeting with the girls.

Fifteen hours later, as the plane started its descent for Abuja, I felt a knot of tension form in my stomach. I dug into my hand luggage and pulled out a dark baseball cap, which I quickly put on and pulled low over my eyes. I wanted to minimize the attention I often found myself subjected to in Nigeria. To my relief and surprise, I made it through immigration without incident. Once my luggage and I were in the car, the driver was off within minutes, racing through traffic toward the CNN workspace.

Adrenaline fuels just about every waking moment a journalist spends out on the road covering a big story. The only thing that matters is the story and how we can bring it to our audience in the most compelling way. The ugly truth is, most television journalists are preternaturally ambitious, which sets up two challenges: First, to outdo the last story you covered. The unacknowledged industry mantra is "You're only as good as your last story." Second, to report the story before anyone else can. Or, at the very least, to gain exclusive access or details that leave fellow journalists kicking themselves and sick with envy.

The driver took me to CNN's temporary communal workspace that we'd set up in one of the big Abuja hotels. When I walked in, it was already packed with bodies, camera equipment, endless reels of cables, and laptops. The medium-size suite felt like it was about to burst wide open.

Our Atlanta bosses had deployed two separate reporting teams so there'd always be one available to provide live updates and analysis across the news shows on CNN USA and CNN International. David McKenzie, one of the network's longtime Africa correspondents, was already there. He'd head up Team McKenzie. The six-foot-plus, sandy-haired South African had flown in from Johannesburg the day before with his producer, Brent Swails, a dark-haired American who'd relocated from Atlanta to South Africa a few years earlier. Running camera for that team was Fridah Okutoyi, a brilliantly talented and wickedly funny Kenyan photojournalist. David was live on the air when I turned up.

Dominique van Heerden, the assigned producer for Team Sesay, would coordinate logistics and liaise with our Atlanta overseers. I'd never worked with her before, but she had a reputation for boundless bravery, and I immediately liked the straight-talking South African. Our cameraman was Fabien "Fabs" Muhire, a softspoken Rwandan I'd enjoyed working with many times before. He'd been home with his family in Kenya when the news of the twenty-one girls broke. Like all of us, he dropped everything and jumped on a plane to Abuja. Rounding out the CNN crew was the digital producer, Stephanie Busari, the only Nigerian among us— her principal focus was writing content for CNN.com. Based in Lagos, she'd also been covering the Chibok girls' story for a long time. Thanks to her dedication and warm, easygoing nature, she'd built deep, well-placed relationships within the Chibok community.

When I entered, the room was already full of frenetic energy. While David provided TV updates from the balcony, everyone else was busy on a phone, on a laptop, or fiddling with a camera. Once the hugs and hellos were out of the way, my team quickly settled down to figure out how we'd get ourselves into the room for the reunion between the twenty-one girls and their parents.

"What are your sources saying about the plan to reunite the girls with their families?" I quizzed Stephanie.

"I haven't been able to get too many details. The only thing we know for sure is that the girls' parents are on their way to the capital right now, and are expected to arrive tomorrow, Saturday. I've been on the phone all morning, but I don't know where or when exactly that meeting is supposed to happen. Right now it seems most likely it will happen at DSS."

The DSS is Nigeria's Department of State Services, the nation's primary domestic intelligence agency.

"We know the girls have been staying in a hospital, there on the grounds of DSS headquarters since yesterday when they arrived in Abuja," she told me.

This was unwelcome news. It was about as easy to stroll into Nigeria's state security complex without an invitation as to simply waltz into the FBI's headquarters in the United States. The situation left us with just one option: we'd have to sneak our way in.

"Can I help you?" the gruff official shouted over to us. Team Sesay had crammed into an SUV and was now parked in front of a make-shift barrier blocking the entrance to the DSS grounds. The official walked toward us, stern faced. He peered through the driver's window. The situation suddenly felt very tense.

Five pairs of eyes stared back at him. None of us moved a limb or said a word. A shiny rifle swung loosely from a strap, slung over his shoulder. Just behind him, a few feet away, stood a group of armed men huddled together with a couple of others sprawled on a bench beside the road. Each was smartly dressed in a button-down shirt and nice trousers, not a single army or police uniform in sight. While they appeared relaxed and nonchalant, it was clear from the multiple times they glanced over at us that they were paying very close attention to our exchange with their burly colleague.

Before we'd left the workspace, we'd learned from one of Stephanie's contacts that the parents and their newly freed daughters were to meet that afternoon at a hospital located somewhere in the sprawling DSS compound, all of which lay on the other side of the entrance barrier we faced. All clearly out of bounds to us.

The burly man stared at our team, waiting for an answer.

In the absence of a better plan, we remained quiet until our driver spoke up. "We're meeting some people at the hospital," he said.

I was crammed uncomfortably between Dominique and Stephanie at the back of the car. I slowly turned my head to the right and glared at Stephanie, prompting her with my eyes to back up the driver's statement with any small detail one of her contacts had given.

She spluttered, "Hello, eh, yes, eh. We're coming to meet some-one at the hospital. They told us to meet them there." She was completely unconvincing.

"Who are you meeting?" the official asked.

"A friend," Stephanie mumbled. "Are we in the right place for the hospital?"

I tried not to squirm. The situation was unraveling. Fast.

The man ignored Stephanie entirely. He looked each of us over, slowly. Then he growled, "You're in the wrong place."

"Let me just call our friend to confirm." Stephanie pulled out her cell phone.

But our interrogator was out of patience. "You can't stay here. You have to leave."

We dared not argue or say another word.

Our driver put the vehicle into reverse and slowly backed away from the entrance. Once out of earshot, we quickly discussed what our next step would be. The agreed plan was to stay in the area and be on the lookout for the Chibok parents' arrival. We settled on a parking spot under a shady tree, still on the main road, but a little way off from the DSS entrance.

It was early afternoon and the heat was unrelenting. Inside the car, things were tense.

"Are you sure we were at the right entrance?" Stephanie asked the driver. "Could there be another way in?"

I was wondering the same thing. Could he have taken us to the wrong place?

"No, this is right. I know it is."

Fabs, who was siting up front in the passenger seat, also pressed the driver.

"Let me just call my friend who works for DSS and confirm," the driver said.

The entire team shouted, "No!"

The last thing we needed was someone we didn't know inform-ing Nigeria's secret police that a bunch of CNN journalists were sitting under a tree outside DSS headquarters, planning to sneak themselves inside. We stressed to him that we didn't want him to do anything. Then we sat in silence and scanned the main road, hoping we'd spot a convoy of vehicles carrying the Chibok parents through the entrance.

"If we can't get inside, then at the very least we need to capture the images of the parents arriving or leaving," I told Fabs.

Meanwhile, Stephanie was still trying to reach her main con-tact to confirm that we were in the right location, but the contact's cell phone was switched off.

I was distressed. For a long time my heart had been set on wit-nessing the moment the girls were reunited with their parents. I wanted to share this new, hopeful beginning, the moment that faith and resilience triumphed over evil and despair, with the world.

"Be sure your camera's ready," I reminded Fabs yet again. "The parents might show up without any prior warning."

If we didn't return with images of the parents arriving or leav-ing, the entire day would be a bust. And there'd be some very un-happy bosses back in Atlanta. Again the vehicle fell silent. Fabs readied his smaller, lighter camera and everyone went back to scan-ning their phones.

Occasionally I looked up, straining to see who was entering or leaving the DSS compound. But there was so little movement in the area, I needn't have bothered.

An hour later, with still no sighting of the parents, the level of anxiety in the car began to rise. "We need a plan B," I said.

Dominique and I talked over our options, while Stephanie tried to reach her numerous Chibok community contacts, and Fabs kept his eyes fixed firmly on the road. We'd all been deep in conversa-tion when we suddenly realized our driver was on his phone talking to someone. It took a moment or two for us to understand what was happening.

"I'm outside with some people and they are trying to get to the hospital. They are looking for the Bring Back Our Girls people. Are they there?" he asked cheerily.

I looked around the car in panic. The driver fell silent a few seconds later, before responding. "We're parked just outside on the side of the road. Okay, we're here." Then he hung up and beamed at the rest of us with pride.

The car erupted.

"What are you doing? We never told you to call your friend!" Fabs screamed.

"Why would you call?" I yelled.

Our rage barely seemed to register with him. "My friend is coming. He's on his way."

We quickly weighed the risk of being exposed to the Nigerian authorities. Maybe it would be best to leave the area now. Before we could reach a decision, though, a sedan headed straight toward us. It quickly pulled off the main road and parked right in front of our vehicle.

Two men leapt out. One made a beeline straight for us; the other remained by the car. The chubby man approaching us was dressed in khaki pants and a dark golf shirt, a handgun nestled in a pouch on his left hip. He had the self-assured air of seniority. The scowl on his face made it clear that this situation had suddenly become very dangerous.

He launched into a heated exchange with our driver in a language none of us understood. As the official's tone grew harsher and the pace of his speech faster, our driver, "his friend," looked more and more afraid.

Then the DSS man suddenly turned to the rest of us in the car, his eyes flashing with anger. "What are you doing here?" he demanded.

"We're just trying to meet up with someone at the hospital over there," replied Fabs, feigning an air of casualness.

"You're breaking national security rules by being here. You could be shot," he replied.

Now it was my turn to be afraid.

As we didn't know his name or where he'd appeared from, Dominique tried to find out more. "Do you work here?" she asked gently.

He swatted away her question. "What I do is of no importance. What I am telling you guys, is you shouldn't be here," he spat back.

He wanted to see our identification cards. We all knew that handing over paperwork revealing we were journalists could well be the tipping point in an already precarious situation. We all mumbled at once and shuffled in our seats as we apologized.

"I'm sorry, but we don't have ID cards," I explained softly.

His eyes bulged in anger. He screamed more unintelligible words at our driver, who shrank into his seat and pleaded with the man in an increasingly strained voice.

"Why would you bring them here? You should know better!" the officer bellowed.

Dominique and I exchanged nervous glances, thinking the same thing. This was getting out of hand. The man with a gun took a step back, and from his facial expression, I could tell he was deciding what to do next. Someone needed to defuse the situation.

"We're so sorry, we had no idea about the rules. It is our mistake. We are so sorry." I spoke slowly and deliberately, doing all I could to convey humility and regret in my tone and with my body language.

Dominique immediately chimed in, underscoring my apology. "We are so sorry, yes. We didn't understand the protocol."

Playing humble, regretful, and dumb was the strategy. We waited nervously to see if it would work.

The officer stood silently for a moment or two, eyeing us

through narrowed eyes. Then he spoke. "You can't just come here, you have to follow official channels."

We sensed a softening. We continued to apologize profusely, even offering to leave the area immediately and to put an end to all the trouble we'd caused. He appeared to be on the verge of buying our act. But then he shifted his attention to Fabs.

"Where are you from? Are you from Nigeria?" he barked at him.

"No." Fabs shook his head.

"He's from Rwanda, not Nigeria," Dominique and I confirmed. The officer retreated into conversation with his partner, who'd been standing next to the car. I felt we were a heartbeat away from being ordered out of the car and detained. Meanwhile Stephanie had remained engrossed in her phone throughout the entire ordeal.

"Get off your phone!" I hissed at her.

By the time the man turned his attention back to us, he'd made a decision. "Leave this place now," he ordered.

Knowing his decision could be reversed just as easily, we told our driver to get moving. But the driver looked back at the officer who, only moments before, had been abusing him. "I will call you later," he said sheepishly.

Alarm bells went off for the whole team. Was our driver an informant for DSS? The truth was, we didn't have a clue about his identity, where he was from, or how he'd come to be our driver that day. As there was so much we didn't know about him, we decided to conceal where the CNN team was staying and instead asked him to drop us off at a decoy hotel.

The roadside encounter left me shaken and reminded me of the risks that come with covering certain stories in Nigeria. I was more discouraged than ever about my chances of seeing the Chibok reunions happen. Unbeknownst to me, the girls had actually been reunited with their parents long before we'd even left our hotel that Sunday. The gathering had taken place early in the morning, far from DSS headquarters, at another DSS location hidden away in Abuja.

On our way back to the hotel, Stephanie found images of the emotional reunion posted all over social media. There was a lump in my throat. I couldn't believe it. We could have been shot or detained trying to gain access to a meeting that had already happened. We weren't even in the right place!

When we walked into our hotel lobby half an hour later, video from the reunion was playing nonstop across all the TV screens. The whole crew stood stunned, watching pictures of the girls singing and dancing while fathers and mothers hugged their long-lost daughters.

This was the climax of the Chibok story. And we'd missed it.

For such a monumental moment to occur and not be there to bear witness to it felt like a colossal failure on my part. We later learned that only China's CCTV, the Associated Press, and various members of the local Nigerian press had been invited to cover the reunions. All other networks, including CNN, had been excluded. I was peeved. As I made my way back to the workspace, I wondered whether CNN had been intentionally kept off the list because of my history with the country's last administration.

I'd missed what was likely my only chance to meet the girls. I was in a foul mood when I walked into the room, but the whole place was abuzz with activity.

"What's going on?" I asked.

Dominique was being redeployed to Iraq, I learned, in preparation for the long-awaited offensive to retake Mosul from ISIS. I was stunned.

She wasn't the only one leaving.

Team McKenzie was also being pulled out. David and Brent were headed back to Johannesburg, and Fridah had been told to stand down because there wasn't enough interest in the story of the released Chibok girls across both CNN USA and CNN International to justify the costs of keeping two reporting teams in place.

Team Sesay was all that was left of CNN's dedicated resources to this story.

I went to bed more despondent than I'd ever been during my time at the network.

CHAPTER TWENTY

I WOKE UP THAT MONDAY IN ABUJA DEEPLY TROUBLED. FABS, STEPHanie, and I met up late in the morning in our suddenly empty workspace to assess our chances of finding another opportunity to meet the girls. It didn't look good.

Stephanie had already started calling some of her contacts and we were busy mulling over other people to reach out to when it dawned on me that another opportunity might be at hand. I remembered the elaborate press opportunity the Nigerian government had fashioned from Amina Ali Nkeki's journey to freedom. She'd been presented to President Buhari in the presence of a bank of cameras, creating a positive news story with the potential to boost the president's flailing political fortunes. If they'd done all of that to show off one girl, it was likely that there'd be another presidential presentation with all the associated fanfare for the twenty-one.

We needed to confirm my hunch. Stephanie and I dug out our cell phones, and with notepads in hand began to call various well-placed individuals to find out. I called government aides, cabinet ministers; I even managed to track down a phone number for President Buhari's daughter Aisha and spoke to her briefly. She confirmed there would be a meeting of the girls and her father, but she didn't know when. We broke for lunch and headed to a popular local restaurant, parking ourselves in a corner away from the few people who dotted the small, sunlit eatery. Given its size and layout, I was worried everyone in the place would be able to hear me on the phone, so I stepped outside to continue my quest. I started each inquiry brightly enough, aware of my reputation for making Nigerian officials uncomfortable.

"Oh hello, it's Isha Sesay from CNN here. How are things?" Within a few seconds it was always obvious which way the call would go. Some responded stiffly and pled ignorance, others talked of plans not yet firmed up, several others just ignored my request for information altogether. Finally my persistence paid off. I eventually got the confirmation I was looking for. The girls and their parents were to be presented to the president the next day, Tuesday. Discovering a second chance to meet the girls overwhelmed me with relief. Now that we'd determined the presentation event was actually happening, we needed permission for the CNN crew to attend. Several phone calls later, I'd pulled it off. My spirits began to rise.

The president of Nigeria has lived and worked in the Aso Rock Presidential Villa since 1991, when Nigeria's capital moved from Lagos to Abuja. This sprawling compound is in the heart of Abuja's central business district and in the shadow of the 1,300-feet rock formation from which the estate gets its name. Variously referred to as the Villa, Aso Rock, and State House, the lush grounds are formidably protected by multiples layers of security, which makes getting in and out of the compound a time-consuming ordeal. Cars must be left on the outskirts of the property, and all bodies and bags are scanned prior to admittance. Surveillance cameras and men with guns are everywhere; all movement is severely restricted. I couldn't help noting, though, that the estate's enormous peacocks are free to wander about at will.

Stephanie, Fabs, and I showed up at the villa early on Tuesday afternoon and headed straight to the reception desk to present our IDs. I was a little surprised when we were told to take a seat so they could track down our contact. While we waited, other journalists gave their names and handed in their IDs, and then whizzed straight past us and out of the building.

For almost half an hour we sat there in the cavernous, dark-tiled room while the team behind the expansive receptionist's counter placed multiple phone calls to officials, attempting to confirm we were actually allowed to be there. When the all clear finally came, it was time for the next stage of security.

We were ushered into another building. Here a bank of small lockers took up most of the room and an unfriendly looking security guard stood watch.

"Put your cell phones in the tray in one of the lockers, and then lock it and take the key," she instructed in no-nonsense fashion.

There was no way I was going to leave my cell phone behind. Not when I knew how important it was to capture pictures of the girls. I could feel the security guard watch my every move, so I slowed down everything I was doing and elaborately searched through my small tan backpack. The bag bulged with makeup, notebooks, phone chargers, an earpiece, and snacks. I pulled out my iPhone with my back turned to the guardian of the vaults and loudly announced I was putting it away in the locker. I secured the small cupboard and pocketed the key. I stepped away and continued to smile sweetly as the guard eyed me with irritation.

My heart was beating violently when I set my overstuffed bag down on the counter to be searched. Clearly overwhelmed by how much I'd crammed into it, the guard merely peered into the corners before pushing it back toward me. With a loud "Thank you," I grabbed my belongings, spun on my heels, and walked briskly through the automated gate—with my second phone stashed away at the bottom of the crowded backpack.

Almost as soon as I exited the building, an official standing on the covered concrete walkway yelled out, "Hello Isha, you're late! The event is starting now. You need to hurry!" I took off running, calling over my shoulder to Fabs and Stephanie, who were following a few steps behind.

The large, stately room with majestic floor-to-ceiling windows and sweeping swathes of brown marble was already full of journalists and VIPs, but President Buhari and his vice-president hadn't appeared. The event had not yet begun.

My blouse and jeans were already sticking to me by the time I walked into the hot room. With well over a hundred people crammed together, the space was loud and it took me a few minutes to gain my bearings. Multiple rows of chairs took up most of the hall. An aisle ran down the middle of the room, creating two separate seating sections.

All the journalists appeared to be standing or sitting on the left; most looked pensive and uncomfortable. A raft of TV cameras mounted on tall legs occupied the aisle area and, as is always the case in these kinds of pressurized public events, the photojournalists lurked protectively by their equipment ready to lose their tempers at the slightest hint that another journalist was trying to encroach on their tiny plot of floor space.

I'd been standing in the room for only a couple of minutes

when an officious individual appeared at my side and started shooing me toward the other journalists. I was tempted to resist, but from the intense look on his face, I already knew there was no point.

As he directed me, I wondered, Where were the girls? Were they in the room? Maybe they'd make an entrance with the president.

Then, out of the corner of my eye, I saw masses of bright, colorfully patterned outfits on the other side of the room, over by the imposing windows.

The twenty-one girls!

They were sitting quietly, almost frozen in their seats. At first I just stared, knowing they'd been through more than most of us could ever imagine. Many of them kept their heads bowed, staring intently at their hands, as others whispered quietly among themselves. They looked serious, uncomfortable in these surroundings—all except for baby Amos, who seemed serene sitting in one of the girl's laps. He had full, round cheeks and bright eyes, and he wore a tiny white T-shirt with blue stripes, under a dusky green button-down vest and beige shorts. His chubby bare feet were exposed to the elements and kicking about. None of the room's commotion seemed to bother him; he just sat there, staring in wonder.

But Amos was the only source of joy in that section. I was pained by the girls' obvious discomfort at the intrusive looks they were being subjected to. The girls occupied the first few rows of seats, while their parents and a handful of Chibok community leaders filled out the rest of the seating area on the right side of the room. At the very front, a handful of senior government officials, including the women's affairs and social development minister, Aisha al-Hassan, who was playing a leading role in the government's efforts to support and rehabilitate the girls, and Lai Mohammed, the country's minister of information and culture, all sat behind a long wooden table. A cherry-red microphone and two gray leather chairs were set out to mark the spot for the president and his deputy.

It was obvious the government had intended to keep the girls away from the assembled media, which is why I was being corralled with other journalists. I had no intention of playing along. I just had to figure out a way to cross the divide and sit beside the girls. I had to make it happen under the watchful gaze of dozens of government officials and journalists and somehow avoid being thrown out of the villa.

I was running out of time. Once President Buhari appeared, I would be stuck, unable to lift a finger, let alone walk across the room in his presence. I scanned the mass of bodies in the room in search of Fabs and Stephanie. They too needed to cross over. Fabs had wedged his camera into a small opening among the dozens of other cameras; he was set up and waiting for the program to begin.

I pushed my way through the dozens of people milling about and whispered to him, "I'm moving across."

Meanwhile, Stephanie was in a conversation with someone toward the back of the room. I caught her eye and used my head to indicate that we needed to move. I couldn't wait any longer. I took a deep breath and stepped into the rows of seats filled by Chibok parents and community elders. I mumbled out loud to no one in particular about needing to find somewhere to sit as I squeezed my way through the barely existent gap. The whole time I feared being yanked from the room by some Nigerian official or falling face-first into the lap of the elderly individuals occupying the surrounding seats. "Excuse me," "I'm sorry," "Apologies," I murmured with each step I took, focusing on not stepping on the numerous pairs of exposed feet I passed.

When I finally plopped myself down on the cold, tiled floor on the far side of the room, I was close enough to touch the twenty-one recently returned Chibok girls. Now that I was this close, I was struck by the haunted look in their dull eyes. Yes, they'd been released from captivity. But from their faraway looks, it seemed they weren't all the way back or totally free. With all the cameras and the people staring at them, it's likely they felt trapped once more. All they could do was sit with pursed lips, occasionally whispering to each other.

Whenever they spoke among themselves, I noted, it was in Kibaku, their local dialect. As I watched them, I glimpsed a host of personalities hidden behind their somber masks. I saw their playful natures, flashes of warm smiles and raised eyebrows accompanying quizzical smirks. Occasionally brief laughter broke out, and I noticed how the chuckling brought down their stiff shoulders, the way their tense muscles relaxed and facial features softened, revealing the young girls they still were. But just a moment later, they'd grow serious and cautious again, replacing their softness with the impenetrable masks once more. Sitting this close, I also noticed that they were all wearing makeup. Dramatic eyebrow arches drawn with black pencil framed their faces and lip gloss illuminated their mouths. I wondered how much these small pleasures like wearing lipstick meant to them after years of hardship and deprivation.

Though much of their ordeal was invisible to prying eyes, the state of their bodies couldn't be completely hidden. I had seen the pictures of their arrival in Abuja and been struck by how thin they were but I was unprepared for this degree of emaciation. Sharp, angular bones pushed against papery skin. Their thin, reedy limbs looked brittle enough to break if too much pressure was applied. The multicolored blouses and matching skirts they wore were too big for most of them and hung loosely from their bony chests and hips.

I stayed in my crouching position and crept slowly toward them. Many in the room, I knew, would be tracking my every move. I wasn't sure what my first words should be. After years of talking about the Chibok girls, I was now a little unsure of what this group of twenty-one would make of a strange woman who suddenly appeared by their side. I tried to ignore my racing pulse. With a big smile on my face, I quietly said, "Hello."

I was unprepared for their reaction, mostly a catalog of cold, blank stares. But a couple of girls sitting closer to me, at the end of the row, smiled shyly at me before quickly dropping their heads and looking down at their laps. Maybe they'd been warned not to speak to any journalists. Half of the group stared at me with wary looks. More nervous now, I pressed on. "Hello, my name is Isha. I'm a journalist with CNN. It is so good to see all of you. I've been telling your story for a very long time. I am so happy you are home." I noticed the surprised looks on some of their faces. Maybe it was actually disbelief that people beyond their families and community cared they were free. I could tell they needed help in making sense of me, so I told them more.

"I'm from nearby Sierra Leone and you are all my African sisters," I explained. At that, the girls on the end let out high-pitched squeals and smiled more warmly. Others in the group also looked at me, but this time their eyes shone a little brighter. Learning that I was African was obviously a pleasant surprise. Still, a couple in the group just stared blankly at me before turning away. Meanwhile, Stephanie, who, like Fabs, had surreptitiously made it across the room, shuffled closer to the girls and also introduced herself.

I turned my attention to the two girls sitting closest to me who continued to smile shyly. Like the others, they wore ankle-length skirts, with blouses in an array of dazzling colors. Theirs were made from a brilliant blue-and-yellow-patterned fabric, and their heads were wrapped in similar material. Looking at their small frames, I found it difficult to believe all these girls were in their late teens. They looked no more than thirteen or fourteen.

"How are you doing?" I asked softly and the girls giggled once more.

With heads bent into their chests they mumbled, barely audible, "Fine."

"How does it feel to be back?"

I just about made out "happy." Their voices were so soft. They continued to smile and cast furtive glances at each other.

I knew from my travels that one surefire way to break the ice with people is to request a selfie. I glanced over to see whether anyone was watching, and then I brought out the cell phone I wasn't supposed to have.

"Would you take a picture with me?"

Many nodded their heads enthusiastically. We huddled together and I snapped several pictures. I showed them the photos. When they saw themselves on my screen, they giggled with obvious delight.

But then, without warning, there was a flurry of activity at the front of the room. I looked up to see the president and vice-president entering. President Buhari, painfully thin due to illness, was clad head to toe in white: a long-sleeved tunic top with billowing sleeves, trousers, and matching white *kufi*, the traditional hat worn by Muslim men. Vice-President Osinbajo was similarly dressed, but in dark hues.

The men took their seats at the center of the table, flanked by other senior officials. The vice-president welcomed everyone with a warm tone that quickly put people at ease. When he finished speaking, one of the twenty-one girls stood and looked around nervously. She'd been given a cue to do something. She gathered herself and then she started to sing. Seconds later, the rest of the group rose to join her in singing a Christian song of thanks. As I listened, all the girls clapped gently and swayed slowly from side to side, the whole time staring blankly into space. It was meant to be a celebratory moment. Instead it was awkward, and the girls' eyes were full of sadness.

When the song ended, the same girl was the only one who remained standing.

"We are happy to see this wonderful day because we didn't

know we would come back to be members of Nigeria. Let us thank God for his love." She spoke slowly and clearly, in halting English, summing up their fears and gratitude. I was struck by how she tamed her obvious nerves and delivered her remarks to the stern-looking president and his officials. I could feel the girls' emotional turmoil there in the room with us, and I wondered what would happen to them after this presidential visit. What would their futures look like?

One of the Chibok leaders then spoke and said that the community and the girls' parents all believed the girls' futures would be best served by keeping them in the care of the government. I felt mixed emotions. I understood the financial difficulties experienced by most of the Chibok families. Handing over their daughters would ease the financial load considerably and possibly position the girls for opportunities their parents could never provide. Even so, this meant the girls were being handed over from Boko Haram to the government, from one group of overseers to another. They weren't actually going home at all. I was deeply troubled.

When President Buhari finally spoke, in his customary low, weak voice, he talked about the government's continuing responsibility to care for the girls.

"These twenty-one girls will be given adequate and comprehensive medical, nutritional, and psychological care and support. The federal government will rehabilitate them and ensure that their reintegration back to the society is done as quickly as possible," he droned on.

"Aside from rescuing them, we are assuming the responsibility for their personal, educational, and professional goals and ambitions in life. Obviously, it is not too late for the girls to go back to school and continue the pursuit of their studies. These dear daughters of ours have seen the worst that the world has to offer. It is now time for them to experience the best that the world can do for them. The government and all Nigerians must encourage them to achieve their desired ambitions."

The girls sat expressionless through it all, their masks firmly back in place, obscuring whatever emotions they were feeling. In the days since, I have replayed this afternoon in my head and always wondered what was going through their minds.

Once the speeches were done, the room sprang to life and officials darted about to coordinate a series of photo ops.

For the parents of the twenty-one girls, meeting President Buhari was clearly a nerve-racking experience. Given Nigeria's highly stratified society, a struggling farmer from a place like Chibok would never in a million years dream of setting foot in the presidential villa, let alone be in the presence of the nation's leader. And now here they were, standing mere feet away from him. The difficulties of day-to-day life in places like Chibok had left many of these parents looking haggard. They edged forward timidly, toward the bespectacled Buhari, who displayed no emotion.

A group of overwrought mothers dropped to their knees in front of him and, with arms aloft, thanked the president profusely for bringing back their daughters. The men from Chibok, meanwhile, bowed deeply. One young father dressed in a burgundy tunic and trousers fell to his knees and reverentially took the president's hand as words of thanks rushed from his lips.

Next it was time for the girls to step up and meet the president. Villa officials directed them to make their way over to the front of the room. They looked every bit as uncomfortable as their parents, and they solemnly shook hands with President Buhari. Once the handshakes were out of the way, the girls were then arranged into two rows for a photograph. The president stood in the middle, flanked by his deputy on one side and baby Amos on the other. It was a joyless scene, without a real smile in sight. The twenty-one girls stared mournfully at the photographers who clicked away.

The only smile I spotted during the entire episode was on the face of the vice-president. He knew these were powerful images being created, especially for an administration that had been lambasted by critics and under pressure to do more to meet the needs of its populace. These photos held the potential of boosting the government's standing both domestically and internationally. The event was a major feather in Buhari's cap. He'd been able to achieve something that his predecessor had been widely assailed for failing. He was the one who'd brought some of the Chibok girls back. Still, the moment the photo-op was over, Buhari was gone.

The twenty-one girls were instructed to fall in line and move outside to board the waiting buses. I told Fabs to follow me, and we both moved quickly to get in beside the procession as it inched its way down the middle of the room. His camera was already rolling when I asked the first question.

"Will you go back to school?" I asked the girls.

To my delight, heads bobbed up and down and several of them said an eager yes.

"What do you want to study?" I asked one of the girls.

"Sciences," she replied shyly.

As soon as we got outside, a beady-eyed official ordered me to step away from the girls. I pretended I hadn't heard him and continued to wave to the girls from a spot they had to pass on their way to the buses. Many waved back hesitantly and smiled. I said "Bye" to each and every one of them. There were still those who looked away from me, refusing to be drawn in.

I lightly rested my left hand on the some of the girls' backs as they moved along. What had happened to their bodies during their two and a half years in captivity was palpable, the feel of their sharp shoulder blades a reminder of the long and difficult road to wholeness for these girls. Meanwhile, the hovering officials wanted the girls swept from public view as quickly as possible. As soon as the last girl boarded the bus, the doors closed immediately, and they were whisked away.

Now my team's sole mission was to rush back to the hotel so we could edit a report and I could make myself available to offer insight and analysis on this presidential villa visit for any of the shows on CNN USA and CNN International. Before we left the Aso Rock, we stopped by the lockers to collect our items. The same surly official was on duty, none the wiser about my secret phone.

Back in our car, I switched on my work phone, expecting a flood of requests for interviews, footage, and information about the girls. But no surge came. Nothing. It was early in the States, I told myself. Eventually my CNN bosses would want me live to discuss the visit and my impressions of the girls. After all, I was the only journalist to actually have gotten close enough to speak to the girls since their release. This was a world exclusive. Little did I know how wrong I was.

There wasn't a single request from CNN USA. Election fever had burned away interest in everything else, even a story the network had been the leader on. In this new world order, the only thing that mattered was the razed-earth election unfolding. Even more disheartening was that CNN International, a channel dedicated to world news, was now airing so many of the shows from CNN USA that there were only a handful of live spots available for me to appear on. After years of reporting for the network alongside some of its finest journalists and winning countless awards for the quality of our work, this was a watershed moment. When one of the most significant moments in the Chibok story arrived, CNN looked the other way. The network wanted to focus all of its attention on Trump. It was galling.

The limited coverage of the girls' release on CNN meant few people saw my reporting that day, but my mother was one of those who did. When we spoke later that evening, I could feel her immense pride. She has always been my biggest cheerleader. Even though the networks' interest in the story fizzled out almost as soon as I arrived in Nigeria, my mother still believed it was an important trip. We were both thrilled that I'd been able to speak to the girls directly. I felt more determined than ever to keep the story alive. More than anything, my mother was relieved my Nigeria assignment was now over, and this time around, unlike countless times in the past, things had unfolded without any new episodes of danger or drama.

I figured it was best to keep the DSS episode to myself.

CHAPTER TWENTY-ONE

WHENEVER ESTHER LONGED FOR HER DAUGHTER DORCAS, SHE DUG out her cell phone and gazed at a photo of her firstborn. Unlike in real life, her child appeared at such moments without fail. Frozen in time on the cusp of her sixteenth birthday, Dorcas was forever a picture of serenity with a vivid purple scarf that concealed her hair from view. The faintest trace of a smile could be seen on her darkly outlined rosebud lips. Her narrow-set eyes always looked back calmly at her mother. Esther sought solace in this image hundreds of times a day.

For the first three months after her daughter's disappearance, Esther refused to eat. In due course she developed a stomach ulcer and high blood pressure. She lived between two realms, preferring to be in her mind among her memories and long-cherished dreams of her baby than with others out in the world. Every day that passed in this painful new reality in which mother and daughter were kept apart, another crack opened up in Esther's heart.

On the second anniversary of the girls' abduction, Pathfinders Justice Initiative, an international NGO working with survivors of sexual abuse, shared letters written by Esther Yakubu, Martha Enoch, and Rebecca Samuel to their missing Chibok daughters. In an accompanying video, Esther reads her letter aloud, her face soaked with tears as she struggles to beat back emotions, to give voice to her grief, a pain still every bit as intense as the day in 2014 when she first learned her beloved was missing.

Letter from Esther Yakubu to Her Daughter, Dorcas Yakubu

Dear Dorcas (Maida),

It has been long I heard from you. How are you and your friends, wherever you are? Hoping that you are doing better, or managing life, and I know that the angel of the Lord Almighty is with you, and He will continue to be with you wherever you are. You don't know—you don't have any idea of the plans I have been planning for you all this while. Since from birth, I've been planning for you, your life, your education, your health, before you were kidnapped. Before marriage, I wanted you to go to the university, because I have not been there. My hope is that you will be a fashion designer, as a woman. I have even bought a sewing machine for you, and a traveling bag, and some set of clothes. But up till now, for two years, I have not seen or heard anything from you. But I would like to advise you, wherever you are, please be strong in the Lord and He will see you through. I know I miss you, but I have the heart and I have the hope that one day I will see you again. I believe that one day I will fulfill my promise to you, and I will see you again, and my happiness, my joy, my life, will be complete with you and I will be a happy mother again. The Lord is your strength, and I have that hope in me that I will see you again and I will rejoice in the Lord Almighty.

From your mum,
Esther Yakubu

Letter from Martha Enoch to Her Daughter, Monica Enoch

Dear Monica,

Life has been difficult without you these last two years. My life is in discomfort and I have been living with hypertension since they stole you from me on April 14, 2014. We miss you whenever we remember the role that you played in our family, especially your sisters. You were so kind and so special because you touched the lives of everyone that met you. Our prayers have never ended for you and we still sing your favorite choruses that you would sing in church. We sing them every morning and every evening in Hausa and we remember your voice. I always end up in tears. I wanted you to be a doctor and in fact, we have nicknamed [our other daughter] "doctor" because of you. Your father had a dream where he saw you walking up a ladder to heaven. My hope is that I will see you here on earth again but if I do not, I know you are in heaven. Please serve God faithfully and I pray that God bring you back to me. I miss you, my daughter.

From your mum,
Martha Enoch

Letter from Rebecca Samuel to Her Daughter, Sarah Samuel

Dear Sarah,

You were only eighteen at the time of your abduction. By now you would be twenty years; that means it's been two years since

you have been taken from me. I am suffering, I am bitter, I cry
every time and I am praying and fasting. Many things are hard
and we are just managing life. I know and believe in God that if
there is still life, one day we will see you again. People say that the
[abduction] is a lie, but it is true. I want to tell them that if it were
their children, how would they feel? The 219 children have not
returned since then. If not because of God's grace, we all would
have died. Some of us [parents] got hypertension, while others
got different illnesses because we are thinking about our abducted
children. If you were dead, we would have cried and been able to
move on. But we do not know if you are still alive or dead. That
is why we are worried. I cry and my heart is bitter every night. I
am praying that if you are alive, God should rescue you. I believe
God will save you. As your mother, I am begging God for you to
continue praying wherever you are. I want to tell you to be strong
and continue praying. I lost everything, I lost everything when I
lost you.

From your mum,
Rebecca

In a town as small and tightly knit as Chibok, everyone felt the
pain expressed by Esther, Martha, and Rebecca. The entire community mourned with the parents of the missing girls, just as it had
done from the very beginning. Many of the parents felt assaulted
by the tragedy, and the tumult of emotions had a terrible effect on
their bodies. Equally injurious was the indifference they felt from
the federal government, the distinct sense that they and their poor
children didn't matter.

By the time that second anniversary came around, more than a
dozen parents of the missing girls had died from stress-related illnesses. Of those remaining, like Esther, many continued to battle
ill health and to ask the same questions they'd asked from the very

beginning: "Where are our girls? What's being done to bring them home?"

But at this point, Esther didn't expect to receive an answer.

"I don't think the government is putting in any effort," she said. "It is in fact only because of the pressure placed on them by Bring Back Our Girls that they make a move. But if they stop, the government just stays where they are."

Esther expressed this opinion loudly and forcefully in countless interviews with journalists from around the world. Her candor brought whispered warnings of government retribution from concerned friends and acquaintances. All of them were worried for her and her family, till finally Esther and her family fled Chibok and relocated in Abuja.

One Sunday afternoon almost four months after the second anniversary, Esther returned from church, feeling unwell. She took her blood pressure medication and retreated to bed. She was drifting off to sleep when her husband's cell phone rang. Groaning with annoyance, she put a pillow over her head and willed herself back to sleep.

"They said they have released some of the girls!" Yakubu came running through the door.

Esther bolted straight up. "Ah! Ah! Which girls?" she demanded. Gone was her desire for sleep—Dorcas was the only thing on her mind.

The news came from Pastor Enoch back in Chibok, whose daughter Monica was also among the missing. The pastor had been trying to reach Esther. She now scrambled for her phone and immediately tried calling a local journalist she knew but couldn't get through. Growing frantic, she quickly called Aunty Becky, a close family friend.

"Is it true that they have released some girls?" Esther's voice was full of expectation.

Becky hadn't heard that news. "But it will be on the Internet, so let me check and I will get back to you."

A list of people to call ran through Esther's head. One after the other, she dialed their numbers: first, Mallam Nkeki, the head of the Chibok Parents' Association; then Madame Yanna, also part of the group, whose her daughter Rifkatu was missing too. Lawan Zannah, the secretary of the organization, was next. But the cell phone network in Chibok was known for being spotty, and she couldn't get through to anyone. She tried her younger brother and couldn't reach him either. She paced up and down, frantic, knowing her blood pressure was climbing. Then Aunty Becky called back.

"They didn't release any girls," Aunty Becky said.

Esther let out the breath she'd been holding.

"It is a video they released and it is showing about fifty girls. Let me put it on my laptop so you can listen."

At first Esther couldn't hear the video clearly because the volume was low, but when Aunty Becky turned it up, Esther heard it: the voice she'd known for nearly sixteen years, one that had been silent for too long.

"That is my daughter!" she screamed.

"No, it can't be," Aunty Becky shot back. "They said this girl's name is Maida."

"My baby's name *is* Maida!" Esther shouted. She'd lost all sensation in her body.

"Esther stop! Stop shouting!" Aunty Becky tried to calm her. "Esther! Esther, stop screaming! Your baby is alive. Now is not the time to cry."

But Esther couldn't have stopped even if she'd wanted to.

Was it true? Was it possible? Could that really be Dorcas? She needed to see the video with her own eyes. But how? Right then she remembered another local journalist and dialed him.

"I was just about to call you," he said, picking up immediately. "Have you seen the video?"

"No, I have only heard it over the phone."

"Okay, I'm coming with it now. Where is your house?"

He was at her front door within the hour with a laptop and his cameraman. Esther and Yakubu gathered around the laptop and then the journalist hit Play. The girl who appeared on screen was thinner, but she was unmistakable. It took only seconds for Esther to let out a piercing scream. The sound panicked her children Ibrahim and Missy, who immediately came running. They were utterly confused by the scene: Esther, Yakubu, the journalist, and his cameraman, all weeping.

Hearing her firstborn child beg the Nigerian government to make a deal for the release was searing. For Yakubu, the shock of seeing his painfully thin daughter standing next to an armed terrorist was a crushing blow. And yet he was relieved, because there she was, his child on the screen, alive. For more than two years she'd been out of sight, but now was right in front of his very eyes. Esther was unable to move on from the images of her daughter in that video; they were all she could think about and she retreated even further into her mind.

Almost nine weeks later, twenty-one of the Chibok schoolgirls along with baby Amos were released, surprising Esther and the entire world. She'd gotten the news from an uncle, but it wasn't immediately clear to any of the Chibok families which of the girls had been set free. Esther and her family spent a sleepless night praying for Dorcas's name to be included on the list. But it wasn't. And the news wounded her.

With all her might, Esther willed herself to be happy for the other Chibok mothers. "If I am a true mother . . . and I don't get mine, but you get yours, I will rejoice with you. Then maybe another time will come and it will be mine to rejoice." Still, the pain of her loss in the face of the other girls' release was searing.

During the two-plus years since the abduction, Esther had refused to enter Dorcas's bedroom, instead leaving it just the way it had been the day her child disappeared in 2014. She didn't want to see any of her daughter's possessions. Her bed, suitcase, books, school bag, and two brand-new school uniforms remained untouched. She forbade the younger children from taking anything out of there.

When Esther and her family moved to Abuja, they'd installed a lodger in the family's Chibok home as a way to stop the numerous break-ins they'd suffered. Unbeknownst to Esther, in a bid for more space, the lodger had moved Dorcas's belongings to Esther's own bedroom in her absence.

A family trip home to Chibok a few months after the August 2016 proof-of-life video was released suddenly brought Esther into contact with Dorcas's possessions for the first time in years. Esther felt the wind knocked out of her. After that one encounter, she moved her mattress into the living room and refused to enter her bedroom again unless absolutely necessary.

Meanwhile, mealtimes continued to be a source of anguish. The entire time, Esther would wonder whether Dorcas was also being fed and nourished. Not knowing if her daughter was being given food to eat left this mother struggling to eat anything herself. All that sustained her was prayer.

Esther and her family held tightly to their faith and willed themselves to believe that it was just a matter of time before the sound of Dorcas's voice once again filled their home. Dorcas had always been the one who led her family in prayer. In her absence, Esther's younger daughter Missy, who was starting to look more like her lost sister with each passing day, now took up those duties during morning and evening devotion. When the twenty-one girls returned, Missy began to alter the daily prayer she gave.

"The twenty-one are back but my sister is not back. Lord, I put my sister in your hands. And one day, I know my sister will be back and she will carry me on her back. She will plait my hair for me. And I know you will do it for me, Lord."

On these occasions, Esther and Yakubu struggled to restrain the tears. With their eyes closed and their remaining children by their side, this broken family weighed down by grief said, "Amen."

CHAPTER TWENTY-TWO

As far back as I can remember I've had nightmares about losing my mum to some act of misfortune. The dreams took different forms. The one I had most often involved intruders bursting into our home in Sierra Leone. I was always there with my mum in her bedroom, and there was a dark cherrywood chest of drawers pushed up against the door—to keep the menacing, unseen forces out. I don't know what happened next, because I always awoke in a panic, but I could never shake the distinct feeling that the standoff was to end badly. Each time I heard a Chibok girl or parent speak of the deep distress he or she felt while separated from a loved one, it resonated, activating a fear buried deep within me I'd always kept hidden.

I got on the plane to Sierra Leone at the end of November 2016.

The twenty-one Chibok girls had been released just six weeks earlier. Even though I spoke to my mum on the phone almost daily—in fact, sometimes multiple times a day—I still couldn't wait to be in her company and hang out with my brother. But I was excited to be going home this time for an additional reason. My nonprofit organization, W.E. Can Lead, was formally launching in seven schools in Sierra Leone, and close to 180 girls were already signed up to join our high school leadership development program. I had suitcases full of journals, T-shirts, and backpacks for my girls. I'd been counting down the days for weeks, impatiently awaiting this momentous trip.

It was after ten o'clock when the car pulled into our family's compound in Freetown on that warm Monday night. But of course, Mum was still awake waiting for me. She pulled open the heavy wooden front door, which set off the funny groaning sound it always makes when it scrapes the hallway tiles. I hugged her close right there in the doorway and then planted a big, noisy kiss on her full cheek, a childish act that always made her laugh. As we walked to the living room, I took great delight in reminding her I was actually taller, a fact she'd developed lightning-quick skills to dismiss whenever it came up—which it did often, because her mock annoyance has always brought me so much joy. It felt so good to be home with her.

At sixty-seven, she looked far younger than her age. The face behind her glasses was still plump and her forehead unlined. Her long black hair, free of gray thanks to hair dye, fell over her shoulders in loose curls. I kicked off my sneakers and felt the coolness of the familiar dark brown floor tiles on the soles of my feet.

"There's food," she said. "Aren't you going to eat?" As usual, the dining table was set with my favorite dishes: roasted spicy chicken, jollof rice, fried plantains, and a hearty salad.

"I'll eat in a minute," I promised her.

We'd fallen right back into our old ways.

She sat in her usual spot—the mustard-colored leather armchair in the corner, with her long, flowing African gown bunched around her knees. Her eyes shone with contentment while I piled a plate high, then settled on the sofa next to her. In between greedy mouthfuls, we caught up on everything. An ardent Hillary Clinton supporter, she was still reeling from the election of Trump earlier that month and worried about what it all meant for America. We talked about the presidential election in Sierra Leone slated for March 2018. She was at the heart of the action once more and, unofficially, had already been named as the vice-presidential pick for the second election in a row. The vote was still sixteen months away, but campaign logistics and internal party machinations were already taking up all her time and energy.

With the political terrain covered, we moved on to stories about my inappropriate suitors and often exceedingly absurd life in the States. Soon the sound of our laughter filled the house. For hours we sat in the living room chatting, the standing fan whirring away and the TV muted in the background, tuned to CNN, as it usually was, where a colleague of mine mouthed away silently.

Suddenly she looked at her watch. "It's past two a.m., Isha Sesay!" She gasped. "It's enough for today! Time to go to bed."

Here I was, a forty-year-old woman. But as far as she was concerned, I was still very much her teenage daughter.

With only a week in Freetown, I'd ensured my schedule would be jam packed. I zigzagged across the overcrowded city to attend back-to-back school visits, where I welcomed dozens of girls with eyes filled of hope, handed out goodie bags loaded with W.E. Can Lead swag, gave lots of hugs, and took tons of pictures. I was in my element, talking to girls about being empowered, achieving their dreams, and becoming leaders.

On Thursday, I was exhausted, and by the time the sun began its journey across the gold, pink, and orange sky, I felt grateful to relax on a hotel patio with my dear cousin Maggie—the baby sister

I never had—and her husband, Mahmoud. We had all attended the Lebanese International School at the same time, and so every get-together was an opportunity to revisit memories of our childhood mischief making. We were in the throes of wild laughter at one of our exploits when my cell phone rang.

Mum was calling. It was six thirty and she wanted to know my plans for the evening. "I'm going to a quick meeting at Maada's," she told me, referring to her presidential running mate. "Are you coming home for dinner?"

"I'm not sure yet. Call me when you're on your way back from the meeting and I'll let you know."

"Okay," she replied, "I won't be long."

When my phone rang a second time, it was a little past seven fifteen. This time it was FA, one of our relatives who lived at home with Mum.

"Isha, come o! Your mummy isn't well."

"What do you mean?" Anxiety tightened my throat.

"They've taken her to Choitram Hospital. Your brother, Mr. Sesay, is on his way."

"I'm ten minutes down the road; I'm coming right away." By the time I said those words, I felt like I'd already left my body. My nightmare was playing out in real time.

Mahmoud drove and Maggie did her best to calm me during the short journey to the hospital. Choitram was the place we went whenever anyone in our family took ill. The standard of care was decent, the facilities basic, and it was considered one of the best in an assortment of terrible hospitals in Freetown.

We sped onto the hospital grounds and I leapt out of the car as soon as Mahmoud parked. I bolted through the courtyard. As I ran I noticed a small crowd of people I recognized. They were my mother's political colleagues, relatives, and family friends. I called out quickly, "Where is she?"

As fast as I was moving, I didn't register who actually answered.

But I did notice the worried look on all their faces. I raced down the walkway, leapt over a handful of steps, passed through the doors of the building housing the ICU ward, and ran straight into a hospital aide. I tried to go around him but he placed his body in front of the door leading to the ward.

"My mother is in there, Dr. Kadi Sesay," I said, gasping for breath.

"You can't go in," he replied. "The doctors are with her."

I tried to get around him but failed. "I need to see her. *Move!*" I screamed and tried to duck past him. He placed his body squarely in front of the door and put his hands out to hold me back. My jaw tightened. "If you don't move, I'm going to punch you in the face!" I had to see her and I was willing to do whatever was necessary to make it happen. The aide faltered for just a moment, enough for me to shove past him and wrench open the ward door.

That's when I saw her. The curtain around the bed was only partially drawn. Something was horribly wrong. She was sitting up on the bed without her glasses. Her head lolled from side to side, and she looked as if she was trying to fight off the handful of medical personnel surrounding her. I could tell she wasn't fully conscious. The situation felt chaotic and the medical team looked overwhelmed. I wanted to call out to her and run over, but I could see they were trying to get her under control. So I just stood there gasping, horrified, while the sound of wildly beeping machines filled my ears. I had only one thought: We need to pray for her. I ran from the room.

By now there were even more people in the courtyard—more politicians, close friends, and relatives, including people from the neighborhood. I called out to an anxious-looking relative hovering close by, summoning all my willpower to speak slowly and clearly.

"Go right now to Alhaji Chernor! Tell him Mum is unwell. I need him to come and pray for her."

Alhaji Chernor was the neighborhood imam and a close family

friend, a constant source of support for my mother, whose faith had deepened as she'd gotten older. He was the person we'd always called if there were burial rites to be performed. Now I needed him to pray over my mother to keep her alive.

My brother turned up a few minutes later. I filled him in on what little I knew and we sat together in a corner, mostly silent, alongside Maggie and her husband.

"Alhaji Chernor is here!" someone shouted. I felt relief sweep through me and my heart was beating a little less violently. He'd come as soon as he heard the news. He walked briskly down the walkway toward me, his Qur'an tucked under the arm of his flowing robe. Gone was the bright, smiling face I was accustomed to. He looked grim, the eyes behind his glasses dark and serious. I led him to my mother. She was lying down now. Her breathing was labored and she was writhing. I was afraid I'd collapse if I stared too long at her, so I hovered with Alhaji Chernor by the horseshoe-shaped nurses' station and tried to catch the eye of one of the doctors huddled by her bedside. A young-looking medic reluctantly came over. I introduced myself quickly. "How is she doing?" I asked nervously.

"We're trying to get her vitals under control," he said matter-of-factly.

"Our imam is here." I pointed to Alhaji Chernor. "I'd like him to come in and pray for her. Is that okay?" I sounded desperate.

He paused for a moment before nodding "That's fine. He just needs to stay out of the way."

Moments later Alhaji Chernor stood beside one of the room's large windows, a few feet away from my mum's head, praying for God to spare her. I said my own prayers under my breath. Surely God would save the life of such a good woman.

The next few hours were the worst of my life. After a great deal of uncertainty, the doctors confirmed that my mother had suffered a massive stroke and there was major bleeding in her brain. It was devastating news. But I told myself that having a diagnosis meant we could at last move forward and deal with her condition. I even felt my spirits lift a little.

"So, who is going to do the surgery to stop the brain bleed?" I asked one of the doctors.

He didn't reply immediately, but when he did, his words made no sense. "There is no neurosurgeon to perform the surgery."

I was confused. "You mean there is no neurosurgeon in this hospital?" I enunciated each word slowly.

"There is no neurosurgeon in the *country*," he responded.

How could that be? There was *no one* to perform this surgery in the *entire* country? No one to help my mum?

"So what do we do?" I asked.

"If you want surgery, you'll have to take her out of the country."

Mum was now lying completely still. Tension rose throughout my body. I nodded to the doctor. If flying her out of Sierra Leone was what needed to happen, then I was going to do that regardless of cost or logistical difficulty. The doctor told me about Aspen Medical, a medical evacuation company with offices thirty minutes away. A pleasant looking Sierra Leonean gentleman had been standing close by and listening intently to our conversation. Dr. Kabia introduced himself as a consultant at Choitram Hospital and offered to show me the way to Aspen Medical.

I emerged from the ward to explain the situation to my brother, Maggie, and her husband. I also had to say something to the crowd of people who'd been waiting in the courtyard for hours.

My legs felt heavy as I walked toward them and everyone stared. When my mother collapsed earlier that evening, she'd been in the home of Maada Bio, her presidential running mate, and a small group of other party faithful. I would later learn he'd caught her in his arms as she fell to ground, complaining of a headache and sweating profusely. Now I stood looking at him and a couple of graying gentlemen in the dark courtyard. They looked disconsolate.

"The scans show a massive stroke. There's no one here who can do the surgery. So I have to take her out of the country. I'm going to arrange that now." There wasn't much else to say.

Brain cells die every minute that goes by after a stroke occurs; or as the experts put it, "Time is brain." It was past ten o'clock and Mum had been bleeding for well over three hours. Time wasn't on her side.

Mr. Claude, who'd been driving for our family since I was a teenager, was parked in the hospital lot. My brother and I ran over to Mum's silver SUV, directing Mr. Claude to follow the vehicle slowly making its way along the gravely path toward the gate, its taillights glaring in the darkness. He nodded, turned the key in the ignition, and nothing happened. The car wouldn't start.

Mr. Claude mumbled, "We've been having car trouble in recent days."

I quickly jumped out to yell, "Dr. Kabia!"

It was after eleven when I discovered in Aspen Medical's startlingly bright reception area that my mother couldn't be airlifted till the next day. The medical aircraft was currently parked across the border in Liberia.

"Where do you want to take her?" a sleepy-looking nurse asked me.

I hadn't even thought about our destination. As I didn't speak French, my choices came down to the two English-speaking options in the region, Ghana and Nigeria. I'd never even visited Ghana before. Nigeria on the other hand, I knew. And for better or worse, they knew me.

"I'm taking her to Lagos," I announced.

But first we needed a doctor in Nigeria to agree to admit her to a local hospital and to organize an ambulance to collect us from the plane the moment we touched down. And all those arrangements needed to be confirmed in writing before Aspen would take us.

The whole way back to the Choitram Hospital, I battled the

grief trying to take over and prayed without end. When I walked back into the hospital courtyard, everyone was still there, looking weary and beaten.

I kept my voice low and unwavering. "I'm taking Mum to Nigeria in the morning, but there are still a lot of arrangements to make. Please go home and rest. There's nothing more any of you can do for her right now. If you want to help, please pray for her to make it through the night. But for now, please go home. Thank you again for being here with us this evening."

Soon I heard the sound of car doors slamming and engines starting.

It was now just my brother, Maggie, her husband, me, and a long list of things to do. Meanwhile my mother's vital signs were weak and the doctors didn't seem confident. I sat on the ground in the corner of the courtyard and went into autopilot. I quickly typed a text to a CNN executive: "My mum has had a stroke. Don't know when I'll be back." I stayed awake through the night making phone calls, sending texts and emails, connecting doctors across borders, finalizing the details, praying. Then I finally packed two small bags, one for her and one for me. I'd gotten help from two Nigerian lifelines, Ayo Otuyalo and Adeniyi Adekoya. They'd buoyed my spirits, mobilized resources, and enlisted a friend from their church, Dr. Marilyn Osanife, to help find the neurosurgeon.

When the sun rose on Friday, December 2, my mother was still alive and all the arrangements were in place.

It was already uncomfortably warm, a few minutes after nine, when we finally left the hospital grounds. There wasn't enough room for me in the ambulance so I followed close behind in Maggie and Mahmoud's car. My brother drove separately, while relatives and close family friends filled the other half dozen cars in the convoy. The roads of Freetown are pitted and scarred by potholes big and small. Every time the ambulance encountered one, I shuddered. My eyes never left the back of the vehicle carrying her as we wove through the congested streets, then boarded the old, lumbering ferry crowded with travelers and traders, packed buses, trucks, cars, motorbikes, and squawking poultry, all of us heading across the wide estuary to the coastal town of Lungi, home to the international airport.

When the creaking behemoth docked, the ambulance with sirens blaring and the rest of the convoy were the first ones off the boat. By now it was almost noon, and the journey to the airport itself took a further thirty minutes. At Lungi International Airport, the ambulance turned off the main thoroughfare and drove past the terminal building onto a short, uneven path I'd never been down before. At the very end was an opening, which took the ambulance directly onto the tarmac where the medical jet was waiting. By this stage, the convoy had grown to include Maada's vehicles and a handful of other cars with more of mum's close party friends. We were all following the ambulance down the same short dirt road when a number of airport officials appeared and ordered the cars to stop. The ambulance kept moving, but the rest of the convoy could go no farther.

An airport official told me I needed to clear immigration in the terminal before boarding the plane. It was time to say goodbye. I hugged my brother tight. "I'll call as soon as we get to Lagos."

He nodded and mumbled "Safe journey," his voice muffled by grief. Maggie and her husband wrapped their arms around me. "God go with you and Aunty Kadi," Maggie whispered. I nodded tearfully and said goodbye to as many family and friends as possible. Then, holding close all their words of comfort and prayer, I sped to the terminal.

On the sunbaked tarmac, two tall, dark-haired South Africans with thick Afrikaans accents were waiting, the pilot and the paramedic. Both looked to be in their midthirties, and when they introduced themselves, I was struck by how gentle they seemed. Mum's stretcher was carefully lifted into the turboprop aircraft.

I was only half-listening to the pilot. His words barely registered until he said, ". . . and the journey will take five hours." Alarm bells went off. The typical flight time of no more than two hours had all of a sudden more than doubled due to the slow pace of the type of aircraft transporting us. I did the calculations. By the time we touched down in Lagos, twenty-four hours would have passed since my mum's stroke.

Before long Freetown was a tiny speck below us. Mum, meanwhile, lay motionless on a stretcher, hooked up to numerous monitors and oxygen tanks. She was so close I could reach over and touch her from my seat. As we flew, the temperature in the plane dropped, and soon I was shivering in my short-sleeved T-shirt. I stared at Mum's still form, worrying she might be cold too.

Every time a machine beeped, my heart bounded, but I was assured repeatedly by the paramedic that everything was okay. Still, I couldn't bring myself to close my eyes. I was too afraid. So I just stared at her and hoped she knew I was present and found the strength to keep fighting.

It was dark by the time Lagos came into view. The lights of the megacity twinkled below, and I'd never been so happy to see Nigeria in my life. When we finally landed, the medics immediately lowered Mum onto the tarmac via an opening in the belly of the plane, while I bolted down the steps at the front.

I stood in the balmy heat surrounded by the sprawling Murtala Muhammed International Airport, searching the darkness for the lights of an ambulance. Nothing. Five minutes later, I felt panic stirring.

A slow-moving figure approached the plane.

The pilot shouted to the man, "Where's the ambulance?"

Though the man's flapping badge indicated he worked for the airport, he was confused by the question.

"An ambulance is supposed to be here!" the pilot insisted. "Where is it?"

"It's coming," the man mumbled, but offered no look of recognition or urgency. Another five minutes went by.

"Where is it?" the paramedic again yelled at the man, who now got on his cell phone while the pilot pulled out his walkie-talkie to repeat our location to air traffic control.

"The ambulance is on the other side," the airport official announced.

"What!?"

Inexplicably, we'd been given permission to land on the international side of the airport when we should have been at the private aviation terminal on the domestic side.

"She's running out of oxygen!" screamed the paramedic.

This couldn't be happening . . . after everything it'd taken to get her to Nigeria. My mum couldn't die here on the tarmac. I kept looking around frantically, as if I could will an ambulance into existence.

Both medics were screaming. "Why can't the ambulance come here?"

"It cannot. You have to go over to the other side."

"We have to get back in the plane and go over to the other side of the airport?"

"Yes."

"If something happens to my patient, it will be your fault!"

The pilot and paramedic rushed to put Mum back on the plane and I ran up the stairs. Less than five minutes of oxygen remained on the tank.

The moment we were all on board, without waiting to close and secure the aircraft door, we were moving, taxiing to the private terminal guided by air traffic control.

The moment we stopped, I heard ambulance sirens approaching, and I whispered a prayer of thanks.

The South African duo leapt from aircraft immediately. "We

need oxygen!" they shouted. Several Nigerian paramedics ran across the tarmac toward us carrying a tank.

I began to sob uncontrollably and gasp for air. I was having an anxiety attack.

"It's okay. She's okay, Isha," the paramedic spoke softly, wrapping his arms around my shoulders.

But I knew it wasn't okay. I'd battled time and lost. His words couldn't stop my tears. I said goodbye to the South African crew and took off in the ambulance.

I've been to Lagos countless times, but I was still shocked by the amount of traffic on the roads as eight o'clock approached on this Friday night. We were headed to a hospital in Apapa, one of the most densely populated areas in this city of twenty-one million. Our vehicle drove between and around cars in the unending, multilane bumper-to-bumper traffic, while pedestrians and street hawkers shared the leftover space on the roads.

"Move out of the way!" yelled Dr. Raji, a dark-skinned, high-spirited anesthesiologist from Lagoon Hospital who'd come with the ambulance, speaking over a loudspeaker and activating an ear-splitting siren. For all his noise, though, it didn't make much difference. A car or two would inch out of our way only to reveal more lines of stationary traffic.

It was ten fifteen by the time we passed through the gates of the hospital. By eleven, Mum was in surgery.

Before disappearing into the operating room, the neurosurgeon, Dr. Tayo Ojo—a tall, thin man with glasses who was not given to unnecessary displays of emotion—informed me the procedure would go on throughout the night.

I was left alone in a doctor's office. The room was sparsely furnished, with only a desk, a couple of uncomfortable-looking chairs, and a black leather examination table. I dumped my bags in a corner and climbed onto the table.

My pulse never stopped racing. I alternated between half sitting and half lying down, too restless to remain in any position for more than a few minutes. My worst fear had come to pass: something had happened to my mum. *Lord, please save her, don't take her away from me.*

My prayers stopped only when Dr. Ojo suddenly came to the room three hours into the procedure.

"Everything is going according to plan. Only a couple more hours," he explained.

I could only nod before I found my voice to thank him for the update. I was on my own once more.

During those long hours I leaned on my faith, and it held me together while my mother lay on that operating table. Born to Muslim parents, I'd been allowed to chart an unregulated religious path while growing up in Freetown. I was allowed to eat pork, went to drama classes instead of Qur'anic classes, and spent my first two years of secondary school attending Saint Joseph's convent—a decidedly Catholic place of learning. As with so much of my life, my mother had allowed me the freedom to experience different things and make my own decisions. She often said, "As long as you have a relationship with God, that's all that matters." So in America I attended Passion—a heart-expanding church in Atlanta led by Louie Giglio, while still being mindful of important dates in the Muslim calendar like Ramadan—the month of fasting and the joyous festivals of Eid. Mine is a faith that is deeply personal—enriched as much by imams as by pastors, unencumbered by the rigid, separatist lines of Islam and Christianity.

That night I prayed, with Christian praise music blaring through my headphones, when the office door opened again. It was four a.m. Dr. Ojo, still wearing his green operating scrubs, came in, his face unreadable. He took a seat by the examination table. It felt like an eternity before he spoke.

"The surgery went very well. I managed to stop the bleeding."

My heart and stomach somersaulted.

"We are now moving her to the ICU. She should be waking up soon."

"I don't know how to thank you, Dr. Ojo! I am so grateful!" I just kept repeating the same words.

When he left the room, a surge of adrenaline and joy swept through me, forcing me off the examination table. I leapt up and down. "Thank you, God!" Minutes later I called my brother. "Hello, Mamud! Surgery went really well . . . she'll be awake in the next couple of hours."

CHAPTER TWENTY-THREE

MORE THAN TWENTY-FOUR HOURS AFTER MY MOTHER'S SURGERY, her eyes still weren't open. The only thing keeping my emotions in check was faith. She was supposed to be awake. That's what Dr. Ojo said would happen when he'd finished draining the blood on her brain in the early hours of Saturday, December 3.

So then why was she still lying unresponsive in ICU?

Dr. Ojo ordered another scan that confirmed my worst fear. Her failure to wake wasn't due to a delayed recovery from the operation's anesthesia, as we'd all hoped. There was more cerebral bleeding; another emergency surgery was needed. When she was wheeled out of the operating room the second time, I waited and prayed for her to open her eyes. Instead, she slipped into a coma.

In her curtained-off cubicle in the ICU, she lay under the white bedcovers with just the tops of her bare caramel-colored shoulders showing. The face I'd known and loved all my life was different, disturbingly bloated. Tubes ran into her nose and mouth, both of which were swollen and raw looking. My mum always took pride in her long, beautiful hair. Now it was mostly gone, shorn down to less than an inch on her scalp. A small piece of gauze rested gently over the deep indentation on the right side of her head, a remnant of the surgeon's efforts to save her life.

Days went by and then weeks. Time merged to create one unending nightmare. There were moments when I became convinced that she was just in the deepest stage of sleep rather than a coma. I shook her forearm gently and called out "Mum" with the child-like belief that I would somehow be able to wake her. Her inert body rocked from side to side, undisturbed by my actions. She was off somewhere else, far beyond my reach. I wondered what she was doing in that other place, whether she was in the sunshine or troubled by shadows. Did she feel at peace, or could she sense the grief of her two children, who were utterly lost without her?

My days quickly became carbon copies of one another. Mornings and afternoons were spent at the hospital, then I was back in my hotel room by early evening. Most nights I cried and agonized about what to do next before falling into a fitful sleep.

My mum had been in a coma for a couple of weeks when I got a tip. It was December 19, and Eric, a well-informed friend from the United States who just happened to be in Lagos, stopped by to see me. He mentioned that the twenty-one girls were going to Chibok to spend Christmas with their families. "They are demanding to go home," he said.

I stared at him intently.

He waved me off. "But don't go asking questions. If you do, the government will know the trip plans leaked out and they might scrap the whole thing."

I nodded, feeling a bolt of excitement. The girls were finally going back to their long-bereft and beloved community, and at such a special time of year!

Once he left, I tried to push the news to the back of my mind, knowing there were far more pressing things to deal with, given my mother's medical situation. But I couldn't let it go. I needed to know if the trip was actually going to happen. So I made some discreet inquiries. The next morning I got my answer. The girls were leaving for Chibok shortly.

I have to go with them.

The thought flashed through my mind, then it was gone almost instantly. I felt ashamed that I'd considered leaving my mother's side, even for a few seconds. I busied myself with her care. But before long the thought was back.

I should take them home. The world should see this homecoming.

My mind was moving fast now, already considering how long the trip to Chibok would take. Could I do it in two days? I reached out to a contact in the Nigerian government and floated the idea of a CNN crew traveling to Chibok with the girls. I got no response.

While I sat in ICU that day, I kept asking myself if it was appropriate to even contemplate leaving my mother to travel to Chibok. Was I interested in going only because of my ego, wanting to be *the* journalist who got the story? What if something happened to her while I was gone? What if something happened to *me* out on the road? Each question produced more guilt and brought into focus my selfishness. I felt wretched and sank deeper into inner turmoil.

But then another question arose: What would my mum say if she knew about my opportunity to take the twenty-one girls home and exclusively bring the world the story? I heard her voice crystal clear in my head. *Go! You should be the one to tell this story!*

Mum had always been my biggest advocate. As a sixteen-year-old, I'd decided I wanted to stay behind in London instead of returning to Freetown with her and my brother. I harbored teenage dreams of becoming an actress. Not once did she undermine or call into question my youthful ambition. "If this is what you really want, then okay, you can stay. I don't want you to ever look back and say I held you back because your dad died young and I was afraid of being on my own."

When I was thirty, I called her from London and announced without warning that I intended to quit the city and move to America to work for CNN.

Her response was characteristically pragmatic. "What's the plan?"

Her encouragement allowed me to move through the world with a fortified confidence, rooted in the knowledge that I had her unfaltering support.

Now, as I wrestled with the guilt of wanting to accompany the twenty-one girls to Chibok, I feared how others might judge me. But deep down inside I could hear her voice. *I may be in a coma, but life has to go on. These are your sisters. No one else should tell this story. You've been covering it since the beginning, you have to make this journey home with them.*

With her words guiding me, I contacted my boss Mike McCarthy in Atlanta to tell him about the girls' return to Chibok and the possibility that CNN could go with them. Given the dangers associated with travel to the region, Mike alerted senior executives. The network's security consultants were placed on standby.

By December 21, Christmas was within touching distance and traffic in Lagos seemed to have increased exponentially overnight. Nigerians coming home for the holidays flew into Murtala Muhammed Airport and then spilled out onto the megacity's already gridlocked roads and bridges, making getting around an ordeal from sunup to sundown.

In fact, when I got word that the Nigerian authorities had agreed to my proposal of traveling with the girls to Chibok, I was trapped in an overcrowded Lagos parking lot, unable to leave because of a broken-down vehicle. The girls would depart from Abuja the very next morning. I would need to fly to the capital that night.

I was thrilled that my bid had been successful. But then I felt anxiety. I was about to leave my mother without knowing what lay ahead. I would have to get to the hospital to say goodbye and pray with her before getting on any flight. I also needed to inform CNN that the trip was on. I made call after call. I discovered that the network's concerns for the crew's safety in northern Nigeria were even greater than I'd initially understood—so much so, that a security consultant was en route from London to Abuja right then to oversee the trip.

At this point, we had approval to travel only as far as Abuja. Tony Maddox, CNN's international's executive vice-president and managing director, wanted many more details about the security and logistical arrangements settled before he'd sign off on the crew moving farther north into Boko Haram–blighted territory.

Now there was just one other problem: I didn't actually have a crew. I still needed a producer and someone to run camera. I contacted Stephanie Busari, CNN's Lagos-based digital producer. I explained the assignment and we divided tasks. She would track down a camera operator and I'd get details on flights from Lagos to Abuja. Call after call, I still sat in the same choked-off parking lot. I dialed the number for Adeniyi (Niyi) Adekoya, a close personal friend and a longtime CNN security contractor, who sprang into action coordinating flights, hotels, and cars. He immediately sent his car to rescue me from the parking lot where the broken-down sedan continued to create a bottleneck and tempers were fraying. Along with Niyi's car came some extra protection in the form of the burly Mel, who, just as in 2014, was assigned the job of watching my every move.

I still needed to get back to my hotel to pack a bag, get across town to the hospital in Apapa, one of the most congested parts of Lagos, and then turn around and make it to the airport by five p.m.

It was chaotic on the roads, which only intensified the stress I felt about leaving my mother. Her condition was unchanged; she was still in a coma. Since her vital signs were all good, though, the chances of something medically happening to her during my absence were low. But I also knew I was taking a huge—some might say unacceptable—risk with my own safety by venturing into northeastern Nigeria. Life for people living in the states of Borno, Yobe, and Adamawa remained fraught with tension, as the fear of Boko Haram attacks remained ever present.

Back in my hotel, I threw clothes, notepads, pens, chargers, and toiletries into my worn duffel, thinking of ways that I could minimize the attention drawn to myself. My standby baseball cap wouldn't be enough, so I settled on wearing an abaya and hijab. I'd worn the long, flowing gown and a headscarf many times during reporting assignments in Saudi Arabia, and I asked Mel to help find a plain black abaya and headscarf before we touched down in the north. He agreed but was far more preoccupied with keeping us on schedule.

"The traffic is very bad. We have to leave the hotel this minute if we are to catch our flight."

Niyi called. The traffic was so bad, he suggested I abandon the effort to reach my mother before heading to the airport. I refused.

"You have less than fifteen minutes," Mel stressed when we arrived at Lagoon Hospital. The driver was still inching forward when I opened the door to jump out. I headed straight for the stairs, taking them two at a time. While I disinfected my hands and carried out the other safety protocols, I went over things with the nurses and begged them to take extra care of my mother in my absence. I couldn't bring myself to explain why I was leaving or where I was going. I was afraid they'd think I was heartless or irresponsible.

Every single time I walked into my mother's cubicle I was shocked. My brain needed to process the sight of my mother lying silently with her eyes closed all over again. I took her hand in mine and spoke slowly.

"Mummy, if you can hear me, it's your Isha. I have to go away for a few days. I am taking the Chibok girls home. You know how important this story has been to us."

I could feel my voice breaking, but I kept going. "So I'm going to take them home, then come right back to you. You're not going to be alone. Niyi and Uncle Ayo and Aunty Tutu will come and see you every day. And I'll be calling to check on you. I'll be back in a couple of days. Everything is going to be okay. I love you." By the time I started praying for her, my cheeks were wet. "Heavenly Father, look over my mother while I'm gone. Keep her safe from harm. Allow me to come back safely to her." I leaned over the bed rail and kissed her gently on the side of her head, surprised as I always was by the warmth of her skin.

Back on the road to the airport, I was stuck in multiple lanes of traffic for over an hour. Niyi, who was flying to Abuja with me, was driving separately and in the same situation. As it was already after five p.m., we'd abandoned hopes of making the six o'clock flight, but were now rushing to make the seven p.m. one. I wasn't sure *that* was even possible given the gridlock.

Lagos's infamous motorcycle taxis, the *okada*, known for their recklessness and horrific accidents, were the only ones making it through the congestion. In 2012, the state's former governor Babatunde Fashola had barred them from hundreds of Lagos's roads in an attempt to minimize traffic accidents and ease the snarl-ups they habitually caused. Four years later, though, the *okada* continued to be a deadly motorized menace—and now they were my only hope of making it to the airport on time.

Mel flagged down a bike. "We need to get to the domestic terminal, fast fast!" he shouted, pointing at me. The young driver looked over and grinned as I clambered onto the back of his bike and nervously wrapped my arms around his waist. Mel grabbed my duffel, which he pulled onto his shoulders like a backpack, and jumped on an *okada* of his own.

I was barely sitting comfortably when my driver took off up the hill. From the whiny sound coming from his machine, it was clearly straining under our weight. The driver accelerated, weaving in and out of lanes of traffic, and without warning dove onto the pavement, narrowly avoiding pedestrians. My screams filled my ears, and my arms, clammy from his sweaty T-shirt, held on even tighter. I worried I was about to lose my life on a Lagos street, all for a story. *I'm an idiot.* Suddenly we were on the other side of the road, driving straight toward oncoming traffic. My stomach was in my constricted throat and the only words I could get out—"Oh my God! Oh my God! Oh my God!"—seemed to greatly amuse the man holding my life in his hands. I prayed the entire way there.

I don't know how they did it, but Niyi and Mel were standing on the airport street corner, looking relaxed, when we pulled up. It was already after six thirty.

"What about the flight?" I asked.

"Delayed," said Niyi.

Of course it was! I'd risked my life to catch a flight that was delayed. By the time we took off at eight o'clock, I was worn out yet still battling anxiety about my mother, who was lying in a hospital bed across town.

The plan was to fly to Abuja, meet the girls there in the morning, then fly with them to Yola. From there, it would be a six-hour drive to Chibok.

But the moment we touched down in Abuja, questions from CNN management started. What kind of security was being provided by the Nigerian authorities? Were we traveling to Chibok by road or air? Were the vehicles to be soft skinned or armored? Would we have bulletproof vests? Satellite phones? I also learned that

Stephanie and Lucky the cameraman were delayed and wouldn't fly to Abuja until six a.m. the next day.

"Steph, you guys have got to be on that first flight." I struggled to sound calm.

The next morning, I had to deal with the final hurdle for getting the CNN green light to proceed to Chibok: We had to supply pages of personal information to the network's security team detailing emergency contacts and next of kin in the event that things went catastrophically wrong. It was the first and only time I'd had to do this, and the forms even included questions about marks that might help distinguish my body. In that moment, I grasped the magnitude of what I was moving toward.

Meanwhile, Andrew Jones, the security risk specialist who'd traveled from London, was downstairs in the hotel lobby. But I still couldn't reach Stephanie. When I finally got ahold of her, I was relieved.

"Are you here in Abuja?" I asked.

"No, we're still in Lagos. There was a problem with the flight."

I froze. It was eight thirty a.m. Our instructions were very clear. We had to leave the hotel at nine with the government escort, who would take us to the twenty-one girls. Together with the girls, we'd leave for Chibok. With less than thirty minutes to departure, there was no way Stephanie and Lucky were going to make it, leaving me without a producer and camera person. When I hung up I wanted to cry.

"Well, that's it. It's over. You can't go anywhere," Niyi said when I told him.

But I was far from ready to give up. Not having a producer wasn't the end of the world, as I could always produce myself. What really mattered was having someone run camera.

I turned to Mel. "Can you help me find someone?"

I called CNN London and told our handler, Sarah Sultoon, about the situation and the need to find a replacement. As we scrambled, the government escort was waiting for the CNN crew downstairs. It was eight forty-five.

A bright-eyed Andrew appeared in the lobby carrying a large first-aid kit and bags filled with essential safety gear, including a bulletproof vest. I couldn't believe how upbeat and energetic he was, having just spent the last couple of hours flying from London to Abuja at a moment's notice.

"We don't have a producer or cameraman," I told him.

"So what now?" he naturally asked.

I was still trying to figure that out when two men in dark suits walked over and quietly introduced themselves—our escorts.

"I need to wrap something up. Please give me a few more minutes," I lied, stalling for time, before I stepped away. There was no good news from Sarah in London; there weren't any CNN photojournalists on the continent who would be able to make it to Abuja on time. I was losing hope, fast.

Then Mel cleared his throat. "I was able to reach a friend who knows someone who's done work for BBC and Al Jazeera. His name is Tim. He's available."

I couldn't believe what I was hearing. "And he is willing to travel to Chibok?"

"Yes."

The detour was unexpected and unwelcomed, but our escorts agreed. The skinny young man was waiting for us on a street corner.

With our cameraman on board, we drove behind the escort car through the capital city. We eventually passed through a security checkpoint and into a large, sprawling complex where we would meet the girls. No one was milling around. Were these buildings for administrative or residential purposes? As I climbed out of the car I suddenly recognized the brick-covered pathway. This was where the joyous Sunday reunion between the girls and their families had happened weeks earlier. On these same bricks the rain and tears had fallen while the girls and their parents danced and celebrated.

I told Tim to start filming immediately as I walked over and introduced myself to a couple of women standing beneath a covered walkway. They were part of the team involved in the rehabilitation of the girls. Dr. Anne Okorafor helped coordinate logistics around the girls' care.

"How are they doing?' I asked her gently.

"They are doing well. We've been working with them, medically, psychologically. And they've been coming up well. They are learning English, putting on weight . . ."

"Have they had much contact with their families? Some are saying the families are being deliberately kept at bay."

"No, that's not true . . ." She dismissed the criticism that the girls had swapped one version of captivity for another, and were isolated from family members and the outside world. Dr. Okorafor said the girls were able to speak to their parents weekly, and she stressed that the girls needed space if they were to pull off a successful recovery.

She was still speaking when the girls themselves suddenly appeared in their brightly colored outfits, pulling candy-colored luggage behind them. I was stunned. They were completely transformed from the silent, morose girls I'd met in the presidential villa just over two months earlier, now appearing as luminous beings with twinkling eyes and faces lit by broad smiles. They'd put on weight, and their now-plump cheeks were what drew my attention, instead of their previously sharp, bony limbs. There was an unmistakably celebratory mood in the air, with the girls chatting excitedly as they neatly placed their bags on the ground.

The mood remained light even when Dr. Okorafor pointed out that they'd gotten a little ahead of themselves. "It's too soon, you can take your bags back in." There was no grumbling. Once all the bags had been cleared, I decided to go inside to see the girls and say hello. When I stepped through the doors, they momentarily stared at me warily till I reminded them we'd met before. "It's me Isha, from CNN. Remember, I met you at the villa a couple of weeks ago?"

Within seconds, their faces relaxed and big smiles took over as they nodded with newfound recognition. They rushed over to welcome me. "Hello, aunty," they chimed one after another. The warm welcome made me emotional.

"Who wants to take a selfie?" I shouted and pulled out my phone.

Back in the villa, only a handful of girls had shown a real interest in posing for a picture. Now I heard feet racing across the tiles to push and jockey for a place on camera. In such a short time there had been so much monumental change in their lives, as well as in my own.

The girls were to fly on a commercial aircraft to Yola, the capital of Adamawa State, and from there drive to Chibok. But there weren't enough seats for the CNN crew on the flight. We needed four seats but had only two. It took pleading, persistence, and prayer, but against all odds, by the time the bus containing the twenty-one girls pulled into the airport parking lot, I had managed to get two more seats. We were all set.

Tim kept the camera rolling as I stood on the steps of the bus and tried to gauge girls' mood now that the journey home was finally under way.

"Are you excited?"

They mostly smiled and nodded, but there were some who looked uneasy. Dr. Okorafor explained they were nervous about the kind of welcome they'd receive once they got home to Chibok. One girl looked absolutely petrified, her eyes brimming with tears.

I knelt in front of her and tried to allay her fears. "Don't be nervous. Don't be nervous," I said to her bowed head while I held her hand. "You must hold on to your faith, that same faith you held on to in captivity." She didn't respond, but I sensed she was listening and that my words were having some effect.

When it was finally time to board the plane, excitement among the girls surged. They giggled and teased each other. This was a moment they'd imagined and reimagined in the dead of night while they lay on the cold, hard ground in Sambisa Forest. Thoughts of this day had provided comfort when they had only each other. Finally, the journey home had actually begun.

As the girls made their way down the narrow aisle of the plane to take their seats, fellow travelers didn't seem to recognize them, or if they did, they made no obvious show of it. On the seventy-five-minute flight, I dug out the abaya and hijab Mel had bought for me. I let out a loud groan as I held it up to the light and saw the eye-catching gold pattern running all over it. I had no choice but to wear it over my jeans and T-shirt.

The CNN team got off the plane before the girls disembarked, allowing Tim to capture their squeals of delight when they laid eyes on the small group of Chibok community leaders waiting for them on the tarmac. I was moved by the lingering warm hugs and loud laughter, struck by how each and every one of the girls began an encounter with these familiar older faces from home with a momentary bend of the knees to show respect.

While we filmed the heartwarming scene, Andrew was busy with more practical matters. He called CNN Atlanta to provide a report on our whereabouts. As part of the security protocol, we had to check in every couple of hours to give our coordinates.

The small Yola airport bustled with unsmiling DSS officials in smart suits huddled in groups and speaking in hushed voices. Once the reunions between the girls and the Chibok elders were complete, the group was led to a restricted VIP area to meet Jibrilla Bindow, the governor of Adamawa State, who was there to welcome the girls with a large contingent of aides and security officials. We hadn't known the governor would be there. I wondered whether it was a matter of coincidence or an orchestrated plan to share in the limelight.

Meanwhile, there was clearly no urgency on the part of the officials to leave the airport and begin the six-hour car journey to Chibok. But I knew that if we didn't leave soon, we'd be driving into Boko Haram territory in the dark. This would never be approved by the network's security team. And at the same time, a brand-new problem was facing us: the DSS officials at the airport hadn't been notified that a CNN crew would be traveling with the girls. In the absence of an official notification, they weren't prepared to let us go any farther.

I tried to get this straightened out, but they only shrugged. "You'll have to call Abuja. We know nothing about it here."

With the airport delay, the original plan to travel to Chibok that same day was shelved. Instead, everyone was headed to a hotel, and the convoy would leave in the morning. I knew that if my team was detained at the airport, it would be extremely difficult to catch up with the girls again. We had to stay together. I needed a lifeline—fast.

The small VIP area was crammed full. The girls were seated on sofas that framed the edges of the room, but gone was the joy from earlier. They were unsmiling and looked uncomfortable. At the center of the room stood Governor Bindow, surrounded by aides, journalists, and a host of cameras.

I balked at the scene, but I knew the governor was my only chance to get my crew out of the airport and alongside the girls on their journey home. So I pushed through the crowd of people, mumbling "Sorry" as I bumped elbows and deliberately moved bodies out of the way. I positioned myself next to the governor, who was in midflow addressing someone when I stepped forward and interrupted.

"Good afternoon Mr. Governor, Isha Sesay, CNN. It is such a pleasure to meet you." I offered a huge smile, my arm outstretched.

I was clearly the last person he expected to see in his state, let alone following the twenty-one girls. As I was dressed in an abaya and hijab, it took him a few moments to recognize me.

Then a wide, warm smile appeared. "Welcome, Isha!" he shouted and took my hand in his, shaking it vigorously. Right at that moment I knew we'd found our lifeline.

I leaned into his shoulder, not wanting the entire contingent of Nigerian media present to hear. "Mr. Governor, do you think you could give me and my crew a lift to the hotel? Right now we don't have a vehicle," I whispered.

"But of course. Not a problem," he replied.

Governor Bindow insisted I travel in his car, while Andrew, Mel, and Tim rode in a different vehicle within his convoy. I was uneasy about being separated, but given our predicament, I wasn't in a position to refuse.

When I stepped out of the VIP area to follow the governor to his vehicle, a host of microphones and cameras closed in on us. To my horror I realized I might end up as part of the story, plastered on the local Nigerian newscasts that night. So much for my goal of keeping a low profile while in the north! Thankfully, most of the questions were directed at Governor Bindow.

As soon as the questioning ended, we sped down Yola's wide, paved roads toward the hotel. The governor chatted away merrily and I spoke up at the appropriate points, asking the right questions to keep him going, while I stared out the window and marveled at how different the landscape was from Abuja. From the deep reddish-brown sandy earth to the straggly straw-like savanna grass, it was clear we had jumped far north and were embracing the desertification of the Sahel. The sunlight had a stark, unrelenting quality and everything looked dry and parched.

The governor's convoy pulled up at the security barrier at the entrance to the American University Hotel. A line of vehicles swept up the long, pristine driveway fringed with well-manicured hedges, palm fronds, and numerous potted plants. When the vehicles stopped, aides appeared to open car doors. No one paid attention to the metal detector that marked the entrance to the lobby.

When I arrived, the girls were already in the hotel's expansive high-ceilinged lobby; their giggling and chatter filled the space. Tim tried to discreetly capture these relaxed scenes on camera and I stood off to the side taking it all in, staring at their relaxed features and carefree movements. In their new, brightly colored clothing, they were like birds of paradise: beautiful, delicate, and radiating pure joy.

CHAPTER TWENTY-FOUR

THE BRIEF PERIOD I SPENT IN THAT YOLA HOTEL ROOM LISTENING TO the soaring voices of the twenty-one girls before we set off for Chibok had a profound impact on me. Long after they'd stopped singing, I was still sorting through the thoughts and feelings they'd aroused while I watched them worship. Being there had opened a window to their faith, and what I glimpsed was transcendent, all-consuming, and resolute. Faith was the never-ending well from which they had drawn the courage to reject religious conversion and marriage during their time in captivity. It was what had kept them going. When separation from their loved ones tested that faith, it not only endured, but grew. That realization kept me in a state of awe.

My mother's stroke had taken her captive and left me wracked by grief. Now I wondered about my own faith and whether it would endure in quite the same way as theirs had.

At dinner in the hotel restaurant that evening, I couldn't stop staring at them. They looked like an ordinary gaggle of girls, unguarded and untouched by life's cruelties. They chatted and their bodies swayed gently as laughter traveled from their bellies and up into their throats. The sound of joy filled the dining room. I couldn't wait to see them reunited with their families in Chibok, back where they belonged.

We'd be on our way there immediately after breakfast the next morning. But before then, I wanted to speak with a couple of the girls on camera for my CNN report to learn more about their lives since being released ten weeks earlier. I turned to Madame Yanna for help because, as a leader of the Chibok parents' association whose own daughter Rifkatu had been taken and remained missing, I knew she'd be able to convince a couple of the girls to speak to me. Cameraman Tim set up for the interview in the sparsely furnished lobby. Realizing that we had only one wireless microphone for three of us on camera, I felt a flash of annoyance but then reminded myself I was lucky to even have a cameraman. The solution was awkward but it was the best we could come up with: I would sit between the two girls and pass the little microphone back and forth during the conversation.

Soon, Madame Yanna appeared with two of the girls, a nervous-looking Rebecca Mallum and Glory Dama. They both smiled broadly but struggled to maintain eye contact. Instead, their heads remained bowed while they awkwardly twisted and flexed their fingers. Even after we took our places on the snug sofa and I explained what to expect from the interview, they still looked uneasy. Seeing how nervous they were and being conscious of all they'd already endured, I wanted them to feel at ease, much more than I wanted to capture every last detail of their story on camera. My prevailing goal was to avoid retraumatizing them.

"What has life been like for you in Abuja? What have you been doing?" I asked.

Rebecca spoke first, her gaze trained on her lap, her English rusty. "In Abuja, we enjoy and very grateful for them . . . because they protect good . . . they have done good for us. And when we are in Abuja we are playing football. We have English classes . . . we are learning how to speak English and writing very well." Her sentences came out slowly. She smiled shyly between pauses, searching for the right English words.

A note of satisfaction accompanied her revelation about playing football and being back in the classroom in Abuja. In captivity, "playing" had been out of the question. The girls had been denied anything and everything that had brought them joy. Meanwhile, the English classes were a reminder that the girls were still hungry to learn, the reason they'd attended the Chibok Government Girls Secondary School to begin with, in defiance of cultural norms. That hunger clearly hadn't been diminished during their years in Boko Haram captivity.

Glory, a pretty girl with a wide, warm smile and plump cheeks, expressed the same joyful gratitude for the care they were receiving in Abuja. Just like Rebecca, when she spoke it felt like she was trying out the new, unfamiliar words of the English language.

When I'd first met these girls in the presidential villa in Abuja, I'd studied their sallow skin and sad eyes. Now, ten weeks later, Rebecca and Glory sat on either side of me with bright skin and their eyes glinted with joy. I was curious about what they saw when they looked at themselves in the mirror. "You look so different, you've put on weight. How are you feeling from that time to now?"

Rebecca responded. "We are feeling beautiful . . . because since we came . . ." Her words trailed off. She laughed nervously, almost as if she suddenly doubted her own perception.

I smiled encouragingly and coaxed her to continue. "You *are* beautiful," I said firmly and lovingly.

She was suddenly overcome with what seemed to be uncertainty. Her face shut down, as did Glory's. Both the girls' eyes narrowed. Neither was comfortable dwelling on this question. Talking about their physical transformations dredged up difficult memories.

"Are you nervous about how you'll be received back in Chibok?"

They both fidgeted. With chins tucked into their chests they mumbled unintelligible words. Clearly this was another gray zone they didn't want to delve into. With each passing moment, I felt them growing tenser. After a few more unsuccessful attempts to encourage them to share more, I brought the interview to a close.

Judging by the speed with which Rebecca and Glory leapt off the sofa, they couldn't have been any more relieved to have the interview over with.

Walking back to my room, I felt anxious about the girls' and my safety for the next day. We would journey by road to Chibok, traversing terrain on which Boko Haram had frequently terrorized travelers with improvised explosive devices and suicide bomb attacks. Even though we'd be in an armed convoy, surrounded by security experts fully prepped with contingency plans, anything could happen. Essentially, the situation was out of our hands.

I felt the same sort of powerlessness with my mum's condition. There was nothing I could do to wake her from the coma. The only thing I had power over were the prayers I said for my safety and everyone making the journey in the next couple of hours, as well as for my mother, who was marooned in a different dimension.

I eventually climbed into bed near midnight, but I found it difficult to sleep. My mind churned and I couldn't get comfortable on the hard hotel mattress.

I was still tired when the sound of singing pervaded my dreams just before dawn. But even through the fog of my fatigue, I knew what I was hearing and was deeply moved by the girls' early-morning devotion. The soothing sounds of their faithfulness filled the hotel's corridors and buoyed my spirits.

I showered and dressed for the journey, but unlike the day before, when I occasionally took the flowing abaya off and wandered throughout the hotel without concern that I'd be recognized or might offend someone, now we were headed beyond the walls of the American University Hotel. I could no longer afford such risks. I put on the gown and headscarf.

The girls were going home to spend the holidays with their families, but I wouldn't be staying. My plan was to drop them off in Chibok and return to Yola that same evening. I grabbed my essentials: a notepad, a couple of pens, my phones, all the Nigerian naira I had with me, and dumped it all in my black backpack. The extra clothing and toiletries I stuffed in my black duffel bag and left it in a corner of the room to await my return from Chibok later that same day.

I was waiting in the mostly deserted lobby when the girls passed through on their way to breakfast. To my surprise, each one of them paused as she walked past, wrapped her arms around me in a gentle embrace, and whispered "Good morning." Twenty-one hugs from these girls who'd been through so much stirred me; I felt tears gathering. I was forming a bond with them, and their gesture reminded me of that and served as an affirmation of my difficult decision to leave my mother in Lagos.

The girls tucked into a morning buffet of fresh fruit, Nigerian breakfast staples of yams, noodles, and spicy stews, as well as eggs, breakfast potatoes, and beef sausage. Meanwhile, outside, multiple trucks—including one with a formidable looking antiaircraft gun—along with buses and other military vehicles moved into place. I was taken aback by the scene spread out across the driveway: a mass of security officials in various colored uniforms, many with rifles slung casually over their shoulders, some in black helmets. Others sported green berets and several wore bulletproof vests. Right in front of the hotel's double doors sat a white minibus to carry the twenty-one girls and their community leaders back home to Chibok.

The Nigerian military and police had readied themselves for this journey of incredibly high stakes. Since the administration of Goodluck Jonathan had faced almost universal condemnation for its response to the Chibok abductions, President Buhari's government understood that even the smallest mishap now would catapult it into the same domestic political abyss. Internationally, the fallout would be swift and damaging if anything went wrong.

Given the concerns of a roadside ambush or some other type of attack, the journey from Yola to Chibok had to be completed before dark. This meant our ten-vehicle convoy needed to be on the move for close to six hours and stop only when absolutely necessary. We'd be racing against the setting sun.

Before we left, Governor Bindow appeared again to say goodbye, as Andrew, the CNN security specialist, finalized our plan. This included securing a separate vehicle for us, specifying our position within the convoy, and preparing our tracking equipment and bulletproof vests.

When I got to the car, my vest was waiting.

"I need you to go ahead and put on your vest now," he said in his usual good-natured way.

I was taken aback and a little confused. "You want me to wear it while I'm in the car?" I casually reached down to scoop it up, shocked by its weight; I needed both hands to lift it. Andrew helped me put it on, and when he finally got it over my head, I groaned from the weight of the two metal plates protecting my chest and back.

While the CNN team readied itself for departure, the twenty-one girls and their assortment of rainbow-colored suitcases on wheels emerged from the hotel. It was time to set off.

As we made our way through Yola, the town's young and old stopped on the side of the road and stared. The sight of such a large convoy crammed with armed soldiers and police triggered looks of apprehension. This town, like many others in Adamawa State, had felt the sting of Boko Haram's deadly violence. With the convoy's weapons brazenly displayed, we proceeded at a steady pace, dominating the uneven roads as we moved.

We passed large tracts of undeveloped land; the fierce northern sun had left the soil baked hard and parched. I sat silent. No one was in the mood for mindless chatter. We all understood the stakes were too high.

We passed through a litany of towns including Gombe, Song, and Hong, all of which had been blighted as recently as 2015 by repeated Boko Haram attacks that had left scores of residents dead, with countless structures—government buildings, schools, shops, and churches—either riddled with bullets or burned to the ground.

As with Chibok, life in these towns looked hard, all efforts centered on working the land and keeping cattle. The few roadside convenience stores we passed were bleak, dust-covered structures. Clusters of mud-walled homes could be glimpsed behind crumbling, sloping fences. Half-finished cement-block buildings dotted the route. Even the trees, gnarled with branches hung low and leaves shriveled and drooping, seemed to add to the sense of desolation.

Just before we crossed into the town of Mararaba Mubi, our security detail shifted from the dozens of soldiers who'd left Yola with us to a new contingent of soldiers who would continue on with us after that boundary area.

After five hours of navigating long stretches of pitted-out roads, we stopped in that small town within the Hong local government area. Just two years earlier, Boko Haram had attacked it and sent its terrified residents fleeing. Now Mararaba Mubi found itself in the terror group's crosshairs whenever it launched an attack on one of several strategically important towns nearby.

We headed straight to a gas station in the middle of a bustling intersection for fuel. A handful of armed soldiers fanned out and formed a loose cordon around the minibus.

The area surrounding the gas station, meanwhile, was a riot

of sound and activity. Roadside tables were loaded with an assort-ment of fresh fruit and local snacks—fried bean cakes and yams. Street sellers hawked household wares, jostling for business next to a strip of small shanty stores loaded with canned goods, soaps, body creams, cookies, noodles, flashlights, drinks, and snacks.

The pause in the journey was a welcome break. My back ached from the weight of the bulletproof vest, and I needed to get more footage to help viewers understand the trip. Before I opened the car door I carefully scanned my surroundings, checked my abaya, and then pulled the folds of my headscarf closer to my face.

As soon as I stepped into the energy-sapping heat, I sensed that something wasn't right. Groups of men were clumped together on the side of the road, staring intently at the convoy. I looked around nervously. There was no time to dwell on my unease. I had to come up with something to say and capture it on camera before the con-voy got moving again. Droplets of sweat gathered under my black abaya and hijab.

When Tim pointed the camera at me, it took me three attempts to say "Mararaba Mubi" correctly.

So the convoy has stopped in a town called Mararaba Mubi, which is about an hour away from Chibok. The movement of the convoy, through these parts, such a well-armed con-voy, is drawing attention from passersby. . . .

I was rattled.

After getting our shot, I checked on the girls, wondering how they were feeling now that Chibok was only an hour away. I stood in the bus doorway and tried to make conversation. The girls seemed pensive, answering my queries with low-key smiles and half nods.

"Does anyone want a drink?" I asked.

Only a few registered the offer. The rest shook their heads or looked away.

Even so, I still wandered over to the shops, moving quickly and keeping my head down. Mel was by my side, his short, stocky body tense and his eyes darting from side to side. The stores were cramped and overwhelming. Items for sale hung from the ceiling, covered the walls, and occupied every space on the floor. Mel talked with the shopkeepers while I stood quietly. We walked back to the minibus with an assortment of soft drinks, potato chips, nuts, and cookies. For all the girls' initial reluctance, their response was as I'd hoped. The treats were happily received.

Thirty minutes later we were back on the road, and before long we came into the girls' home state of Borno, which, alongside Adamawa and Yobe, had been under the state of emergency imposed by President Jonathan back in 2013 when the conflict with Boko Haram was at its bloodiest high point. Signs of the long-running conflict were impossible to ignore. Rusted tanks and artillery sat conspicuously idle on the side of the road.

As we neared the outskirts of Chibok, bulbous rock formations dominated the horizon. Their appearance gave the arid landscape an otherworldly feel and intensified my sense of being far off the beaten track. The closer we got to Chibok town, the more the road conditions deteriorated, the gouges growing deeper and wider, forcing the convoy to slow considerably.

Before arriving in Chibok for the first time that day, I'd been reporting on the town for two and a half years. I'd seen the images of the town, read and reread accounts of what had happened when Boko Haram brought terror to these parts on April 14, 2014. I'd spoken to parents, young girls, and others who hailed from this community.

And yet Chibok had remained a vague, almost illusory place in my mind. Now actually arriving there, and seeing with my own eyes the faded matchbox cement houses with roofs made out of rusted corrugated-iron sheets, the collectives of mud and thatched dwellings all lining the sandy road, was surreal.

The few cars lumbered past slowly, mindful of the treacherous road surface. A far more common sight was a man wearing traditional floor-length robes over flowing trousers with opened-toed sandals pushing an aged bicycle with strangely large wheels. A young boy, probably eight or nine, in a faded yellow open-neck shirt sat on a worn wooden bench behind a compact table displaying his wares: six little off-white sticks of yam. He watched the vehicles of our convoy pass with a sad expression that didn't change. Groups of men lounged in front of houses as sheep grazed in front yards or amid inhospitable-looking fields.

As the military convoy appeared in Chibok town, residents noticed. People looked up from their spots in front of their homes, traders manning small roadside tables strained necks to see what was happening. People waved excitedly, children squealed as the community realized their girls were finally home. The excitement grew as we made our way through town to a large house behind compound walls, which belonged to a local politician. It was midafternoon when the girls disembarked and were ushered inside. Beyond the compound's walls, I noticed a large pile of sand in one corner, as well as an open pit in the middle of the yard with an eight- to ten-foot drop, at which point I realized that parts of the house were still being constructed. Past the front door, we found ourselves in a large room with no other furniture apart from white plastic chairs. The walls of the room were painted a curious mix of cream from ceiling to halfway down, then a pink-toned lilac from midway to the dark concrete floor.

The girls eagerly seated themselves, grinning widely, chatting excitedly as they looked about. Peals of laughter rang out, giving the room a celebratory feel. They were finally back and everyone was ecstatic, all of us savoring this homecoming, which had been years in the making.

We'd been waiting for half an hour when a soldier stepped into the middle of the room. Brigadier General Omoigui, of medium height with a muscular physique, moved in a self-assured way. He gave the distinct impression that he was the man in charge and more than comfortable with the authority he wielded. He cleared his throat and introduced himself. I was prepared for a warm welcome, but not for what he said next, addressing the girls.

"Due to ongoing military operations in and around your homes and the lack of security, we will not be able to let you go home."

The faces of the girls changed as his words registered.

"We have made arrangements for you to spend the Christmas period here in this house. Your families will have free access to come here and spend time with you."

By the time he'd finished speaking, every girl in the room was wailing. In the blink of an eye the joyous homecoming had become a nightmare.

All around me girls doubled up in grief. It felt like an emergency.

I tried to console them. "Don't cry, we'll work something out."

Nothing made any difference. They were too far gone. Having traveled so far, having held out hope for so long, they couldn't hold their emotions in check.

The Nigerian military was wrecking the girls' homecoming. I stood up, searching for the brigadier general. I spotted him on the patio surrounded by other soldiers. When I stepped outside, the men stared at me, perplexed looks on their faces.

I calmly introduced myself and then launched into my complaint. "These girls have been waiting for two and half years to come home and now they get here, and you tell them they can't go home?" I was struggling to keep my composure.

"It is for their own safety," the brigadier general responded. "We are still conducting operations in various parts of Chibok. It just is not safe for them."

"But you see how distraught they are. They got on the bus expecting one thing and now this?" My frustration was making it difficult for me to get the words out.

"We are assessing which areas are safe for the girls and once we know, those girls will be allowed home to their families."

"You obviously knew all of this before the girls got on the bus," I protested. "I don't understand why you let them travel all the way here believing they were going to their homes. This was obviously your plan all along. It's very painful, what you have done." I hoped I'd somehow be able to change his mind.

"They will be safe here. And their families will be able to come and stay here with them. As I said, those areas we deem to be safe, the girls can go home to those places." Though Omoigui had a kind face, he spoke firmly.

I felt deflated; this was not the homecoming any of us had imagined, one where only *some* of the girls could actually go home. Meanwhile, inside the big room, the scene remained unchanged, the girls were still wailing.

It was late in the day, that time when the sun casts a warm, golden glow on everything, including the long line of parents gathered outside the compound, waiting to see their daughters. The fathers huddled together at the front, while the women dutifully took their places behind them. The mix of vivid patterned fabrics—reds, greens, oranges, and yellows—on the mothers brought much-needed relief to a blanched and wizened landscape. The harshness of life was inscribed in the deep furrows on the faces of these parents. The mothers and fathers stood quietly, staring at the compound that separated them from their children. Their eyes brightened as General Omoigui arrived to address them, and a murmur rippled through the crowd. He stood there for a few seconds, sizing them up, his face relaxed and his lips set in a slight smile, taking measure of the situation. He seemed friendly and nonthreatening.

Mallam Nkeki, the chairman of the Chibok Parents' Association whose niece had also been kidnapped from the Chibok school, stood by the general's side ready to translate his speech into Hausa and Kibaku, the dominant languages in this corner of Nigeria. He told the parents that their daughters would not be heading home with them. Remarkably, any anger they felt remained concealed. They listened with grim-faced stoicism, laughing only when Omoigui told them he understood how much the mothers wanted to smother their babies with affection and keep them close morning, noon, and night. "But I'm sure it is more important to you that they remain safe," he said.

All the parents nodded in agreement. There were no objections, no requests for further explanation or discussion. The parents had been waiting years to see their girls back home in Chibok, and they had no appetite to wrangle with the Nigerian military. They just wanted to be with their children. They began shuffling slowly toward the compound gate, where they were lightly frisked before being allowed to enter. I trailed the group, still stunned by how easily these parents had taken the bombshell news, unlike their daughters. Soon, whoops and screams of joy erupted as families laid eyes on each other. Within seconds, the girls were out of their chairs and rushing toward outstretched arms. It was only then, within these loving embraces, that the daughters could exhale and finally accept that they were home.

I did my best to stand out of the way as loved ones rushed all around me and more people poured in. Before long the large space was full. There were scenes of overjoyed girls surrounded by parents, unbridled love and relief on all the faces everywhere I looked. Every few minutes the joyful sounds of celebration would peak as fresh reunions took place, and I was soon overwhelmed by noise. So much so that, at first, the new sounds didn't register. I heard the high-pitched voices, but it took a couple of minutes before my senses detected that something wasn't right. I looked through the throng of people and saw Madame Yanna, one of the Chibok community elders, weeping bitterly and being propped up by the arms of those around her. I moved over to see what was wrong. As women's leader of the association of Chibok girls, she had to be present for this momentous occasion, but the reality of watching joyful parents and children reunite was simply too much for this aching mother who yearned for the return of her daughter Rifkatu and now simply couldn't control her grief.

I made my way through the crowd and put an arm around her to draw her close. Her chest rose and fell heavily as she sobbed. Hands of the women around us reached out and smeared away her tears as they fell. I knew from the few conversations we'd had before this journey to Chibok that she was a woman of immense faith.

"You have to be strong, Madame Yanna, and believe that Rifkatu will come back, the same way these girls did. Your faith must remain strong," I said.

She listened and nodded gently, but the tears still came.

More strange sounds drew me to the next room. At the far end, a handful of women were on the ground. It took a few seconds to realize they were crying out in pain. They too were mothers of Chibok schoolgirls who were still lost.

I learned that somehow, when word had reached Chibok about the girls' homecoming for Christmas, it triggered the mistaken belief that *all* the hundreds of girls in Boko Haram's captivity had been released and that the entire group was headed home. And because there was no process to screen and verify family members before they entered the compound, these women had walked right past the military into the house to be reunited with their kids. Only now did they learn their daughters were still in captivity.

I crouched down in an attempt to comfort these mothers, but this time my words sounded hollow. "Don't cry. Your daughters will come back soon." I wanted to believe in the same way they did—I just didn't know how long it would take for their daughters to return to them.

It was a strange and uncomfortable scene: pockets of suffocating grief surrounded by family members laughing, bright eyed, hugging and squealing with delight. Tim turned on his camera so I could record another piece.

"There has been such an outpouring of grief amid the joy. The piercing screams of mothers realizing that indeed, they are not to be reunited with their daughters on this day, which has turned what should have been an overwhelmingly happy moment into a bittersweet one."

Andrew looked over at me and pointed to his watch. We needed to wrap things up and get going. The girls were now spread out among the different empty rooms, some sprawled out on the floor, others with their backs against the walls and their shoes off, all surrounded by relatives. Among the returned, their anger seemed to have melted away. I wandered about to say goodbye and share warm embraces with "my sisters," as my mother always called them.

In a corner of the main room, I found Priscilla kneeing beside her father's feet, her head bowed. When I reached her side, she looked up. It was clear she'd been crying.

"What's wrong?" I gently touched her shoulder.

She refused to explain, pressing her lips shut and shaking her head. I later learned she was upset that her mother wasn't there with her father.

Her father, a painfully thin man with angular features and dressed head to toe in white, took my hand in both of his and held it there, speaking a language I didn't understand. I could read the warmth in his eyes, though, and the phrase he kept repeating touched my heart. He was saying thank you again and again. He said the words and shook my hand vigorously to emphasize his gratitude.

"You're welcome." I smiled in return. "You're welcome."

My team had stayed longer in Chibok than we were supposed to. It was already five p.m. The families were all happily engrossed in each other, so no one looked up as I left. In a flash, I was back at our car parked outside the compound gate, my bulletproof vest in place.

I'd had no time to process what had just happened. The mix of emotions had been overwhelming. I had left my mother in a hospital bed in Lagos, on the promise of a joyous homecoming and the page being turned on years of horror and heartbreak. And I wasn't entirely sure of what I'd actually found in Chibok. The girls had been denied the one thing they wanted above all—the chance to return to their own homes, to sleep and worship among their loved ones. And if anything, I had encountered much more pain, with the sharper, deeper sting of mothers trying to remain hopeful as they watched other families reunited while their daughters remained out of reach. I was grateful when our car doors slammed shut, and the open-backed vehicles of our police escort took off flying down the road. We followed the trail of dust. Despite our breakneck speed, the skies above us grew dark while we were still driving to Yola. But by this point, fatigue had gone a long way toward numbing my fears, and I simply refused to worry.

The next evening, the traffic around the Lagos airport was just as horrific as it had been when I'd left for Chibok a few days earlier. It took well over an hour to reach the hospital. When I finally saw my mother, nothing had changed. Her eyes remained closed and she lay on her back, the tops of her bare shoulders peeking out from under the off-white sheets, her arms solidly by her sides. My eyes burned with tears that wanted to fall but were stuck. I reached for her hand. "Mum, I'm back from Chibok," I told her. "I'm safe." Standing by her side once more, I felt gratitude. She was safe and I'd been able to take a story full circle—one that would always mean a great deal to us. The trip to Chibok hadn't been the emotional high I'd hoped it would be, but I had come back with a heart that was full. I'd seen the indescribable joy of parents and their children reunited, and I'd done something that would have pleased my mother and pushed my heart toward bursting with joy. "Mum, I took the Chibok girls back, and now I have come back to you."

I longed for a miracle, a sign, no matter how small, to show me she heard my voice, but there was nothing.

CHAPTER TWENTY-FIVE

MY MUM WAS FINALLY STABLE ENOUGH TO BE MOVED TO THE UNITED States a couple of months after my trip to Chibok. We left Lagos on February 26, 2017. She'd spent almost twelve weeks in Lagoon Hospital's intensive care unit and had been in a coma for more than half that time. When we finally boarded our flight, I found myself altered immeasurably. I knew that some of the changes only I was aware of, and others you could spot from a mile off, like my strengthened faith. Then there were other smaller, subtler alterations that emerged later, once we were settled in Los Angeles and my life slowly shifted to a new version of "normal."

While I juggled hospital visits, consultations with doctors, and seemingly endless hours of covering the Trump presidency for CNN, which at times felt like covering a raging Dumpster fire, I thought a lot about Priscilla, Bernice, and the other nineteen girls from Chibok. Thanks to relationships I'd formed over the years with several people in their orbit, I could keep track of their progress. Once I started work on this book, trips back to Nigeria for interviews and research allowed me to see for myself the ways in which the girls were adjusting to life far from the forest and their captors. With their straitened circumstances undoubtedly front of mind, the parents of the twenty-one girls turned over to the Nigerian government the cost and responsibility of educating their freed daughters after they were released in October 2016. For almost a year they were kept in a government-run rehabilitation center in Abuja, where a staff of teachers, doctors, psychologists, and others made their academic studies, as well each girls' physical, emotional, and psychological well-being, the priority.

Every time I saw Priscilla, she was a little more whole. I could see the sadness receding, while joy and confidence showed more of themselves in her personality. She was increasingly able to hold eye contact, and her voice was no longer just a faltering whisper. During our interviews, we would invariably collapse into a fit of giggles after she subjected me to a long, quizzical look or a sideways glance loaded with ridicule—her response to a question I'd asked. I called those our "lost in translation moments," but as her understanding of English improved and she became more capable of fully expressing herself, these moments occurred less often. Eventually Priscilla would hug me warmly every time I turned up. There were always selfies to be taken with wide smiles and beaming eyes before another warm hug, and she would then disappear out the door. Then and now, I struggle to fully make sense of the warmth and openness this girl from Chibok still possesses after all she has endured.

For Esther Yakubu, there has been no progress; she doesn't have stories of her daughter's healing to share. More than four years have passed since Dorcas disappeared, and Esther continues to count the days until her beloved returns. During these long years of separation, this mother of five has slowly morphed into a ghost of her former self. All joy has ebbed away, leaving her lifeless. She laments that God keeps her in a world without her firstborn by her side. She does her best to wade through the unending anguish, to be present for her remaining four children, all of whom miss their big sister terribly. They also mourn the mother they lost the day that Dorcas disappeared.

When Esther learned her Dorcas wasn't among the twenty-one girls released on October 13, 2016, she was heartsick, but her faith steadied her through the tears. She continued to profess that her daughter would return to her soon. But she was as surprised as the rest of us when the Nigerian army announced the sudden appearance of two more Chibok schoolgirls within weeks of each other. Maryam Ali Maiyanga and her ten-month-old son, Ali, were discovered by the military on November 5, 2016, among a larger group of men, women, and children—all of them escapees from Boko Haram captivity. Eight weeks later, on January 5, 2017, Rakiya Abubakar Gali and her six-month-old baby were found among a group of more than one thousand Boko Haram suspects detained by the Nigerian military during raids on camps in Sambisa Forest. Rakiya was the twenty-fourth Chibok girl to gain her freedom. Like Amina Ali Nkeki, who escaped in 2016 with her young baby, all of these girls are believed to have once been wives of Boko Haram fighters and their children the products of those unions.

On every occasion that Esther learned of more freed girls, she wept bitterly but consoled herself with the thought they might bring with them some news of Dorcas. But once photos of Maryam and Rakiya were made public, the young women disappeared from view. No further information was ever released.

When on Sunday, May 7, 2017, the Nigerian government broke the news on Twitter that another eighty-two Chibok girls had been set free, as part of an exchange deal "for some Boko Haram suspects held by the authorities" after "lengthy negotiations,"

Esther and those closest to her felt hopeful again. The tweet by the presidential spokesman Garba Shehu announced, "The released #ChibokGirls are due to arrive in Abuja today Sunday May 7, and will be received by the President." Maybe this time Dorcas was on her way home. They all held out hope for better odds because the group of girls being released was so much larger than before. Everyone in the small, tightly knit community of Chibok, where so many people were related to each other, joined in prayer as they waited for the girls' names to be made public. Esther, now living in Abuja, sought comfort from the Bring Back Our Girls family that day, which had gathered at the Unity Fountain in Abuja for its daily sit-in. The hours went by. No names emerged.

Esther was interviewed by the BBC and sounded decidedly sanguine. "Whether she is among the freed ones or not, I am very happy," she said. "We started this year with twenty-four [returned girls] and now we have one hundred and six. It is a large number, and we have hoped that, if they are alive, they will come back. I have never been happy in my life like today. I am a mother. I accept any child that is back. My baby will be back soon, if she is among them or if she isn't."

It was late Sunday night by the time the office of the president put the eighty-two names on Twitter, a somewhat curious move given that many people in a place like Chibok have limited access to social media.

Filled with anxiety, Esther immediately went through the list. Her baby's name was not there. Again. She looked several more times before her hope turned to sand. She had to accept that her girl was still someplace else, far from home.

To a woman whose public grief had in many ways come to represent the agony felt by the hundreds of Chibok mothers, it was another monumental blow. A few days after the world learned that eighty-two schoolgirls had been exchanged for five Boko Haram commanders who had been in Nigerian custody, we also learned

through another video released on May 12, 2017, by a Nigerian journalist, Ahmad Salkida, that a number of other girls in captivity had
actually rejected the opportunity to return home. Roughly three-
and-a-half minutes long, the video features four girls in full-length
black veils who are completely covered except for their eyes. One
of the girls casually holds an AK-47 and answers questions posed to
her in Hausa by a man off camera, said to be Shuaibu Moni, one of
the five commanders handed over by the Nigerian government in
exchange for the eighty-two girls.

Moni: Which school were you attending?

Girl: GSS Chibok.

Moni: Why don't you want to return to your parents?

Girl: I don't want to return because they are living in the city of
infidels; we want them to come and follow this religion for us to
have rest in heaven.

Moni: Some people are saying that you are being forced into
marriage, is this so?

Girl: No. It is not so. Among us are those who agree and accept
to get married.

Moni: What is your message to your parents?

Girl: My message to them is for them to repent and follow Allah's religion for our salvation.

Moni: What is your appeal to Nigerians?

Girl: My call to Nigerians is that they should leave the book
that is not that of Allah and follow the Sunna [the sayings
and deeds of the prophet]. Allah's religion will move forward
whether you like it or not. If you don't agree you will die in
your misery.

The girl in the video, calmly wielding the AK-47 and speaking
in a clear, steady voice, was asked her name.

"Maida Yakubu," she readily replied.

But Esther had only needed to hear the voice from behind the veil for a split second to know without a doubt it was indeed her Dorcas. The very first time she laid eyes on the images, Esther crumbled.

"For me, this video is torture." She spoke plainly to the media about what she was going through. "I haven't slept since I watched it. The tie that binds us is unbreakable. It's just not possible that my daughter prefers her kidnappers to me."

The searing image of her daughter so completely transformed initially erased all hope of her ever holding her child again. Since then, though, she has fallen back on her steadfast faith. It continues to be her defense against hopelessness. Esther repeats to herself and to anyone who will listen that her daughter's statements must have been made under duress.

Aside from seeing Dorcas looking and sounding like an alien being to her own mother, most painful of all for Esther was watching the freed Chibok girls go back to school. On September 15, 2017, a total of 106 Chibok girls—Priscilla plus nineteen of the girls she was freed with, alongside the group of eighty-two released just a few months earlier in May and Amina Ali Nkeki, Maryam Ali Maiyanga, and Rakiya Abubakar (the three girls who escaped with babies)—all headed to the American University of Nigeria (AUN) in Yola. Only one girl, Deborah, baby Amos's mother, refused to return to school, choosing to return to her husband and family instead. This private institution, founded by Atiku Abubakar, a former Nigerian vice-president, in partnership with the American University in Washington, DC, is their home for the foreseeable future. They are enrolled in the New Foundation School (NFS) Chibok Education Initiative—a university preparatory program specially designed for the Chibok girls. Their school fees and a monthly allowance is paid by the Nigerian federal government. The program was actually established in August 2014 with eleven students who escaped in the immediate aftermath of the mass abduction that

April night and rose to twenty-four escaped students by the end of 2014. The New Foundation School academic courses include twelve subjects—English, math, business studies, basic technology, civic education, biology, physics, chemistry, agricultural science, social studies, and computer studies, according to school officials. This is paired with extracurricular activities such as singing, dancing, drama, yoga, and an array of competitions in spelling, debate, and public speaking, all designed to help students "discover their talents, voices, literacy, leadership and critical thinking." Given the trauma Priscilla and her schoolmates have suffered, each one of them is also part of a psychological health support program. They live together on campus, separate from the rest of the AUN students, and they head home during the Christmas and summer breaks. For Esther, seeing these girls advance toward a dream she'd long held for her Dorcas was gut wrenching. She still imagines a future for her baby. Except these days, with images of a dark-veiled Dorcas rooted in her thoughts, dreams of college no longer shine quite as brightly as they once did.

For Bring Back Our Girls' Aisha Yesufu, one of the cruelest parts of this sprawling tragedy has been the Buhari administration's "victimization" of outspoken parents like Esther. The government, angered by Esther's public calls to rescue Dorcas, sent her a warning. "If you have anything to do with BBOG, we will not bring back your daughter." Initially Esther dismissed the words. But as the years went by and Dorcas remained lost even as other parents were reunited with their girls, Aisha watched Esther slowly internalize the threat. Aisha visited the Yakubu home on June 8, 2018, the day Dorcas turned twenty in Boko Haram captivity. By then, Esther had fully internalized the guilt. "It is my fault my baby is still not back," she told Aisha.

Aisha has watched grief consume not only Esther, but also countless other Chibok families, moving like a disease through the community. Chibok, in northeastern Nigeria, is located in perhaps the most educationally regressive region in the country. In this part of the world, the girls who make it into school and manage to keep going do so, more often than not, because of their mothers. Women fight and cajole fathers to allow their daughters to have a decent shot at life and an education. When the 219 Chibok girls disappeared in the middle of the night, many of those fathers turned to their wives with accusatory looks. In some cases, they said without hesitation, "This is your fault." As a result, blame and guilt have moved through Chibok with a destructive force, leaving heartbroken mothers struggling to find their footing in shattered families.

In this landscape of fear, pain, and brokenness, Aisha Yesufu and others from Bring Back Our Girls remain committed to fighting until Dorcas and every one of the 111 other girls have been accounted for.

"The rescue of the Chibok girls is not a privilege. It is their right as enshrined in the constitution of the Federal Republic of Nigeria. We want all our girls to be accounted for so we can move on with our lives." Time and again, Aisha spoke with her trademark passion.

Meanwhile the Buhari government's animosity toward the Bring Back Our Girls movement remains as intense as ever. Upon the release of the twenty-one Chibok girls in October 2016 and the group of eighty-two in May 2017, no active members of BBOG were invited to any of the state-run events marking those joyous occasions. To this day, Aisha Yesufu still has not met a single one of the freed girls for whom she and the other members of BBOG have tirelessly fought.

She remains unfazed.

When the Nigerian military announced on January 4, 2018, that Salomi Pogu, another missing Chibok girl, had been found in northeastern Borno, bringing the total number of freed schoolgirls to 107, Aisha and the rest of Bring Back Our Girls promptly thanked the troops for their actions. But BBOG refuses to turn its gaze away from the 112 girls still in captivity.

The Buhari government, for its part, maintains that it is committed to securing the girls' release. According to a presidential statement released by his spokesman on April 14, 2018, the fourth anniversary of the Chibok abductions:

"This government it is not relenting. We will continue to persist, and the parents should please not give up. Don't give up hope of seeing our daughters back home again. Don't lose faith in this government's ability to fulfil our promise of reuniting you with your daughters. Don't imagine for a moment that we have forgotten about our daughters or that we consider their freedom a lost cause."

The truth is, though, that there is little to indicate the Buhari government is being driven by a sense of urgency to end the nightmare for these girls and their families. President Buhari acknowledged in that same statement that efforts have stalled, saying, "Unfortunately, the negotiations between the government and Boko Haram suffered some unexpected setbacks, owing mainly to a lack of agreement among their abductors, whose internal differences have led to a divergence of voices regarding the outcome of the talks."

Bring Back Our Girls' marches, sit-ins, media interviews, and public advocacy for the lost Chibok girls went on, even as the first prosecutions in relation to the mass kidnapping were secured in 2018. Haruna Yahaya and Banzana Yusuf, two abductors who were both swept up in Nigerian military operations, were brought up before a special court established to try hundreds of Boko Haram suspects. The thirty-five-year-old Yahaya admitted his involvement in the mass kidnapping and was given two fifteen-year jail sentences. Yusuf, whose age is unknown, received a twenty-year sentence for "planning and kidnapping" the girls.

In fact, BBOG's focus has expanded, and the group has become a voice for the easily marginalized girl in Nigeria. When a Boko Haram faction kidnapped 112 schoolgirls between the ages of eleven and nineteen from the Government Girls' Science and Technical College and one boy from the town of Dapchi on February 19, 2018, the movement took up the cry and mounted a public pressure campaign for their safe return, which happened a couple of weeks later, on March 21, 2018. The release of the Dapchi schoolgirl Leah Sharibu, the only Christian among them and the sole abductee still in captivity at the time of this writing in 2018 (reportedly because of her ongoing refusal to convert to Islam), is now a another key BBOG demand.

That's not to say that the movement's public advocacy hasn't taken a toll on Aisha and many of the other members, like cofounder Oby Ezekwesili. It has, greatly. Unlike Oby, before the events in Chibok, Aisha Yesufu was unknown to most Nigerians. Back then, she made a quiet living from her business interests and focused the rest of her energies on caring for her husband and children. These days her trademark red hijab and soul-stirring speeches at the Unity Fountain have made her one of the country's most recognizable and polarizing public figures. This notoriety is unwelcomed by Aliyyah, who's made no secret of her displeasure.

"Mummy, since the Chibok girls, you have changed," Aisha's daughter said to her. "You used to be more fun and now you worry so much. I can't wait for the Chibok girls to be back, so I can have my mummy back." Aliyyah's words haven't lost their power to sting, but the fight for the Chibok girls isn't one she feels she can ever abandon.

"Even if it takes twenty years of my life, I am ready to give it to Chibok because if I give up on the Chibok girls, it means I have given up on the little girl who was crying to be educated."

By the time I saw Priscilla again, it was August 2018. She was twenty-one years old and nine months had passed since our last interview. I flew to Abuja to spend a week with her, Bernice, and Azizat, their school-dorm mother, with the hope of asking the handful of outstanding questions I needed answered before I could finish this book. When we met on the first day, I found myself speechless for a minute or two while we sat in my hotel room. Priscilla, Bernice, and Azizat occupied the room's three armchairs by the windows, leaving me to sit on the twin bed, closest to them. The changes in Priscilla were impossible to ignore. Her makeup and jewelry were bolder, and though her clothing remained modest, here too I noticed things had shifted. The neckline of her blouse sat a little more off the shoulders, quietly signaling a young woman's growing physical confidence. But by far the biggest change of all was her grasp of English, which I grew more impressed with as the week went on. Bernice too was evolving and sported similar changes in appearance, though when she spoke English there was still a hint of uncertainty as she expressed herself. I made a comment about how much they'd changed, both grinned back at me, giggling happily with a mix of self-consciousness and pride.

I found myself wanting to stomp my feet and cheer for the power of education to transform, for its ability to refashion a girl like Priscilla into an Aisha Yesufu or my own mother. At some point when I hadn't been paying attention, Priscilla had shed the "Chibok girl" moniker and eased into becoming a young woman. I couldn't help but smile when I pictured the shy, nervous girl she had been during my last visit to the American University in November 2017. Back then she'd tenderly cradled the chocolate cupcake I'd handed her, refusing to eat it in my presence. Now in my hotel room, she sat cradling a cell phone, scrolling through its contents, opening and closing its case.

We methodically worked through my list of questions, with Priscilla confirming and expanding on elements she'd shared in past interviews. This was the first time I'd spoken to Bernice in depth. Back in December 2016, when I traveled home to Chibok with them, she'd pointedly refused to answer or even acknowledge my questions. Now, as Priscilla sank deeper into her memories, Bernice nudged her toward more details and greater clarity. At certain points, while they were speaking about what they'd endured in the forest, they both twisted and flopped backward and forward in the hotel armchairs, as if physically wrestling with memories they were reluctant to share with another who hadn't been with them in the forest underneath that giant tree, or in the house in Gwoza where they'd faced constant pressure to marry their captors. In these moments, I repeatedly asked if they wanted to stop and take a break. Priscilla always said no with a faraway look in her eyes.

Midweek I returned to a question we'd talked about before: "How did it feel to know you were finally heading home?" In an earlier interview, Priscilla's answer had been a brief mishmash about joy and faith. This time around, though, she said nothing. Her body slumped forward so that I couldn't see her face clearly. The room fell into silence. I looked over at their chaperone, Azizat.

"Priscilla, are you okay?" I called out softly.

"Priscilla, what's wrong?" asked Azizat.

Priscilla's head remained lowered and she stayed silent. It was only when she raised her hand up to her face that I knew she was crying. In an instant I felt sick to my stomach and guilty. I'd upset her. I'd done the one thing I promised never to do. Within seconds I was off the bed, sitting at her feet and looking up at Priscilla.

I tried to make her tears stop.

"Everything is okay. You made it. You're okay. You're free."

The tears still fell.

I didn't see Bernice get up, but suddenly she was standing by Priscilla's side, while I remained on the floor. I looked over at Azizat, who was intently watching the scene with a knowing look on her face. I was a little puzzled at first, but soon understood.

Within seconds, Bernice was comforting her best friend in their native Kibaku, forcefully drying her tears. Without warning, Bernice pulled the scarf from her best friend's head. This last action made the crying young woman yell out in frustration. Clearly enjoying herself, Bernice slapped Priscilla's hands away and laughed, while she strained in vain to snatch back her head covering.

In that instant, a window opened, and I saw them together in the forest, huddled under that grand tamarind tree. They'd been each other's mother, sister, and best friend, sharing whatever they had and caring for one another during bouts of illness or when despair threatened to take over. I grew emotional watching Bernice ease Priscilla's distress in a hotel room in Abuja, though I didn't understand her words. I could tell from her tone and the look on her face that she was tenderly chiding Priscilla, who was still trying unsuccessfully to break free from Bernice's efforts to wrap the sheath of fabric around her best friend's head.

During our eighteen months of conversations I'd never before seen Priscilla cry. I'd often thought the strength she projected seemed almost superhuman. I accepted it when I thought of the deep, abiding faith that had seen her through. But now, for first time, I began to make out her hidden wounds.

Within fifteen minutes the tears were gone. I was perched on the bed, Bernice was back in her armchair, and Azizat now had an "I told you so" look on her smiling face. Bernice had wound the fabric around her best friend's head to create an elegant wrap, the folds of cloth reminiscent of petals. The new creation Priscilla sported was the only outward sign something had been disturbed within her. Calm returned to the room, and I asked a question I continued to be puzzled by.

"Have you forgiven the boys who took you?"

"Yes, always," said Priscilla matter-of-factly with a genuine smile. "There isn't any three days that I don't pray for them."

"Pray for them for what?" I was incredulous.

"For them to repent on what they're doing. Maybe they don't understand what they are doing, that's why. Because they say what they do is worshipping God and they say killing people is good to God. So we say these people don't know what they are doing."

"And you pray for God to show them?"

"Yes."

I looked over at Bernice, who nodded in agreement. "I forgave them on the first day," Bernice said.

They could tell I was confused. I have struggled to understand the wholesale forgiveness of hundreds of men who stole them from their school, then beat, starved, and terrorized them for months on end. I stared at their faces, searching for any hint of insincerity, but there was none to be found. I looked over at the clock sitting on the table between the twin beds. It was already past four p.m., which meant I was running very late. This was the girls' last day in Abuja, and I'd promised to be finished by three so they could drive around the city and take in the sights. Priscilla was getting restless, groaning and starting to roll her eyes. I pushed on with my last few questions.

"Do you want to travel? Do you have any interest in going abroad?"

Priscilla perked up. "You know, when we were released, there was one place that me and Bernice made a promise, here in Abuja, that by God's grace in life, we will be there . . . one day . . ." Then she suddenly paused.

"Where?" I asked. London or New York? What excited these two?

Priscilla and Bernice looked at each other and giggled uncontrollably before shouting in unison, "Jerusalem!"

It made perfect sense. Both girls were lovers of the Bible; I understood how they'd arrived at the point of wanting to visit the very place they read about almost daily.

"I knew you would say Jerusalem!" Azizat shouted gleefully. "They are completely fascinated by the place, its history, and want to experience it."

Their attention was waning. I asked quickly about their futures, schooling, and marriage. Shrieks filled the room. They told me adamantly that they weren't interested in marriage any time soon, especially after seeing the girls who had married their captors and then instantly regretted it. Bernice dreamed of being a doctor, the same dream Priscilla once had. But for Priscilla, more had shifted within her than I'd realized. She didn't know what career path she desired at that moment, only that she wanted to be "a somebody" and a good person.

I hugged them tightly when it was finally time to say goodbye. Both Priscilla and Bernice are at least a head taller than me, but I felt protective of them. There were selfies and more hugs, and then they were off to find early-evening fun in Abuja.

Hours later as I checked the audio recording of the day's interview, I found myself smiling as I listened to Priscilla singing her favorite song.

Take it away from me
Jesus, take it away from me
Anything that will make me not to serve you
Take it away from me
Anything that will make me not to honor you
Take it away from me

As she sang, her voice carried me back to the dark forest, and there I pictured Priscilla beneath the overbearing tamarind tree. For nearly two and a half years, she had been cut off from everyone she loved and all that she knew. But through it all she never believed she was truly lost. Her faith then and now is her north star, guiding her back to Chibok and toward a future that will touch the hearts of many. For the more than one hundred girls who remain missing, one can only hope that they are still buoyed by a faith that comforts them and that will one day bring them back to their loved ones—home once again, where they belong.

ACKNOWLEDGMENTS

This book would never have become a reality were it not for the bravery of the abducted Chibok schoolgirls and the wider Chibok community—thank you for opening up your hearts and worlds to me. To all those who helped facilitate interviews with the girls, parents, community leaders and deepen my understanding of this subject matter, among them Emmanuel Ogebe, Paul and Becky Gadzama, Zannah Mustapha, Oby Ozekwesili, Reginald Braggs, Kirsti Zitar, Jeremy Anderson, Malea Martin, Rebecca Shane, and Hilary Appel—I owe you a huge debt of thanks. Aisha Yesufu, you continue to use your voice even as others try to silence you—I am grateful for your candor and the faith you have long expressed in this project.

There have been many who have kept me on the path to completing this book, especially while I was juggling my on-air duties at CNN, with caring for my mother—Kwasi Atuah, Ayo Otuyalo, Niyi Adekoya, my baby sister Maggie Kadi, my B-I-L Mamoud Kadi, my baby brother Mamud Sesay, Stacey Brice—each of you were indispensable. My fairy godmother Kathy Eldon who opened up her heart and home, allowing me to write for days on end uninterrupted—you are a gift from God. I love you, Michael, and the Turtletaub clan enormously.

The team at UTA who listens to every idea I have ever had and works to set them in motion—Ryan Hayden, Marc Gerald, Byrd Leavell, and my attorney Nina Shaw, who is always willing to go an extra round for me—thank you. And the amazing team at Dey Street—Jessica Sindler, Lynn Grady—you are literary guardian angels. Bernadette Murphy, you were my editorial rock throughout this journey, asking questions and challenging me to write with more honesty and heart. Every author would be lucky to have you pushing them on—thank you for reading and rereading my pages. This process would not have been as much fun without you.

In some ways, I have been working on *Beneath the Tamarind Tree* since April 15, 2014, from the first moment I learned that Boko Haram had targeted 276 schoolgirls huddled together in their northern Nigeria boarding school. At the time, I had no idea that this would become a book. Back then, I simply felt compelled to fully understand how that night had unfolded, and to put pressure on Nigerian authorities to find the girls and to bring them home. What followed were hundreds of hours of conversations about what happened that night, and in the days and months after, with some of the girls who managed to escape, with the distraught parents of the missing, and with Nigerian government officials. I also spoke with celebrities, global leaders, human rights activists, political analysts, humanitarian workers, fellow journalists, and a wealth of

Nigerians from all walks of life, in order to fully understand this event and its repercussions. My total immersion in this story and the years I spent reporting on it in the field have allowed me to build my own unique perspective on what happened and the conditions that gave rise to this tragedy.

By the time the idea for a book began to take shape in 2016, "the 21" had been released. At that point, I knew I wanted to prick the world's conscience and to write an account of that fateful night, and what unfolded once the group of kidnapped girls and their captors disappeared into Sambisa forest. And so began my efforts to slowly build a relationship with the traumatized girls. They shared with me their individual, highly personal stories in confidence, but also with the understanding that the material would be used in this book. The bond we developed yielded the accounts you have read in the pages of this book. Prior to our discussions, much of what they told me had only ever been shared with family members and with officials tasked with helping them recover from their ordeal. As a result, despite my best efforts, there is simply no way of corroborating all that they have chosen to disclose. The reality is, the girls, who are in fact now young women, have steadfastly refused to speak with such specificity to other journalists. I am deeply humbled by the fact that they have allowed me to share their experiences with the world. My hope, and theirs, is that by sharing these stories, we can create a groundswell of interest, and exert pressure on the Nigerian government to do whatever is necessary to see that the remaining girls are reunited with their families.

A WORD ON DATES AND HOURS

On that night in Chibok in 2014, Boko Haram swept in and whisked hundreds of terrified schoolgirls away into the darkness of a forest full of terrifying sights and sounds. The conditions they faced left them disoriented, traumatized, and unable to firmly keep track of the passage of time. As such, there is some element of confusion surrounding when certain things happened during their captivity. Despite carefully note-taking and repeated questioning, discrepancies remain between accounts provided by the abducted—which is to be expected given the horrific nature of all they endured in a strange place, far from their loved ones.

A WORD ON TRANSLATION

The majority of interviews and conversations that took place as I covered this story for CNN and researched this book were conducted in English. However, at points along the way it was necessary to have individuals close at hand serve as translators. This was the case on a number of occasions when I spent time with some of the twenty-one freed girls. Given the periodic use of translators, there may be slight differences of opinion in what was shared with me and how I have chosen to present the dramatic details of this story to a global audience.

SOURCE NOTES

CHAPTER 1

much of the world had been stunned by their sudden release:
Stephanie Busari, Jason Hanna, and Faith Karimi, "Boko Haram
releases 21 Chibok girls to Nigerian government," *CNN*, October 13, 2016, https://www.cnn.com/2016/10/13/africa/nigeria
-chibok-girls-released.

their plight held the gaze of celebrities worldwide: Margaret Eby,
"#BringBackOurGirls: Anne Hathaway, Angelina Jolie, other stars
rally for kidnapped Nigerian girls," *New York Daily News*, May 08,
2014, https://www.nydailynews.com/entertainment/gossip
/bringbackourgirls-campaign-attracts-hollywood-star-power
-article-1.1785054.

Zannah Mustapha, a former Nigerian lawyer: Yemisi Adegoke and

Torera Idowu, "Zannah Mustapha: The Nigerian man saving Boko Haram orphans," *CNN*, September 21, 2017, https://www.cnn.com/2017/09/21/africa/boko-haram-orphans-zannah-mustapha/index.html.

the release of 82 more girls: Stephanie Busari and Kelly McCleary, "82 Chibok schoolgirls released in Nigeria," *CNN*, May 7, 2017, https://www.cnn.com/2017/05/06/africa/chibok-girls-released/index.html.

Ruth Maclean and Alice Ross, "82 Chibok schoolgirls freed in exchange for five Boko Haram leaders," *The Guardian*, May 7, 2017, https://www.theguardian.com/world/2017/ may/07/chibok-schoolgirls-familes-await-as-82-are-freed-by-boko-haram-exchange-prison.

Felix Onuah and Ahmed Kingimi, "Nigeria exchanges 82 Chibok girls kidnapped by Boko Haram for prisoners," *Reuters*, https://www.reuters.com/article/us-nigeria-security-idUSKBN1820P1.

I'd be traveling in a convoy along a route that had seen several ambushes in the recent past: Jason Burke, "Nigerian clashes cast doubt on claim that Boko Haram is on its knees," *The Guardian*, November 20, 2016, https://www.theguardian.com/world/2016/nov/20/nigerian-clashes-doubt-boko-haram-technically-defeated.

CHAPTER 2

Nigeria isn't some far-flung, insignificant, or forgettable nation: Patrick Meehan, "Boko Haram: An Overlooked Threat to U.S. Security," *The Heritage Foundation*, July 24, 2012, https://www.heritage.org/terrorism/report/boko-haram-overlooked-threat-us-security.

President Muhammadu Buhari was one of only two African leaders known to have spoken by phone to President Trump in the early days of his new U.S. administration: Stephanie Busari, "Trump calls presidents of Nigeria, South Africa," *CNN*, February 13, 2017, https://edition.cnn.com/2017/02/13/africa/buhari-zuma-trump-call-africa/index.html.

the United States is the largest foreign investor in Nigeria: a wealth of information on the state of the bilateral trade relationship

between the United States and Nigeria can be found on the U.S. Department of State, Commerce, and the U.S. Energy Information Administration websites: "How much petroleum does the United States import and export?," *U.S. Energy Information Administration*, last modified October 3, 2018, https://www.eia.gov/tools/faqs/faq.php?id=727&t=6.

"U.S. Imports from Nigeria of Crude Oil and Petroleum Products," *U.S. Energy Information Administration*, last modified November 30, 2018, https://www.eia.gov/dnav/pet/hist/LeafHandler.ashx?n=pet&s=mttimusni1&f=m.

"U.S. Imports by Country of Origin," *U.S. Energy Information Administration*, last modified November 30, 2018, https://www.eia.gov/dnav/pet/pet_move_impcus_a2_nus_ep00_im0_mbbl_m.htm.

U.S. Department of State, Bureau of Democracy, Human Rights and Labor, *Nigeria 2017 Human Rights Report*, 2017, https://www.state.gov/documents/organization/277277.pdf.

"U.S. Relations With Nigeria," *U.S. Department of State, Bureau Of African Affairs*, last modified December 4, 2018, https://www.state.gov/r/pa/ei/bgn/2836.htm.

"FACT SHEET: U.S.-Africa Cooperation on Trade and Investment Under the Obama Administration," *Office of the White House Press Secretary*, September 21, 2016, https://obamawhitehouse.archives.gov/the-press-office/2016/09/21/fact-sheet-us-africa-cooperation-trade-and-investment-under-obama.

"Exporting to Nigeria—Market Overview," *U.S. Department of Commerce,* last modified November 29, 2018, https://www.export.gov/apex/article2?id=Nigeria-Market-Overview.

many of us learned for the first time about the concept of "ungoverned spaces": Seema Habib, "Is Afghanistan A Failed State? A Brief Overview Of Indicators In The Context Of Afghanistan," *Global Public Policy Watch*, May 26, 2014, https://globalpublicpolicywatch.org/2014/05/26/is-afghanistan-a-failed-state-a-brief-overview-of-indicators-in-the-context-of-afghanistan.

Joe Havely, "Afghanistan: Rebuilding a 'failed' state," *CNN,* September 10, 2002, https://edition.cnn.com/2002/WORLD/asiapcf/central/09/08/afghan.gov.feat/index.html.

Turning to North Africa, we see how a local Islamist militant

group borne out of the 1990s fight against Algeria's secular government aligned itself with Al Qaeda to become Al Qaeda in the Islamic Magreb (AQIM): Zachary Laub and Jonathan Masters, "Al-Qaeda in the Islamic Maghreb," *Council on Foreign Relations*, March 27, 2015, https://www.cfr.org/backgrounder/al -qaeda-islamic-maghreb.

In the years since 9/11, this Al Qaeda affiliate expanded to Mali, Mauritania, and Niger, entrenching itself in large tracts of land in the Sahara and the Sahel: Caleb Weiss, "Al Qaeda maintains operational tempo in West Africa in 2017," *The Long War Journal*, January 5, 2018, https://www.longwarjournal.org /archives/2018/01/al-qaeda-maintains-operational-tempo-in-west -africa-in-2017.php.

As the Airbus 330 descended towards Detroit: David Ariosto and Deborah Feyerick, "Christmas Day bomber sentenced to life in prison," *CNN*, February 17, 2012, https://edition.cnn.com/2012 /02/16/justice/michigan-underwear-bomber-sentencing/index .html.

Al Qaeda's links to Yemen go all the way back to the Afghan jihad against the Soviets in the 1980s. But it was Yemen's fractious civil war that cleared a path for the offshoot AQAP to flourish: "Yemen's al-Qaeda: Expanding the Base," *International Crisis Group*, February 2, 2017, https://www.crisisgroup.org/middle-east -north-africa/gulf-and-arabian-peninsula/yemen/174-yemen-s-al -qaeda-expanding-base.

Abdulmutallab traveled to Yemen to receive his training: Mark Hosenball, "Islamic Radicalization: Umar Farouk Abdulmutallab," *Newsweek*, January 1, 2010, http://www.newsweek.com/islamic -radicalization-umar-farouk-abdulmutallab-70905.

"Documents Reaffirm Awlaki's Role in Radicalizing "Underwear Bomber" Umar Farouk Abdulmutallab," *Counter Extremism Project*, February 23, 2017, https://www.counterextremism.com /press/documents-reaffirm-awlaki's-role-radicalizing-"underwear -bomber"-umar-farouk-abdulmutallab.

Scott Shane, "Inside Al Qaeda's Plot to Blow Up an American Airliner," *New York Times*, February 22, 2017, https://www.nytimes .com/2017/02/22/us/politics/anwar-awlaki-underwear

-bomber-abdulmutallab.html?hp&action=click&pgtype=Ho
mepage&clickSource=story-heading&module=first-column-
region&region=top-news&WT.nav=top-news.

**On the second day of his trial in Detroit, this attempted bomber
suddenly pleaded guilty to all charges:** Laura Dolan, "Accused
Christmas Day bomber pleads guilty to all counts," *CNN*, October
12, 2011, http://edition.cnn.com/2011/US/10/12/michigan.under
wear.bomber/index.html.

Monica Davey, "Would-Be Plane Bomber Pleads Guilty, Ending Trial,"
New York Times, October 12, 2011, https://www.nytimes.com
/2011/10/13/us/umar-farouk-abdulmutallab-pleads-guilty-in
-plane-bomb-attempt.html.

**It gave the rest of us travelling through the nation's airports the
full body x-ray scanner:** Jayshree Bajoria, "The Debate Over
Airport Security," *Council on Foreign Relations*, December 22, 2010,
https://www.cfr.org/backgrounder/debate-over-airport-security.

**Boko Haram has similarly been able to successfully exploit a sense
of alienation amongst northern Nigeria's youth: For accounts
on the rise of Boko Haram see the excellent book:** Hilary Matfess, *Women And The War On Boko Haram: Wives, Weapons, Witnesses* (London: Zed Books, 2016).

As well as the extensive writings by Alex Thurston: Alex Thurston,
'*The Disease Is Unbelief': Boko Haram's Religious And Political Worldview*, The Brookings Institution, January 2016, https://www
.brookings.edu/wp-content/uploads/2016/07/Brookings-Analysis
-Paper_Alex-Thurston_Final_Web.pdf.

And BBC's years long in-depth reporting on the terror group:
"Who are Nigeria's Boko Haram Islamist group?," *BBC News*, November 24, 2016, https://www.bbc.com/news/world-africa
-13809501.

in 2014 in the aftermath of their capture of Gwoza: "Boko Haram
declares 'Islamic state' in northern Nigeria," *BBC News*, August 25,
2014, https://www.bbc.com/news/world-africa-28925484.

**By some estimates at one point the group controlled an area of
twenty thousand square miles—roughly the size of Belgium:**
David Blair, "Boko Haram is now a mini-Islamic State, with its
own territory," *The Telegraph*, January 10, 2015, https://www

.telegraph.co.uk/news/worldnews/africaandindianocean/nigeria
/11337722/Boko-Haram-is-now-a-mini-Islamic-State-with-its-own
-territory.html.

Farouk Chothia, Boko Haram crisis: How have Nigeria's militants
become so strong?," *BBC News*, January 26, 2015, https://www.bbc
.com/news/world-africa-30933860.

Matt Broomfield, "Boko Haram 'crushed' by Nigerian army in final
forest stronghold," *The Independent*, December 24, 2016, https://
www.independent.co.uk/news/world/africa/boko-haram
-nigerian-army-sambisa-forest-a7494176.html.

In 2015, a year after the girls disappeared, Boko Haram pledged allegiance to ISIS: Hamdi Alkhshali and Steve Almasy, "ISIS leader
purportedly accepts Boko Haram's pledge of allegiance," *CNN*,
March 13, 2015, https://edition.cnn.com/2015/03/12/middleeast
/isis-boko-haram/index.html.

**In 2016, ideological differences led to the splintering of Boko
Haram into two distinct jihadist movements: A great deal has
been written about the split in Boko Haram's leadership ranks,
as analysts and journalists from around the globe, try to assess
the scope of the resulting fallout":** Omar Mahmood, "The Potentially More Sinister Threat In Boko Haram's Split," *Institute for
Security Studies*, July 12, 2018, https://reliefweb.int/report/nigeria
/potentially-more-sinister-threat-boko-haram-s-split.

Loveday Wright, "Boko Haram split in leadership crisis," *Deutsche
Welle*, April 8, 2016, http://www.dw.com/en/boko-haram-split-in
-leadership-crisis/a-19449738.

President Buhari has said over and over that Boko Haram is defeated: Jason Burke, "Nigerian clashes cast doubt on claim that
Boko Haram is on its knees," *The Guardian*, November 20, 2016,
https://www.theguardian.com/world/2016/nov/20/nigerian
-clashes-doubt-boko-haram-technically-defeated.

Ben Ezeamalu, "Is President Buhari correct that Boko Haram are 'not
holding any territory' in Nigeria?," *Africa Check*, February 1, 2016,
https://africacheck.org/reports/is-president-buhari-correct-that
-boko-haram-are-not-holding-any-territory-in-nigeria.

Daniel Mumbere, "Pres. Buhari insists that Boko Haram has been
defeated," *Africa News*, January 2, 2018, http://www.africanews

.com/2018/01/02/pres-buhari-insists-that-boko-haram-has-been
-defeated.

According to BBC Monitoring, in 2017 the militant group targeted all four countries in 150 attacks: Mark Wilson, "Nigeria's Boko Haram attacks in numbers—as lethal as ever," *BBC News*, January 25, 2018, https://www.bbc.com/news/world-africa-42735414.

Islamic State West Africa Province (ISWAP), stormed the northeastern Nigerian town of Dapchi: Jonathan Gopep et al., "Boko Haram's Seizure of 110 Girls Taunts Nigeria, and Its Leader," *New York Times*, March 18, 2018, https://www.nytimes.com/2018/03/18/world/africa/boko-haram-dapchi-girls-nigeria.html.

25-year old Khorsa was executed on September 16: Amanda Erickson, "At least one kidnapped aid worker in Nigeria has been killed by Boko Haram," *The Washington Post*, October 15, 2018, https://www.washingtonpost.com/world/2018/10/15/frantic-plea-red-cross-warns-kidnapped-aid-workers-nigeria-may-be-killed-hours/?utm_term=.ec5796ecaa5d.

On October 16 ICRC received word that Liman had been executed: "Boko Haram kills Red Cross staff member in Nigeria after kidnapping three aid workers," *The Telegraph*, October 16, 2018, https://www.telegraph.co.uk/news/2018/10/16/boko-haram-kills-red-cross-staff-member-nigeria-kidnapping-three.

The group also threatened to keep Alice and Leah as their "slaves for life.": Lindy Lowry, "Boko Haram Sect Vows To Keep Leah Sharibu 'Slave For Life'," *Open Doors*, October 16, 2018, https://www.opendoorsusa.org/christian-persecution/stories/boko-haram-sect-vows-to-keep-leah-sharibu-slave-for-life.

Coalition forces in Iraq have driven ISIS militants from Mosul. Meanwhile, across the border, the Syrian Defense Forces routed them: Jacob Wirtschafter and Karim John Gadiaga, "Africa becomes the new battleground for ISIS and al-Qaeda as they lose ground in Mideast," *USA Today*, October 25, 2017, https://www.usatoday.com/story/news/world/2017/10/25/africa-becomes-new-battleground-isis-and-al-qaeda-they-lose-ground-mideast/796148001.

More than two million people have been displaced in the region: Conor Gaffey, "Why Are Over 1 Million Displaced Persons In

Nigeria Too Scared To Go Home?," *Newsweek*, October 12, 2017, https://www.newsweek.com/boko-haram-idps-refugees-nigeria-683001.

numerous reports of women and girls being sexually assaulted and exploited by the very officials meant to protect them: Dionne Searcey, "They Fled Boko Haram, Only to Be Raped by Nigeria's Security Forces," *New York Times*, December 8, 2017, https://www.nytimes.com/2017/12/08/world/africa/boko-haram-nigeria-security-forces-rape.html.

Radina Gigova, "Nigeria investigates reports that officials raped displaced women," *CNN*, November 4, 2016, https://www.cnn.com/2016/11/04/africa/nigeria-displaced-women-rape-report/index.html.

"'They Betrayed Us': Women Who Survived Boko Haram Raped, Starved And Detained In Nigeria," *Amnesty International*, 2018, https://www.amnestyusa.org/wp-content/uploads/2018/05/THEY-BETRAYED-US-WOMEN-WHO-SURVIVED-IN-NIGERIA.pdf.

the Trump administration's repeated efforts to slash foreign aid budgets by up to 37%, though money sent abroad makes up a mere 1% of federal spending: Those who work in the Development sector and many in the State Dept and USAID have been taken aback by Trump adminstration's limited understanding of the benefits of foreign aid—not only to the recipients, but also for long term security of US and its interests

David Hong, "Trump Plan To Cut Foreign Aid Endangers U.S. Interests," *One Acre Fund*, 2018, https://oneacrefund.org/blog/trump-plan-cut-foreign-aid-endangers-us-interests.

Molli Ferrarello, "What "America First" means for US foreign aid," *The Brookings Institution*, July 27, 2017, https://www.brookings.edu/blog/brookings-now/2017/07/27/what-america-first-means-for-us-foreign-aid.

Marcela Escobari, "How foreign aid helps Grand Rapids, Michigan," *The Brookings Institution*, July 11, 2017, https://www.brookings.edu/articles/how-foreign-aid-helps-grand-rapids-michigan.

At the time of writing there are 6,000 U.S. troops spread across 53 African countries: Caitlin Vito, "Shifting US counter-terrorism strategy plays out in the Horn of Africa," *International Institute for Strategic Studies*, June 30, 2018, https://www.iiss.org/blogs/analysis/2018/06/us-counter-terrorism-strategy-horn-of-africa.

Steven Feldstein, "Do Terrorist Trends in Africa Justify the U.S. Military's Expansion?," *Carnegie Endowment for International Peace*, February 9, 2018, http://carnegieendowment.org/2018/02/09/do-terrorist-trends-in-africa-justify-u.s.-military-s-expansion-pub-75476.

Greg Myre, "The U.S. Military In Africa: A Discreet Presence In Many Places," *National Public Radio*, October 20, 2017, https://www.npr.org/sections/thetwo-way/2017/10/20/558757043/the-u-s-military-in-africa-a-discreet-presence-in-many-places.

October 2017, when four U.S. soldiers were killed and two others wounded alongside their Nigerien counterparts: Madison Park, "Niger ambush: Timeline of attack that killed 4 US soldiers," *CNN*, October 25, 2017, https://edition.cnn.com/2017/10/24/politics/niger-ambush-timeline/index.html.

"They are afraid of books and pens": Words from a headline making speech given by a then 16 year old Malala Yousafzai at the U.N. in 2013.

Fazal Khaliq, "World Malala Day: Extremists are afraid of books and pens, says Malala," *The Express Tribune*, July 13, 2013, https://tribune.com.pk/story/576389/world-malala-day-extremists-are-afraid-of-books-and-pens-malala.

Malala Yousafzai, "Our books and our pens are the most powerful weapons," *The Guardian*, July 12, 2013, https://www.theguardian.com/commentisfree/2013/jul/12/malala-yousafzai-united-nations-education-speech-text.

CHAPTER 3

its population of just under 70,000: "CHIBOK Local Government Area in Nigeria," *City Population*, November 7, 2017, https://www.citypopulation.de/php/nigeria-admin.php?adm2id=NGA008006.

four telecom masts: Helon Habila's short book, **The Chibok Girls, The Boko Haram Kidnappings, and Islamist Militancy in Nigeria, Columbia Global Reports, provides an atmospheric**

account of life in Chibok and the impact of the mass kidnapping on this small mainly Christian community.

Helon Habila, *The Chibok Girls: The Boko Haram Kidnappings and Islamist Militancy in Nigeria* (New York: Columbia Global Reports, 2016).

this area of approximately 1,350 square kilometers: Ola' Audu and Ibanga Isine, "Welcome to world famous Chibok, home of over 250 abducted schoolgirls," *Premium Times*, May 10, 2014, https://www.premiumtimesng.com/news/160455-welcome-to-world-famous-chibok-home-of-over-250-abducted-schoolgirls.html.

Christians, who make up 90% of this community: Ola' Audu and Ibanga Isine, "Welcome to world famous Chibok, home of over 250 abducted schoolgirls," *Premium Times*, May 10, 2014, https://www.premiumtimesng.com/news/160455-welcome-to-world-famous-chibok-home-of-over-250-abducted-schoolgirls.html.

built in the 1940s by American missionaries: from various articles, photographs, plus a host of interviews with Chibok locals and others from northern Nigeria I pieced together the origins and conditions in the Government Girls Secondary School in Chibok

Carla Barber, "Nigerian missionaries recall region of stolen schoolgirls," *McPherson Sentinel*, May 13, 2014, https://www.mcphersonsentinel.com/article/20140513/News/140519814.

"Our Church & the Kidnapped Girls of Chibok, Nigeria," Midland Church of the Brethren, http://www.midlandbrethren.org/id24.html.

Gloria Casas, "Church of the Brethren, headquartered in Elgin, hosting Nigerian choir," *The Chicago Tribune*, June 19, 2015, http://www.chicagotribune.com/suburbs/elgin-courier-news/lifestyles/ct-ecn-nigerian-chior-elgin-st-0621-20150619-story.html.

Emenike Ezedani, *Boko Haram Chibok Girls and All Matters Nigeria Security* (Amazon Digital Services, 2015).

"Chibok school falls into ruin," *eNCA*, April 4, 2016, https://www.enca.com/africa/chibok-school-falls-ruin.

Michael Daly, "We Built a School in Boko Haram's Heartland," *The Daily Beast*, May 13, 2014, https://www.thedailybeast.com/we-built-a-school-in-boko-harams-heartland.

more than 70% of primary school-aged girls are out of school: it is worth noting that access to reliable and complete information on education and the out-of-school population in northern Nigeria has long been difficult. As a result I have relied on data from a number of sources including reports released by the United Nations and other education focused organizations

E.W., "Boko Haram's impact on Nigeria: Education in crisis," *The Economist*, May 9 2014, https://www.economist.com/baobab /2014/05/09/education-in-crisis.

Chimaraoke Izugbara et al., "Maternal Health in Nigeria: A situation update," *African Population and Health Research Center*, 2016, https:// www.researchgate.net/publication/303752425_Maternal_Health _in_Nigeria_A_situation_update.

Rachel Hatch, "Schooling in northern Nigeria: Challenges for girls' education," *Education Policy Data Center*, 2012, https://www.epdc .org/epdc-data-points/schooling-northern-nigeria-challenges-girls -education.

Temitope Mustapha, "27 percent of girls in Nigeria not in school," *Voice of Nigeria*, March 19, 2018, https://www.von.gov.ng/27 -percent-school-age-girls-nigeria-not-enrolled.

"Girls' Education in Nigeria," *British Council*, 2004, https://www .britishcouncil.org/sites/default/files/british-council-girls -education-nigeria-report.pdf.

David Ajikobi, "FACTSHEET: Grading Nigeria's progress in education," *Africa Check*, July 16, 2018, https://africacheck.org/factsheets /factsheet-grading-nigerias-progress-in-education.

"Education for the Girl Child in Northern Nigeria," *Africa Check*, July 3, 2017, https://africacheck.org/wp-content/uploads/2017/03/July -info-graphic.pdf.

"UNICEF Targets One Million Girls Enrollment In Northern Nigeria," *Quick News Africa*, December 2017, https://www.quicknews-africa .net/unicef-targets-one-million-girls-enrollment-northern-nigeria.

"Nigeria: The situation," *UNICEF*, https://www.unicef.org/nigeria /education_2161.html.

Uju Peace Okeke, "Child Marriage: A Breach of Human Rights," *Women's UN Report Network*, August 19, 2013, http://www.wunrn .org/news/2013/08_13/08_19/081913_nigeria.htm.

after the Hebrew woman: "Bible Verses About Tabitha," *King James*

Bible Online, 2018, https://www.kingjamesbibleonline.org/Bible
-Verses-About-Tabitha.

"100 Bible Verses about Tabitha," *Open Bible*, December 1, 2018,
https://www.openbible.info/topics/tabitha.

caused by the insurgents in Borno, Yola, and Adamawa states:
"Country Profile: Nigeria," *Global Coalition to Protect Education from
Attack*, 2018, http://www.protectingeducation.org/country
-profile/nigeria.

CHAPTER 4

**The country has faced a "multi-dimensional crisis" in education
according to the U.K.'s Department for International Development report released in 2009:** Hilary Matfess, *Women And
The War On Boko Haram: Wives, Weapons, Witnesses* (London:
Zed Books, 2016) was a critical source of the data used in this
section.

more than 450 other girls, plus 70 boys: Talatu Usman, "How Borno
Governor caused kidnap of Chibok schoolgirls—WAEC," *Premium
Times*, May 3, 2014, https://www.premiumtimesng.com
/news/160062-how-borno-governor-caused-kidnap-of-chibok
-schoolgirls-waec.html.

Segun Odeleye, "#BringBackOurGirls: WAEC gives details on number of students writing exams at Chibok school," *The ScoopNG*,
May 3, 2014, http://www.thescoopng.com/2014/05/03
/bringbackourgirls-waec-gives-details-on-number-of-students
-writing-exams-at-chibok-school.

Governor Kashim Shettima to the BBC Hausa Language Service:
Haruna Umar, "Nigeria: Borno schools closed fearing extremists,"
Associated Press, March 18, 2014, https://www.apnews.com/4402e4
3d1571415980bf0e17d4573893.

**Boko Haram had attacked the Federal Government College in
Buni Yadi:** Adam Nossiter, "Islamist Militants Blamed for Deadly
College Attack in Nigeria," *New York Times*, February 25, 2014,
https://www.nytimes.com/2014/02/26/world/africa/dozens
-killed-in-nigeria-school-assault-attributed-to-islamist-militant
-group.html.

Joe Hemba, "Nigerian Islamists kill 59 pupils in boarding school attack," *Reuters*, February 26, 2014, https://www.reuters.com /article/us-nigeria-violence/nigerian-islamists-kill-59-pupils-in -boarding-school-attack-idUSBREA1P10M20140226.

"'Boko Haram killed 29 students and lined up their bodies in front of the hostel' — Buni Yadi massacre revisited," *The Radar*, February 22, 2018, https://www.thecable.ng/boko-haram-killed-29-students -lined-bodies-front-hostel-buni-yadi-massacre-revisited.

CHAPTER 5

The reporting on violence against women during conflict is well established. There is no shortage of sources detailing the horrors faced by women in various hotspots around the globe. "'Comfort women': Researchers claim first known film," *BBC News*, July 10, 2017, https://www.bbc.com/news/world-asia-40552812.

European Parliament, *Sexual violence in the Democratic Republic of Congo*, November 2014, http://www.europarl.europa.eu/EPRS /EPRS-AaG-542155-Sexual-violence-in-DRC-FINAL.pdf.

Jocelyn Kelly, "The ICC's New Precedent for Sexual Violence as a War Crime," *Council on Foreign Relations*, April 4, 2016, https://www .cfr.org/blog/iccs-new-precedent-sexual-violence-war-crime.

"'All of My Body Was Pain': Sexual Violence against Rohingya Women and Girls in Burma," *Human Rights Watch*, November 16, 2017, https://www.hrw.org/report/2017/11/16/all-my-body-was-pain /sexual-violence-against-rohingya-women-and-girls-burma.

Rukmini Callimachi, "Freed From ISIS, Yazidi Women Return in 'Severe Shock'," *New York Times*, July 27, 2017, https://www .nytimes.com/2017/07/27/world/middleeast/isis-yazidi-women -rape-iraq-mosul-slavery.html.

Major General Chris Olukolade, announced the rescue of all "129 girls, except eight": "Nigerian government says most kidnapped girls rescued," *Al Jazeera*, April 16, 2014, http://america.aljazeera .com/articles/2014/4/16/nigeria-kidnap-rescue.html.

"Chronicle Of False Narratives And Inconsistencies By The Nigerian Government Over The Rescue Of The Abducted Chibok Schoolgirls," *Bring Back Our Girls*, October 13, 2014, http://

www.bringbackourgirls.ng/chronicle-of-false-narratives-and
-inconsistencies-by-the-nigerian-government-over-the-rescue-of
-the-abducted-chibok-schoolgirls.

He followed up with a retraction: Aminu Abubakar et al., "Nigerian
military retracts claim that nearly all abducted students were released," *CNN*, April 18, 2014, https://edition.cnn.com/2014/04/17
/world/africa/nigeria-abducted-girls/index.html.

CHAPTER 6

Reports date back to 2009 of women and girls being snatched: "Nigeria: Chibok anniversary a chilling reminder of Boko Haram's
ongoing scourge of abductions," *Amnesty International*, April 13,
2017, https://www.amnesty.org/en/latest/news/2017/04/nigeria
-chibok-anniversary-a-chilling-reminder-of-boko-harams-ongoing
-scourge-of-abductions.

"Those Terrible Weeks in their Camp: Boko Haram Violence against
Women and Girls in Northeast Nigeria," *Human Rights Watch*, Oc-
tober 2014, http://features.hrw.org/features/HRW_2014_report
/Those_Terrible_Weeks_in_Their_Camp/index.html.

**Christian town of Konduga and disappeared with dozens of
women:** Jacob Zenn And Elizabeth Pearson, "Boko Haram And
The Kidnapping Of Women: A Troubled Tactic," *War On The
Rocks*, March 11, 2014, https://warontherocks.com/2014/03/boko
-haram-and-the-kidnapping-of-women.

**The group was founded in Maiduguri back in 2002: There has been
a great deal of deeply researched writing on the origins of
Boko Haram and the socio-political conditions that gave rise
to Mohammed Yusuf and upon his death, his successor Abubakar Shekau:** Hilary Matfess, *Women And The War On Boko Haram:
Wives, Weapons, Witnesses* (London: Zed Books, 2016).

Hilary Matfess, "Boko Haram: History and Context," *Oxford Research
Encyclopedia*, October 2017, http://africanhistory.oxfordre
.com/view/10.1093/acrefore/9780190277734.001.0001/acrefore
-9780190277734-e-119.

"Boko Haram: Behind the Rise of Nigeria's Armed Group," *Al Jazeera*,

December 22, 2016, https://www.aljazeera.com/programmes
/specialseries/2016/11/boko-haram-rise-nigeria-armed-group
-161101145500150.html.

Karin Brulliard, "For Many, Nigeria's Moderate Form of Sharia Fails
to Deliver on Promises," *The Washington Post*, August 12, 2009,
http://www.washingtonpost.com/wp-dyn/content/article
/2009/08/11/AR2009081103257.html?noredirect=on.

**Elodie Apard's scholarly writings about speeches given by Yusuf
and Shekau provide keen insight into the motivations and evolution of both men:** Élodie Apard, "The Words of Boko Haram,"
Afrique contemporaine 255, no. 3 (2015): 41-69, https://www.cairn
-int.info/article-E_AFCO_255_0043—the-words-of-boko-haram
.htm.

the killing of Yusuf's former mentor Sheikh Adam: Ahmad Salkida,
"Muhammad Yusuf: Teaching and preaching controversies,"
Salkida, February 28, 2009, http://salkida.com/muhammad-yusuf
-teaching-and-preaching-controversies.

Atta Barkindo, "An introduction to Boko Haram's ideologues: from
Yusuf to Shekau," *Africa Research Institute*, February 2, 2017,
https://www.africaresearchinstitute.org/newsite/blog
/introduction-boko-harams-ideologues-yusuf-shekau.

Misbahu Ahmed, "Nigeria: Boko Haram raises more questions than
answers," *The Final Call*, February 2, 2012, http://www.finalcall
.com/artman/publish/Perspectives_1/article_8582.shtml.

Will Ross, "Boko Haram Kano attack: Loss of life on staggering scale,"
BBC News, November 30, 2014, https://www.bbc.com/news
/world-africa-30266868.

Alex Thurston, "Salafism in Northern Nigeria Beyond Boko Haram,"
Council on Foreign Relations, January 27, 2017, https://www.cfr.org
/blog/salafism-northern-nigeria-beyond-boko-haram.

Alex Thurston, *"The Disease Is Unbelief": Boko Haram's Religious And Political Worldview*, The Brookings Institution, January 2016, https://
www.brookings.edu/wp-content/uploads/2016/07/Brookings
-Analysis-Paper_Alex-Thurston_Final_Web.pdf.

**schools at all levels had been closed for months in 22 out of 27 local
government areas:** "'They Set the Classrooms on Fire': Attacks

on Education in Northeast Nigeria," *Human Rights Watch*, April 11, 2016, https://www.hrw.org/report/2016/04/11/they-set-classrooms-fire/attacks-education-northeast-nigeria.

CHAPTER 7

the unfamiliar notes of Kanuri, the language: Michael Baca, "Boko Haram and the Kanuri Factor," *African Arguments*, February 16, 2015, http://africanarguments.org/2015/02/16/boko-haram-and-the-kanuri-factor-by-michael-baca/.

Jeremy Weate, "Boko Haram's roots in Nigeria long predate Al-Qaeda era," *Al Jazeera*, April 23, 2014, http://america.aljazeera.com/articles/2014/4/23/boko-haram-s-rootsinnigerialongpredatetheal qaedaera.html.

Nomadic Fulani herdsmen: "Displacement of herdsmen from Sambisa heightens farmers-harders conflicts-Zwingina," *Vanguard News Nigeria*, July 11, 2018, https://www.vanguardngr.com/2018/07/displacement-of-herdsmen-from-sambisa-heightens-farmers-harders-conflicts-zwingina.

"How to resolve herdsmen crisis—Nigerian Working Group," *Premium Times*, January 12, 2018, https://www.premiumtimesng.com/news/top-news/255364-resolve-herdsmen-crisis-nigerian-working-group.html.

Bodunrin Kayode, "Inside Nigeria's Sambisa forest, the Boko Haram hideout where kidnapped school girls are believed to be held," *The Guardian*, April 29, 2014, https://www.theguardian.com/world/2014/apr/29/nigeria-sambisa-forest-boko-haram-hideout-kidnapped-school-girls-believed-to-be-held.

CHAPTER 9

Almost three weeks went by before: "Nigeria missing girls: President makes first comments," *BBC News*, May 4, 2014, https://www.bbc.com/news/world-africa-27280187.

Naina Bajekal, "Inside the Search for the Chibok Schoolgirls Abducted by Boko Haram," *Time Magazine*, April 23, 2015, http://time.com/3833024/chibok-boko-haram.

the historic tensions that beset: Alexander Thurston, "Divinely Divided: How Christianity and Islam Coexist in Nigeria," *Council on Foreign Relations*, June 21, 2018, https://www.cfr.org/event /divinely-divided-how-christianity-and-islam-coexist-nigeria.

Moses Ochonu, "The roots of Nigeria's religious and ethnic conflict," *Public Radio International*, March 10, 2014, https://www.pri.org /stories/2014-03-10/roots-nigerias-religious-and-ethnic-conflict.

Tolu Ogunlesi, "Nigeria's Internal Struggles," *New York Times*, March 23, 2015, https://www.nytimes.com/2015/03/24/opinion/nigerias -internal-struggles.html.

Shobana Shankar, "The complicated politics of conversion in Northern Nigeria," *Africa Is A Country*, May 2014, https://africasacountry .com/2014/05/the-complicated-politics-of-conversion-in-northern -nigeria.

the nation's powerbrokers reached a critical agreement: Max Siol-lun, "The Gentleman's Agreement That Could Break Apart Nigeria," *Foreign Policy*, June 1, 2017, https://foreignpolicy.com/2017 /06/01/the-gentlemans-agreement-that-could-break-apart-nigeria -buhari-health-rumors.

Walter Mead, "Religious Conflict in Nigeria: Religion and the Nigerian Elections - Session 1," *Council on Foreign Relations*, May 8, 2007, https://www.cfr.org/event/religious-conflict-nigeria-religion-and -nigerian-elections-session-1.

CHAPTER 10

she addressed an audience gathered to honor UNESCO's selection of the Nigerian city of Port Harcourt as the World Book Capital: Brian Ries, "Bring Back Our Girls: Why the World Is Finally Talking About Nigeria's Kidnapped Students," *Mashable*, May 6, 2014, https://mashable.com/2014/05/06/nigeria-girls-bringbackourgirls /#Gqu6hzeddiqE.

impassioned remarks also struck Ibrahim M. Abdullahi: Nnenna Ibeh, "INTERVIEW: Meet the man who generated #BringBackOurGirls hashtag," *Premium Times*, June 14, 2014, https://www.premiumtimesng.com/news/162803-interview-meet -man-generated-bringbackourgirls-hashtag.html.

social media analytics firm Topsy: Miranda Neubauer, "#BringBackOurGirls: How a Hashtag Took Hold," *Tech President*, May 7, 2014, http://techpresident.com/news/24996/bringbackourgirls-how-hashtag-took-hold.

"a million woman march":

Agence France-Presse, "Hundreds march over Nigeria schoolgirl kidnappings," *The Guardian*, April 30, 2014, https://www.theguardian.com/world/2014/apr/30/hundreds-march-nigeria-chibok-schoolgirl-kidnappings-boko-haram.

child brides for a sum of approximately $12 each: "Kidnapped Nigeria school girls reportedly sold as brides to Islamic Boko Haram militants," *CBS News*, April 30, 2014, https://www.cbsnews.com/news/kidnapped-nigeria-school-girls-reportedly-sold-as-brides-to-islamic-boko-haram-militants.

"Boko Haram: Nigerian Terror Group Sells Girls Into Slavery," *NBC News*, April 30, 2014, https://www.nbcnews.com/storyline/missing-nigeria-schoolgirls/boko-haram-nigerian-terror-group-sells-girls-slavery-n93951.

CHAPTER 11

Sambisa forest, hidden away: the enduring myths surrounding Sambisa forest and its recent occupation by Boko Haram have created a dearth of extensive writings about the enclave. What exists are best described as snapshots of the terrain and details of what it used to be during the days of Nigeria's colonial past. Most influential to my writing has been the accounts provided by the girls themselves of what they saw and heard while in this no-go zone

Moki Edwin Kindzeka, "Sambisa Forest: An Ideal Hiding Place for Boko Haram," *Voice of America News*, May 24, 2016, http://www.voanews.com/a/the-forest-concealing-boko-haram/3343895.html.

Bodunrin Kayode, "Inside Nigeria's Sambisa forest, the Boko Haram hideout where kidnapped school girls are believed to be held," *The Guardian*, April 29, 2014, https://www.theguardian.com/world/2014/apr/29/nigeria-sambisa-forest-boko-haram-hideout-kidnapped-school-girls-believed-to-be-held.

Muhammed Adamu, "Boko Haram and the legend of Sambisa Forest," *Blueprint*, January 19, 2017, https://blueprint.ng/boko-haram-and -the-legend-of-sambisa-forest.

"Sambisa Forest," *Wikipedia*, https://en.wikipedia.org/wiki/Sambisa _Forest.

"Sahel," *Encyclopædia Britannica*, October 09, 2018, https://www .britannica.com/place/Sahel.

Alexis Okeowo, "As the Year Ends, Where Are Nigeria's Kidnapped Girls?," *New Yorker*, December 17, 2014, https://www.newyorker .com/news/daily-comment/year-ends-nigerias-kidnapped-girls.

"Nigeria says troops invade last Boko Haram stronghold," *Al Jazeera*, April 23, 2015, https://www.aljazeera.com/news/2015/04/nigeria -boko-haram-sambisa-forest-150423090548354.html.

Azeez Olaniyan, "Once Upon a Game Reserve: Sambisa and the Tragedy of a Forested Landscape," *Environment & Society*, 2018, http:// www.environmentandsociety.org/arcadia/once-upon-game -reserve-sambisa-and-tragedy-forested-landscape.

"See photos of Nigerian troops camouflage as trees in Sambisa forest," *P.M. News*, March 28, 2017, https://www.pmnewsnigeria .com/2017/03/28/see-photos-nigerian-troops-camouflage-trees -sambisa-forest.

Bodunrin Kayode, "Inside Nigeria's Sambisa forest, the Boko Haram hideout where kidnapped school girls are believed to be held," *The Guardian*, April 29, 2014, https://www.theguardian.com /world/2014/apr/29/nigeria-sambisa-forest-boko-haram-hideout -kidnapped-school-girls-believed-to-be-held.

In early 2013, the terror group—It is difficult to say definitively when exactly Boko Haram relocated to Sambisa, making it the group's base. But it is clear that from at least 2013 it had become ground zero for the terrorists

Azeez Olaniyan, "Once Upon a Game Reserve: Sambisa and the Tragedy of a Forested Landscape," *Environment & Society*, 2018, http:// www.environmentandsociety.org/arcadia/once-upon-game -reserve-sambisa-and-tragedy-forested-landscape.

"Who are Nigeria's Boko Haram Islamist group?," *BBC News*, November 24, 2016, https://www.bbc.com/news/world-africa-13809501.

Moki Edwin Kindzeka, "Sambisa Forest: An Ideal Hiding Place for

Boko Haram," Voice of America News, May 24, 2016, http://www
.voanews.com/a/the-forest-concealing-boko-haram/3343895.html.

Bodunrin Kayode, "Inside Nigeria's Sambisa forest, the Boko Haram
hideout where kidnapped school girls are believed to be held,"
The Guardian, April 29, 2014, https://www.theguardian.com
/world/2014/apr/29/nigeria-sambisa-forest-boko-haram-hideout
-kidnapped-school-girls-believed-to-be-held.

"What do you know about Sambisa near Chibok?," *The Cable,* May 7,
2014, https://www.thecable.ng/what-do-you-know-about-sambisa
-near-chibok.

among the 57 girls who fled: "Nigeria Chibok abductions: What we
know," *BBC News,* May 8, 2017, https://www.bbc.com/news
/world-africa-32299943.

CHAPTER 12

Nigeria had been chosen to host this: Bassey Udo, "Nigeria relishes
right to host WEF 2014, says Okonjo-Iweala," *Premium Times,* November 11, 2013, https://www.premiumtimesng.com/business
/149427-nigeria-relishes-right-host-wef-2014-says-okonjo-iweala
.html.

the Nigerian Minister of Information, Labaran Maku: "CNN's Isha
Sesay Interviews Information Minister Labaran Maku On Slow
Response To Chibok Aduction," *360nobs,* May 10, 2014, https://
www.360nobs.com/2014/05/cnns-isha-sesay-interviews-information
-minister-labaran-maku-on-slow-response-to-chibok-aduction-video
/?utm_source=feedburner&utm_medium=feed&utm_campaign=
Feed%3A+360nobscom+%28360Nobs.com%29.

**CNN interview May 2014: Tensions rose further when Amnesty
International released a report on May 9:** "Nigerian authorities
failed to act on warnings about Boko Haram raid on school,"
Amnesty International, May 9, 2014, https://www.amnesty.org
/en/latest/news/2014/05/nigerian-authorities-failed-act-warnings
-about-boko-haram-raid-school.

**The Senior Special Assistant on Public Affairs to the President,
Doyin Okupe:** May 2014

exclusive CNN sit-down interview: "Transcript: CNN interviews

Nigerian President Goodluck Jonathan," *CNN*, October 1, 2010, http://edition.cnn.com/2010/WORLD/africa/09/30/goodluck .jonathan.transcript/index.html.

CHAPTER 13

the Civilian Joint Task Force (JTF): Alex Thurston, 'The Disease Is Unbelief': Boko Haram's Religious And Political Worldview, The Brookings Institution, January 2016, https://www.brookings.edu /wp-content/uploads/2016/07/Brookings-Analysis-Paper_Alex -Thurston_Final_Web.pdf.

Alexis Okeowo, "Inside the Vigilante Fight Against Boko Haram," *New York Times Magazine*, November 5, 2014 https://www.nytimes .com/2014/11/09/magazine/inside-the-vigilante-fight-against -boko-haram.html.

CHAPTER 14

nearly hour-long video on May 5 2014: Aminu Abubakar and Josh Levs, "'I will sell them,' Boko Haram leader says of kidnapped Nigerian girls," *CNN*, May 6, 2014, https://edition.cnn .com/2014/05/05/world/africa/nigeria-abducted-girls/index .html.

quickly stepped up with offers of support: Catrina Stewart, "World pledges help to Nigeria in hunt for girls kidnapped by Boko Haram," *The Independent*, May 8, 2014, https://www.independent .co.uk/news/world/africa/world-pledges-help-to-nigeria-in-hunt -for-girls-kidnapped-by-boko-haram-9340967.html.

May 12, 2014, Boko Haram released a twenty-seven-minute video: Adam Nossiter, "Nigerian Girls Seen in Video From Militants," *New York Times*, May 12, 2014, https://www.nytimes.com/2014 /05/13/world/africa/boko-haram-video-kidnapped-nigerian-girls .html.

"Nigerian kidnapped girls 'shown in Boko Haram footage'," *The Guardian* video, 1:16, May 12, 2014, https://www.theguardian .com/world/video/2014/may/12/nigeria-kidnapped-girls-boko -haram-video.

"Nigeria kidnapped girls 'shown in Boko Haram video'," *BBC News*,
    May 12, 2014, https://www.bbc.com/news/world-africa-27373287.

parents couldn't immediately watch: Ndahi Marama and Emmanuel
    Elebeke, "#BringBackourGirls: Doubts, hope as parents watch
    B-Haram video," *Vanguard News Nigeria*, May 13, 2014, https://
    www.vanguardngr.com/2014/05/bringbackourgirls-doubts-hope
    -parents-watch-b-haram-video.

Paris Security summit: John Irish and Bate Felix, "Paris summit to
    try to rally region against Nigeria's Boko Haram," *Reuters*, May 16,
    2014, https://www.reuters.com/article/us-nigeria-girls-summit
    /paris-summit-to-try-to-rally-region-against-nigerias-boko-haram
    -idUSBREA4F0BQ20140516.

Sam Frizell, "West African Leaders Agree on Plan to 'Crush' Boko
    Haram," *Time Magazine*, May 17, 2014, http://time.com/103835
    /boko-haram-nigeria-africa-summit.

Maïa de la Baume and Alissa J. Rubin, "West African Nations Set Aside
    Their Old Suspicions to Combat Boko Haram," *New York Times*,
    May 17, 2014, https://www.nytimes.com/2014/05/18/world/africa
    /west-african-nations-set-aside-their-old-suspicions-to-combat
    -boko-haram.html?hp.

CHAPTER 16

President Jonathan had been seen out in public, happily singing:
    David Smith, "Nigerian president faces increasing pressure over
    kidnapped schoolgirls," *The Guardian*, May 18, 2014, https://www
    .theguardian.com/world/2014/may/18/nigerian-president-under
    -increasing-pressure-over-schoolgirls.

"Nigeria refused help to search for kidnapped girls," *The Times of Israel*,
    May 11, 2014, http://www.timesofisrael.com/nigeria-refused-help
    -to-search-for-kidnapped-girls/?fb_comment_id=713467175377679
    _713487772042286.

Nicholas Ibekwe, "Nigerians lambast Jonathan for singing, dancing at
    campaign rally while nation mourns bomb blast victims," *Premium
    Times*, April 16, 2014, https://www.premiumtimesng.com
    /news/158836-nigerians-lambast-jonathan-for-singing-dancing-at
    -campaign-rally-while-nation-mourns-bomb-blast-victims.html.

done her part to sow discord: "Nigeria: First Lady Orders Arrest of 'Bring Back Our Girls' Protest Leader," *The Burton Wire*, May 8, 2014, http://theburtonwire.com/2014/05/08/politics/nigeria-first-lady-orders-arrest-of-bring-back-our-girls-protest-leader.

Ogala Emmanuel, "Patience Jonathan did not order arrest of #BringBackOurGirls protest leader – Aide," *Premium Times*, May 5, 2014, https://www.premiumtimesng.com/news/160163-patience-jonathan-order-arrest-bringbackourgirls-protest-leader-aide.html.

"Patience Jonathan Orders Arrest Of #Bringbackourgirls Abuja Protest Leaders, You Won't Believe Why," *Information Nigeria*, May 5, 2014, http://www.informationng.com/2014/05/patience-jonathan-orders-arrest-of-bringbackourgirls-abuja-protest-leaders-you-wont-believe-why.html.

"Nigeria schoolgirl abductions: Protest leader detained," *BBC News*, May 5, 2014, https://www.bbc.com/news/world-africa-27283278.

Alex Badeh, proudly announced: "We know where abducted Chibok girls —Chief of Defence Staff Alex Badeh," *News Express* video, 0:46, May 26, 2014, https://newsexpressngr.com/videos/video_details.php?title=We-know-where-abducted-Chibok-girls-Chief-of-Defence-Staff-Alex-Badeh&id=10&cat=Video-News.

Muhammadu Buhari was sworn in as the fifteenth President: "Nigeria's President Buhari promises change at inauguration," *BBC News*, May 29, 2015, https://www.bbc.com/news/world-africa-32927311.

"technically . . . won the war": Daniel Mumbere, "Pres. Buhari insists that Boko Haram has been defeated," *Africa News*, January 2, 2018, http://www.africanews.com/2018/01/02/pres-buhari-insists-that-boko-haram-has-been-defeated.

CHAPTER 17

known as female genital mutilation or cutting—long-standing tensions around the practice of FGM continue to make it difficult for anti-FGM campaigners to collect data of cases. What is not in doubt is this "coming of age" rite is still very much a part of Sierra Leonean culture.

"Fighting genital mutilation in Sierra Leone," *World Health Organization*, November 2005, http://www.who.int/bulletin/volumes /83/11/news21105/en.

Umaru Fofana, "Captured and cut: FGM returns to Sierra Leone despite official ban," *The Guardian*, September 29, 2016, https://www .theguardian.com/global-development/2016/sep/29/female -genital-mutilation-returns-sierra-leone-official-ban.

Lisa O'Carroll, "Sierra Leone's secret FGM societies spread silent fear and sleepless nights," *The Guardian*, August 24, 2015, https://www .theguardian.com/global-development/2015/aug/24/sierra-leone -female-genital-mutilation-soweis-secret-societies-fear.

Sharmila Devi, "FGM in Sierra Leone," *World Report* 391 (February 2018): 415. https://doi.org/10.1016/S0140-6736(18)30189-2.

"Sierra Leone: The practice of female genital mutilation (FGM); the government's position with respect to the practice; consequences of refusing to become an FGM practitioner in Bondo Society, specifically, if a daughter of a practitioner refuses to succeed her mother," *Research Directorate, Immigration and Refugee Board of Canada*, March 27, 2009, https://www.refworld.org/docid/4b20f02bc.html.

CHAPTER 18

the BBC reported the accounts of four unnamed eyewitnesses: "Nigeria's Chibok girls 'seen with Boko Haram in Gwoza'," *BBC News*, April 14, 2015, https://www.bbc.com/news/world-africa-32292854.

Samuel Malik, "Chibok girls are in Gwoza, says freed Boko Haram abductee," *Premium Times*, March 25, 2015, https://www.premium timesng.com/news/headlines/179106-chibok-girls-are-in-gwoza -says-freed-boko-haram-abductee.html.

Jola Sotubo, "No sign of Chibok girls as soldiers recover Gwoza from terrorists," *Pulse News*, March 27, 2015, https://www.pulse .ng/news/local/boko-haram-no-sign-of-chibok-girls-as-soldiers -recover-gwoza-from-terrorists-photos-id3608122.html.

David Blair, "Nigeria's army captures Boko Haram HQ," *The Telegraph*, March 27, 2015, https://www.telegraph.co.uk/news/worldnews /africaandindianocean/nigeria/11500457/Nigerias-army-captures -Boko-Haram-HQ.html.

"Nigeria: A tale of survival in Gwoza town," *United Nations Office for the Coordination of Humanitarian Affairs*, October 31, 2016, https://www.unocha.org/story/nigeria-tale-survival-gwoza-town.

"Boko Haram HQ Gwoza in Nigeria 'retaken'," *BBC News*, March 27, 2015, https://www.bbc.com/news/world-africa-32087211.

on the outskirts of Banki: "Nigeria's Boko Haram 'seize Banki town near Cameroon'," *BBC News*, September 3, 2014, http://www.bbc.com/news/world-africa-29048394.

"Banki: a Nigerian border town choked by Boko Haram homeless," *Daily Mail*, May 3, 2017, http://www.dailymail.co.uk/wires/afp/article-4472054/Banki-Nigerian-border-town-choked-Boko-Haram-homeless.html.

negotiations with Boko Haram for the release of these 21 girls: From my interviews with Zannah Mustapha, I learned he was undoubtedly the lynchpin of the talks that took place to secure the release of the 21 Chibok girls. But to date he refuses to be drawn on the specific details of the deal that resulted in their freedom.

Yemisi Adegoke and Torera Idowu, "Zannah Mustapha: The Nigerian man saving Boko Haram orphans," *CNN*, September 21, 2017, https://www.cnn.com/2017/09/21/africa/boko-haram-orphans-zannah-mustapha/index.html.

Abdulkareem Haruna, "INTERVIEW: My role in negotiation with Boko Haram, release of Chibok Girls—Zannah Mustapha," *Premium Times*, January 15, 2018, https://www.premiumtimesng.com/news/headlines/255539-interview-my-role-in-negotiation-with-boko-haram-release-of-chibok-girls-zannah-mustapha.html.

"The man who brokered the deal to release the Chibok girls," *BBC News*, May 17, 2017 https://www.bbc.com/news/world-africa-39928628.

John Campbell, "The Ransom of Nigeria's Chibok School Girls," *Council on Foreign Relations*, April 15, 2016, https://www.cfr.org/blog/ransom-nigerias-chibok-school-girls.

Joe Parkinson and Drew Hinshaw, "Freedom for the World's Most Famous Hostages Came at a Heavy Price," *The Wall Street Journal*, December 24, 2017, https://www.wsj.com/articles/two-bags-of-cash-for-boko-haram-the-untold-story-of-how-nigeria-freed-its-kidnapped-girls-1513957354.

the release of the 21 girls was triggered by President Buhari's 2016 statement at the United Nations: Curt Mills, "Nigeria Seeks U.N. Help to Get Back Chibok Girls," *US News & World Report*, September 22, 2016, https://www.usnews.com/news/articles/2016-09-22 /nigerias-muhammadu-buhari-asks-for-un-help-with-boko-haram -chibok-girls.

CHAPTER 19

CNN's release of a never before publicly seen proof of life video: "Chibok kidnapping: New 'proof of life' video," *CNN* video, 0:54, April 13, 2016, https://edition.cnn.com/videos/world/2016/04/13 /chibok-girls-boko-haram-proof-of-life-video-sdg-orig.cnn.

J. Weston Phippen, "Proof of Life For Nigeria's Kidnapped Girls," *The Atlantic*, April 14, 2016, https://www.theatlantic.com/international /archive/2016/04/nigeria-boko-haram-girls/478239.

the first of the missing Chibok schoolgirls—Amina Ali Nkeki: "Rescued Chibok girl: Who is Amina Ali Nkeki?," *BBC News*, May 19, 2016, http://www.bbc.com/news/world-africa-36330379.

Stephanie Busari and Bryony Jones, "Escaped Chibok girl: I miss my Boko Haram husband," *CNN*, August 17, 2016, http://www.cnn .com/2016/08/16/africa/chibok-girl-amina-ali-nkeki-boko-haram -husband/index.html.

Michelle Faul, "Family demands news of Nigerian girl who escaped Boko Haram," *The Independent*, June 24, 2016, http://www .independent.co.uk/news/world/africa/boko-haram-amina -ali-nkeki-escaped-chibok-schoolgirls-a7098786.html.

Brigadier General Rabe Abubakar, announced: Michelle Faul, "Family demands news of Nigerian girl who escaped Boko Haram," *The Independent*, June 24, 2016, http://www.independent.co.uk/news /world/africa/boko-haram-amina-ali-nkeki-escaped-chibok -schoolgirls-a7098786.html.

CHAPTER 21

an international NGO working with survivors of sexual abuse, shared letters: "'Letters To Our Daughters: Hope Endures' Photo

Essay," *Pathfinders Justice Initiative*, April 14, 2016, http://pathfinders ji.org/letters-to-our-daughters-hopeendures-photo-essay.

CHAPTER 25

Maryam Ali Maiyanga and her 10-month-old son, Ali: Chandrika Narayan, "Missing Chibok schoolgirl found with baby, Nigerian army says," *CNN*, November 5, 2016, https://www.cnn.com /2016/11/05/africa/nigeria-chibok-girl-found/index.html.

Oludare Richards, "Chibok Girl, Maryam, discovered with baby in Northern Borno," *The Guardian*, November 13, 2016, https:// guardian.ng/sunday-magazine/chibok-girl-maryam-discovered -with-baby-in-northern-borno.

Rakiya Abubakar Gali and her 6-month-old baby: "Another Chibok girl, Rakiya Abubakar, baby rescued by troops," *Vanguard News Nigeria*, January 5, 2017, https://www.vanguardngr.com/2017/01 /breaking-another-chibok-girl-rakiya-abubakar-baby-rescued -troops.

Karls Tsokar et al., "Another Chibok girl found with baby," *The Guardian*, January 6, 2017, https://guardian.ng/news/another-chibok -girl-found-with-baby.

"Nigerian girl kidnapped by Boko Haram, now a mother, found with baby," *CBS News*, January 5, 2017, https://www.cbsnews.com /news/nigerian-chibok-girl-kidnapped-by-boko-haram-found -baby-nearly-200-still-missing.

the Nigerian government broke the news on Twitter: Associated Press, "Nigeria presidency releases names of 82 freed Chibok girls," *Daily Mail*, May 8, 2017, http://www.dailymail.co.uk/wires /ap/article-4484180/Nigeria-presidency-releases-names-82-freed -Chibok-girls.html.

Bashir Adigun and Sunday Alamba, "Nigeria identifies 82 freed Chibok girls; parents await word," *The Seattle Times*, May 8, 2017, https://www.seattletimes.com/nation-world/nigeria-presidency -releases-names-of-82-freed-chibok-girls.

"Chibok girls reunited with families after three years," *The National*, May 20, 2017, https://www.thenational.ae/world/chibok-girls -reunited-with-families-after-three-years-1.32393.

we also learned through another video: "Girl in Boko Haram video refuses to return, pledges loyalty to group," *Deccan Chronicle*, May 14, 2017, https://www.deccanchronicle.com/world/africa/140517/chibok-girl-in-boko-haram-video-refuses-return-pledges-loyalty-to-group.html.

"Boko Haram releases video of purported Chibok girls," *Al Jazeera*, May 12, 2017, https://www.aljazeera.com/news/2017/05/boko-haram-releases-video-purported-chibok-girl-170513025720253.html.

"'Chibok girl' wields AK-47 in new Boko Haram video," *The Cable*, May 13, 2017, https://www.thecable.ng/chibok-girl-wields-ak-47-new-boko-haram-video.

Abdur Rahman Alfa Shaban, "Boko Haram video confirms some Chibok girls against release," *Africa News*, May 15, 2017, http://www.africanews.com/2017/05/13/boko-haram-video-confirms-some-chibok-girls-against-release.

"How 15-year-old Chibok abduction victim became 20-year-old Boko Haram 'wife'," *Pulse News*, June 8, 2018, https://www.pulse.ng/news/local/chibok-girl-dorcas-yakubu-turns-20-in-boko-haram-custody-id8470760.html.

"Boko Haram video of purported Chibok girl worries parents," *Channel News Asia*, May 14, 2017, https://www.channelnewsasia.com/news/world/boko-haram-video-of-purported-chibok-girl-worries-parents-8844882.

They are enrolled in the "New Foundation School (NFS) Chibok Education Initiative: Over the course of a number of visits and calls with school officials I've learned about the girls' new lives at the American University. Far from the gaze of a global public many of the abducted are embracing this exciting chapter and throwing themselves into the academic and extracurricular activities on offer.

Salomi Pogu: Casey Quackenbush, "A Chibok Schoolgirl Kidnapped By Boko Haram Has Been Found in Nigeria," *Time Magazine*, January 5, 2018, http://time.com/5089293/nigeria-boko-haram-chibok-schoolgirl-found.

Abdur Rahman Alfa Shaban, "Nigeria army finds another Chibok girl abducted by Boko Haram in 2014," *Africa News*, January 4, 2018,

http://www.africanews.com/2018/01/04/nigeria-army-finds
-another-chibok-girl-abducted-by-boko-haram-in-2014.

The Buhari government for its part, maintains that it is commit-ted: Samson Toromade, "What has happened to schoolgirls 4 years after Boko Haram abduction?," *Pulse News*, April 14, 2018, https://www.pulse.ng/news/local/what-has-happened-to-chibok -girls-4-years-after-abduction-id8251598.html.

Felix Onuah and Alexis Akwagyiram, "Nigeria plans to negotiate for release of 110 abducted Dapchi girls," *Reuters*, March 12, 2018, https://www.reuters.com/article/us-nigeria-security/nigeria -plans-to-negotiate-for-release-of-110-abducted-dapchi-girls-idUSK CN1GO2BZ.

the first prosecutions in relation to the mass kidnapping: "Chibok girls' kidnapper jailed for 15 years: Nigeria," *News24*, February 13, 2018, https://www.news24.com/Africa/News/chibok-girls -kidnapper-jailed-for-15-years-nigeria-20180213.

Ola Lanre and Ahmed Kingimi, "Nigerian police say eight Boko Ha-ram suspects confess to Chibok abduction," *Reuters*, July 18, 2018, https://www.reuters.com/article/us-nigeria-violence-girls /nigerian-police-say-eight-boko-haram-suspects-confess-to-chibok -abduction-idUSKBN1K81QL.

"Boko Haram terrorist, who planned abduction, sentenced to 20 years imprisonment," *Pulse News*, July 13, 2018, https://www.pulse .ng/news/local/court-sentences-terrorist-to-20-years-for-chibok -abduction-id8613651.html.

Bukola Adebayo, "Nigeria court jails second man involved in Chibok girls kidnapping," *CNN*, July 13, 2018, https://www.cnn.com /2018/07/13/africa/chibok-girls-kidnapper-jailed/index.html.

When a Boko Haram faction kidnapped 112 schoolgirls: "Nigeria Dapchi abductions: Schoolgirls finally home," *BBC News*, March 25, 2018, https://www.bbc.com/news/world-africa-43535872.

"Dapchi girls: Freed Nigerian girls tell of kidnap ordeal," *BBC News*, March 22, 2018, https://www.bbc.com/news/43489217.

Jonathan Gopep et al., "Boko Haram's Seizure of 110 Girls Taunts Nigeria, and Its Leader," *New York Times*, March 18, 2018, https://www.nytimes.com/2018/03/18/world/africa/boko-haram-dapchi -girls-nigeria.html.

PHOTO INSERT CREDITS

INDEX

Isha Sesay is an award-winning journalist who has covered global events and major breaking news with a focus on stories of social injustice and their impact on women and girls. Sesay led the CNN team that won a 2014 Peabody Award for coverage of the missing Chibok girls, hosted *CNN NewsCenter*, and headed the network's Africa reporting for ten years. She received a Gracie Award for Outstanding Anchor for her coverage of the Chibok girls story, in addition to other accolades during her tenure at CNN. She is the founder of W.E. (Women Everywhere) Can Lead, a nonprofit organization dedicated to nurturing and empowering teenage girls to become Africa's next generation of leaders. Of Sierra Leonean descent, Sesay grew up in Britain and holds a BA with honors in English from Trinity College, Cambridge University. She lives in Los Angeles.